COYOTE

COYOTE

LYNN VANNUCCI

THE BODLEY HEAD
LONDON

British Library Cataloguing in Publication Data

Vannucci, Lynn
Coyote.
I. Title
813'.54[F]   PS3572.A6/

ISBN 0-370-31080-2

Copyright © Lynn Vannucci 1987
Printed and bound in Great Britain for
The Bodley Head Ltd,
32 Bedford Square,
London WC1B 3EL
by
St Edmundsbury Press Ltd,
Bury St Edmunds, Suffolk

First published by Bantam, New York, 1987
First published in Great Britain 1987

For my grandparents,
the late Albertina and Philip Vannucci

A second chance—that's the delusion. There never was to be but one. We work in the dark—we do what we can—we give what we have. Our doubt is our passion and our passion is our task.

—HENRY JAMES
The Middle Years

I tried to run away myself,
To run away and wrestle with my ego,
And with this flame
You put here in this Eskimo . . .

—JONI MITCHELL
"Coyote"

PART ONE

Of course I'd been thinking about Coyote when it happened: when I'd put my car into forward instead of reverse; when I'd plowed my silver-gray Mercedes 450SL up and over the hood of the metallic-gold Porsche Targa that had been parked head-to-head with me in the parking garage of the Beverly Hills Neiman-Marcus.

Another time, when the song had come on the radio, I'd merely locked my keys in the car, with the engine running. The parking attendant had been charmed by what I'd done, by the cuteness of my dilemma. My being young and blond had helped, too, as had my being a minor television personality, whom he'd recognize even if he hadn't known my name. But in the Neiman-Marcus garage, when I'd heard Joni Mitchell's voice over the radio—"No regrets, Coyote . . ."—I'd wrecked my car.

Oh, who was I kidding? I didn't need a song to make me think about him. I thought about Coyote all the time. And when I thought about him I was distracted, and when I was distracted I did dumb things. Like wrecking my car. People had begun to characterize me as dumb. And ditsy.

Ditsy over Coyote, who loved me best because I was cool and levelheaded.

The wreck had been actually very pretty, almost classic: the streaks of Mercedes silver etched across the gold of the Porsche; the broken glass of the headlights glittering on the black pavement, under the fluorescent lights.

The owner of the Porsche had approached, shrieking: nasty, hasty generalizations about women drivers. Clearly, he hadn't shared my aesthetic appreciation of the accident; he'd demanded my insurance information. Obviously, no amount of cuteness, youngness, blondness, or celebrity could have gotten me off the hook with that guy. I'd fished around in my purse to find my wallet and my Allstate card.

Every so often you needed to straighten things out.
Like regret.
"No regrets, Coyote."
Like Coyote.
I couldn't put him out of my mind. After a year with him and over four years without him, he was still there, every damned day, in my mind. And every night; I dreamed him and had him, like in the old days, when things had been hopeful.

There was, in my life, a plenitude of everything and no hope whatsoever. Hope died when he left. When I left, actually. I know that sounds melodramatic, but even he admitted upon a few occasions that we had a very melodramatic relationship: lots of fun and anger and lots of laughing and screaming. Lots of highs and lows and no reality at all.

At the time of the car wreck, I had a good deal of reality in my life, and no hope.

That sounds morose. I had no reason to sound morose, because my reality was a very nice one. Nice: typical, normal, middle-of-the-road, moderate, even, level. No great highs or lows in my life at all. Nice.

God, I hate the word *nice*. I remember when I didn't have that word in my vocabulary. Things were either awful or fantastic, but never ever nice. I hadn't realized how nice my life was until I wrecked my car.

The guy who owned the Porsche had raved at me, about what an idiot I was, didn't I know forward from reverse? Of course I did, I'd told him, but I knew I'd crashed the cars because I'd wanted to, and not because I didn't know any better. I didn't tell him I'd done it on purpose. I'd let him think I was stupid. It was easier.

I'd driven my mangled car away from the wreck and tried to analyze my need to crash it. Dissatisfaction. Plodding through life down the middle of the road instead of skating on the edge. Sometimes things just needed to be straightened out. And put in their place.

The wreck was going to make me late picking up Katie. She was going to be pissed. I honked my horn. The other drivers on the San Diego Freeway seemed to know that it was a New Yorker honking her horn; Californians don't honk their horns when they get stuck in traffic, so I honked proudly. I could direct all my anger toward the passive Californians, and never have to face any other kind of anger as long as I lived in L.A. California is very therapeutic that way for New Yorkers.

It was the first week of the new year. What the hell business did California have being as hot as it was? I wrecked my car the first week of the new year. New

3

beginnings. As with all beginnings, I couldn't see its promise, but regretted that something else had ended.

And that New Year's, having turned twenty-four, I felt regret all the more. A quarter of my life (expecting, as I always had, that my life would be a long one) was almost over. My youth was over. Even the commercials for skin cream reminded me that I would soon have "skin over twenty-five," and skin that old needed special protection.

There was so much regret. And it wasn't diminishing. No, all the past regrets were holding their own. I wondered, if I had that much to regret at twenty-four, how was I ever going to survive the next quarter century?

What I regretted most was the loss of love. The loss of New York. I'd been brash and pragmatic about love when I was held in its thrall. Living in reality and being secure outside of love made me see things differently. I was without love, without someone who thought I was beautiful and intense and flawless. I was desperate for that kind of love.

A silly romantic, that's what I'd become. And I lived in reality and had no hope. But my heart still dreamed. Dreams, however, couldn't be confused with hope. Hope was for the possible. Dreams were for the never-to-be. Dreams were for regrets.

The traffic moved a little and I honked my horn again, in approval.

We were sitting at a bar that faced the ocean at Malibu, drinking Lite beers. It was January; the sun was burning our faces. Katie leaned her face and lower arms out beyond the bar's white canvas awning into the sun. I leaned back, the one who would remain in lush, lethargic

Los Angeles after Katie had returned to New York, and I lamented my fate.

"No sympathy," said Katie. Katie had wrecked her car that day too. She'd wrecked it on the icy BQE getting to the airport, getting to me, getting to the sun and Lite beer in Malibu.

"Besides the weather, Katie. Besides the climate, what has L.A. got going for it? Why am I here, Katie?" I shooed away a dusty-looking gull that was walking down the vinyl bar with eyes for our bowl of corn chips.

"You're such a snob," Katie said, not opening her eyes, not turning her face away, for one moment, from the sun.

"You can afford to say that. You can afford to be generous. You live in New York. You teach at NYU. You live in a real place and do serious things."

"Every one of my serious students would give an integral part of their body to be you: living in Malibu and playing one of the leads on a soap opera."

"This isn't what I planned, Katie." My monologue about what I'd planned takes approximately half an hour to get through.

Katie, tall and gorgeous and blond, who dressed as if she sprang from the pages of *Vogue* and who kept lovers (until the divorce) to supplement her husband, and who was as cynically funny, and unnarcissistic, and openhearted as anyone that beautiful could possibly be, had not turned her face away from the sun for all that time. But she was listening to me, I knew, because when I paused she punctuated my monologue with a knowledgeable grunt.

". . . and I can't stop thinking that it was the wrong thing to do. . . . Each day I wake up and feel . . . displaced. I hurt, Katie. I hurt. And, damn, I know I shouldn't, but I do. I miss New York, the whole life I had there. . . ."

Katie drew back into the shade and looked at me and said, "Bullshit." She stared me down. I loved Katie, and I trusted her with my very life, but she had eyes that read my soul and scared the shit out of me.

"If you still love Coyote, why did you move all the way across the country and move in with Ben?"

I hadn't mentioned Coyote at all.

"I love Ben."

"Company for your misery. If you didn't love misery you wouldn't have given Coyote all the time you gave him. You wouldn't be thinking about him now, not when you're all settled with Ben."

"Don't you think I know I shouldn't be thinking about one lover when I'm living with another? Christ, Katie, you may live well with your bent for collecting lovers, but I really love Coyote, and not having him, and having to try to love Ben, is, shit, it's ripping me apart!"

Katie smiled. We'd known each other far too long and well to be sentimental. "Then go back to New York and give Coyote a second chance."

"Not necessary. Even after all this time . . . changes . . . Coyote and I don't need a second chance. We're still on the same one."

"If you think like that, you're really crazy not to go back to him."

"Except, God, except, maybe Coyote isn't my one true love. Maybe he's just an obsession."

"Mick, you can keep screwing up your life and stay in Los Angeles, or you can go back east and try sorting out New York, and Coyote. Go back to him, his pain, instead of manufacturing your own and heaping the vast surplus on Ben . . . and me, and everyone else. You're not happy, I know that. Honestly, you've been a depressing little fuck to be around for a few years now."

Oh, shit. I couldn't continue to screw up my life, Ben's life, possibly (hopefully) Coyote's life. It was essential I straighten things out, put things in their place, like I had with that damned, limping Mercedes that afternoon. I had to confront the rest of it. I had to contact Coyote. I had to confide in Ben. I had to mess up my life again. I supposed it was better than wrecking cars.

"Oh, Katie."

"What are you going to do?"

"I don't know. Having you know is enough right now. You saying I can. Go back . . . and see Coyote, I mean." The panic of not being safe with Ben collided with the thrill of just being with Coyote and I had to gasp to get any air.

PART TWO

Coyote (I'd nicknamed him that, after the Joni Mitchell song) and I were walking up Fifth Avenue, to the Seventy-second Street entrance to Central Park, the boat pond, and Alice's toadstool.

Coyote was walking with a slight limp from a child-hood injury that I did not yet know about and for which I would later refer to him as "my cripple." He was small (not so small really, at five feet nine inches, but small for a man) and skinny (but not painfully skinny because underneath his skin he was solid lean long muscle). His skin was dark, Semitic, and he was tanned too. He had long, wild, coarse black hair with strands of white in it and lines on his face. He had sparkling gray-green eyes, and his complexion was flawed only by a small oval scar on his right temple. His teeth were small and white and his lips were skinny and silk-smooth and his hands were dark, square, with short white nails, and they were strong-looking. He smelled good, crisp, like leaves in the fall, or a new book. He was wearing a white Brooks Brothers button-down and tight Calvin Klein jeans (over Giancarlo Giannini hips), and no belt and a navy-blue blazer from

Bloomingdale's, and white socks and Weejuns and a silver band on the middle finger of his left hand, and those dark glasses.

He pushed his Ray-Bans up to his forehead and squinted at me. "Shrimpton, you walk so slow!" He called me Shrimpton because he thought I looked like Jean Shrimpton, whom he had a crush on in the sixties.

I'd been turning and smelling the red carnation he'd given me and thinking whether Coyote looked more like Woody Allen or Dustin Hoffman. When we were in class and he was lecturing and wearing his brown horn-rimmed glasses and being witty and gesturing with his hands, he looked like Woody Allen. When we were outdoors and he was wearing his dark Ray-Bans, and looking sexy, he looked like Dustin Hoffman. No matter who he looked like, he walked too fast. But I forgave him this nervous idiosyncrasy: it was his body trying to keep pace with his mind.

I sped up my walk and caught up with him; we were falling, tentatively, in love.

Who wouldn't fall in love, with the love begun in the crispness of the leaves turning yellow-red in Central Park? With the wind blowing very cold in your face and the leaves very crunchy under your feet?

Falling in love should be done in the summer. From our earliest summer-camp years and high-school summer romances we're conditioned that summer loves invariably end, and summer lovers go home to play on rival football teams in the fall. There is never an appropriate season for a romance begun in fall to end, because whenever it does, it's too difficult to discern the ending's sadness from the beginning's, from the mood of fall itself. New Yorkers would understand. Nothing is so much New York as

Central Park in the fall. And nothing but Central Park in the fall is so seductive in its melancholy.

Coyote was a lot of firsts for me: my first older man (he was thirty-eight; I was nineteen), my first professor, my first Ph.D., my first New Yorker, my first Jew, my first married man. I was thrilled by all of it. Thrilled to have this sexy, intelligent, older, worldly man falling, tentatively, in love with me.

Aline Bernstein once wondered, of her love for Thomas Wolfe, why she put so much energy into such a destructive relationship. I know, Aline. When you met Tom aboard that ship and felt for the first time your heart really beat, you felt as I did when I first met Coyote at the Friday screening. Michele Marie Azzi, meet David Nathan Hellerman and the feeling to which you will devote an enormous amount of energy.

Professor Hellerman stood on the stage of the City College auditorium, his thumbs hooked through the belt loops of gray corduroy pants which hung casually over his slim, delicious hips, and called to the darkness of the balcony: "Can you fix it?"

It was the first time I heard his voice: fluid, smooth, slightly nasal, just slightly urgent.

"Yeah," came the answer.

"Film broke," he mumbled and walked behind the podium. It was the first time I saw the hurry in his step, the slight limp, the glide of his hips. The blurb in the Student Guide to City College had described Professor Hellerman as a Ph.D. from Columbia, the author of two books on film history (*Symbolism in Cinema*, and *Samuel Fuller: His Symbols and Their Meanings*) among other

11

various, impressive accomplishments. It had not mentioned those hips.

Professor Hellerman stood behind the podium and wrestled with one of those cumbersome green computer printouts. "I have to take a roll call. I hate to do this, but the registrar needs to make sure you all showed up. I'll never do it again. No one cares if you show up after this or not. Just if you take the tests.

"Azzi, Michele Marie." He pronounced it wrong: Ozzie, as in Ozzie and Harriet. Not as it should be: with a T-Z sound, like in pizza.

"It's Ought-Z," I answered.

"Ought-Z"—he stressed the correct pronunciation—"is here." He rolled his eyes. "Barkowski, Richard."

"Here."

And so on.

Whoever else made up the hundred-odd occupants of the auditorium didn't concern me. I was there and so was Professor Hellerman. I concentrated on the electric energy in Professor Hellerman's gray corduroys. Michele Azzi, better known as Mickey, sometimes as Mick, was here, Professor Hellerman. So talk to her. Ask her how she came to be taking Cinema History One from you at City College in New York City on this crisp fall day. She wasn't your typical inner-city undergraduate. She was an honor graduate of a small Catholic girls' high school. She'd spent a year at a small Catholic girls' college, as a drama major, and she'd moved to New York to become an actress. She'd taken your course because she was really interested in cinema history and not just because she wanted to have fun while fulfilling a City College breadth requirement. She was dying to touch your hips.

Did young girls really sleep with older men? Did professors really have affairs with their students? What would a Ph.D., not to mention a Jew, be like in bed?

Professor Hellerman stood before the class, addressing us on the film to be screened that afternoon. He stood before me as a symbol of credibility: If I could have an affair with Professor Hellerman, then a lot of things were possible. And, if I was going to be an actress, I'd better find out what was possible.

The auditorium grew dark; the day's film, King Vidor's *Our Daily Bread,* began to roll. Professor Hellerman let a slice of light from the hallway into the dark auditorium as he left by a side door.

I was in the cafeteria having a glass of milk and a chocolate chip cookie and recopying my notes from the *Our Daily Bread* lecture.

"Hey, Ought-Z!"

Professor Hellerman walked up to my table and I stood and spilled my milk.

We mopped the milk from my lecture notes and the table and his gray corduroys.

"Would you like to go for coffee?" he asked.

Over our cups at a coffee shop near the school, I told him that I'd just moved to New York and was fixing up my studio apartment in Greenwich Village and was nineteen years old.

He snorted at that last bit of information, surprised, and told me most people in the Continuing Education program were a little older than that. I told him I couldn't afford to take classes full time.

He told me he'd just gotten back from Arizona, where he'd spent the summer teaching and making a last-ditch effort to get his marriage back together.

So I found out he was married. Soon after, I told him I'd see him in class next Wednesday and caught the Number 6 for Astor Place. Married. Shit. How much credibility could I swallow all at once?

"Why are you so tired?" he asked.

We were walking on Sixty-eighth Street; it was the next Wednesday after class. I'd spent the previous five days thinking about him and had decided to go along with whatever he pursued: I was after credibility and he was devastating.

"I was out late."

"Why?"

"I just was. I went dancing."

"You went dancing? On a Tuesday night? What time did you get home?"

"Three. Or so. Why are you so upset?"

"I never go dancing. I will never take you dancing."

"Good. I'll know never to ask you."

"I'm in bed by ten, eleven. Three in the morning you got home?" He shook his head: awe and contempt. "Well, here we are."

"What's here?"

"My apartment."

"I thought you lived in a high-rise, on the West Side."

"I do. But I keep an apartment here too."

I looked at him and didn't believe him.

"I do!" he said.

"Sure."

What if he did? I was suddenly panicked: He was taking me to his apartment. What if his wife walked in? What if she was *there*? No, surely he wouldn't be taking

14

me home to meet his wife. I'd been developing an affair with him in my naïve little mind, and to him I was just a sweet student he could take home to meet his wife.

"Come on." He took my hand and started to lead me up the stoop, seven steps to the front door.

Nobody keeps two apartments in New York. Who can afford two apartments? I could hardly afford my five-flight walk-up. He was a professor; professors have minds, maybe, but not money. I'd gathered that his wife wasn't employed, and I was sure they couldn't afford a high-rise on the West Side and a brownstone on the East, on a professor's salary. And why would they want two homes? An apartment in the city and a summer place upstate, maybe, but two apartments in the city?

He opened the front door and led me into a red-carpeted hallway with a massive dark wooden curving banister I held on to as he led me upward. "It's on the second floor," he said.

On the second step I realized that the only reason he would keep two apartments was to have one in which to keep his wife and one in which to have afternoon trysts. From a silly schoolgirl to an afternoon tryst from the sidewalk to the second step. If I was an afternoon tryst, then I was sleazy, easy. I would have stopped then, but the alternative was to be a schoolgirl, unsophisticated, and not credible, so I followed him.

By the tenth step I was excited. An afternoon tryst meant finally getting to touch those hips, and not only to see but to feel them glide. At the top of the staircase I waited while he inserted the key, turned the lock, and opened the door.

"Hi!" he shouted when the door opened.

Hi? Who was there? I should have felt relief, maybe

anger, but I felt only disappointment. What were all those people doing in his apartment where he'd brought me to have an afternoon tryst?

I got introduced around to the people, five in all: young, creative-looking, the men with rustic, smoky beards, the women in leotards and batiked wraparound skirts. It sunk in, when Professor Hellerman winked at me, that this was not an afternoon tryst; it was a joke. And during the introductions, that this was not an apartment; it was an art gallery. It was an art gallery where Professor Hellerman's friends were hanging an exhibition. We were there because Professor Hellerman wanted to meet the artist being exhibited, a very old, crumpled man in a khaki suit, with a white beard and a red nose. I missed his name, and decided he should be named Santa Claus anyway.

Santa Claus used both of his hands to welcome Professor Hellerman and led us to look at his paintings. He was jolly as he asked me what I thought of his work. I told him I liked the colors, hoping he couldn't tell that was the only thing I liked.

"I'm not sure I like them much myself." He laughed and I was mortified. I was searching my brain for appropriate phrases learned in art appreciation class in high school. I wanted to say something intelligent, pertinent, about form, shape, texture. Before I could redeem myself, Santa Claus was leading us to another room.

"Oil is just an experiment. Something I thought I'd like to try. I'm really a photographer."

On the walls of the other room were hung photographs, simple black-and-whites: an open window, a sheer white curtain blowing inside, a pasture outside; a grainy oval, an egg on closer inspection; the shadow of an old bentwood rocker on the floorboards of a farmhouse porch. Those I loved.

"They're beautiful." I wandered around the room to look at them. Santa Claus was telling Professor Hellerman in a fatherly tone that he admired his work; apparently Professor Hellerman had written about the artist's photographs.

One of the photos was of a gnarled old tree on a roll of pasture. The bark of the tree looked as if it had been sanded and would be smooth to the touch. The leaves were crinkled and falling away. The tree looked somehow like the artist himself. I couldn't stop looking at that photograph until I heard the artist say, "I thought the article was very flattering, David. What I mean is for you to stop analyzing. Just absorb them. As she is doing."

I turned. The artist's hand was outstretched, indicating me. My face turned red, embarrassed that I'd been absorbing so intently, and been caught. The artist chuckled and Professor Hellerman said we had to go.

On the street he handed me a book: *Panama* by Thomas McGuane.

"Ever read any McGuane?"

"No."

"You should. I just picked this up to replace my other copy, which is shredded, but I think you should read it."

"Okay."

"If it doesn't interfere with your dancing, I mean."

"I'll fit it in somewhere."

Friday we were seeing Polanski's *Repulsion*. Before the screening started, Professor Hellerman ran to my seat and dropped two books in my lap: his books. I sat through the movie alone. After class I waited in the lobby of the auditorium to see if he'd ask me for coffee or a walk. On the student message board was a list of names of people with phone messages; my name was included. Shit. I ran downstairs to the information desk. Now I couldn't wait for Professor Hellerman. Still, something had to be really wrong. Bloody wrong. Why would someone leave a phone message for me at school if there was no blood?

"Message for Azzi," I told the obese black woman in the orange polyester staff jacket. She flipped through a stack of yellow message slips and handed one to me.

"Here you go, honey."

"Thanks." I opened the paper at the fold.

"Have you finished reading *Panama* yet?" the note said.

Jesus Christ.

Back upstairs, Professor Hellerman was holding court in the auditorium lobby. I waited until the rest of the students dispersed.

"What the hell is this?"

"Oh, you got the note."

"What . . . I thought someone had had an accident . . . when I got this note . . . why would you leave me a phone message?"

"I see you are 'self-owned,' but are you 'fiercely cheerful, and ready to rock and roll'?" That was how the hero of *Panama* described his girlfriend in the book. Was he comparing me to her, or testing to see if I'd read the book?

"Did you finish it?"

"Yes!"

"You didn't go dancing last night?"

"No, I stayed home and read this book." I shoved the copy of *Panama* at him.

18

"Good," he said, delighted, I think, that he'd kept me in, kept my attention for an evening, via Thomas McGuane.

Monday was rainy. I'd agreed to meet Professor Hellerman at the Thalia on Ninety-fifth Street, where they were showing *The Last Waltz*, the film about The Band's last concert at Winterland. I took a cab uptown. It was expensive, but I was dry when I got there. He opened the cab door for me and ushered me into the Thalia's lobby, under an umbrella.

He shoved the copy of Rita Mae Brown's *Rubyfruit Jungle* in my book bag as he fought to close his umbrella.

"This book stinks," he said. "Nobody in this book's a good person. Except Molly. Depressing. And the end's a total copout."

"Look, you drag me to the student bookstore Friday afternoon and give me five minutes to pick a book I want you to read from a crummy selection, and disappear to your meeting."

"I had to go to that meeting. The film faculty was deciding what new films to get for the library."

"Fine. Just don't bitch at me. I knew it probably wasn't your type of book. I yelled after you that you probably wouldn't like it."

"God! It is so poorly written."

"But the spirit of the book is wonderful."

"I can't believe you gave it to me to read. Where did you ever get to read it anyway? I thought you were a good Catholic girl."

"Good Catholic girls are not necessarily completely uninformed."

"Since when?"

19

———————

" 'Coyote's up early on the ranch,' " he sang, badly out of tune.

"And when you're just getting up, I'm just getting home," I answered.

We shared a salty pretzel and a can of Coke and walked toward the subway stop.

"That book. You weren't trying to tell me you're a lesbo, were you?"

"No, I wasn't."

"You're not, are you?"

"I'm not."

"You're sure?"

"I'm sure I'm not a lesbian."

"So why'd you give me that dyke book to read? It certainly wasn't for the literary value."

We argued on the subway until Coyote got off at the Sixty-sixth Street stop to go home. I rode to Sheridan Square in peace.

When I got home there was a postcard in my mailbox. "McGuane for Brown is not a fair trade," it said.

I listened to "Coyote" all night long.

Mondays and Wednesdays after his lecture we went to the movies, foreign films with subtitles. Fridays we watched the movie I had to see for his class and he brought us Cokes and falafel sandwiches to share while we watched.

Once, in the auditorium, while we were watching Eisenstein's *October* for the next week's lecture, our hands brushed very close together and I stopped breathing for a moment: I wanted him to hold my hand, but if he touched me, I wasn't sure it would be comfortable. I didn't know where the relationship was going, if it was even going anywhere, or if I wanted it to. Were we teacher/student, developing a very special, but unbreachable, teacher/student bond? Or were we potential lovers? If we were potential lovers how long would it take us to reach our potential? Not since I was fourteen had it taken someone so long to get up the nerve to hold my hand, nor had the idea of just holding someone's hand appealed to me so much. Not since I was fourteen and experienced my first touch of flesh-on-flesh had the idea of a simple palm-to-palm been so tantalizing, so intimate, so scary.

Toward the beginning of October, on a Friday afternoon, just before he left me at my subway stop to go home, he leaned over and kissed both of my cheeks. Quick, proper, almost Victorian kisses; he lingered just long enough so that I could feel his breath on my face. He'd never gotten so close to me before, and he left a trace of his special smell on my sweater. All weekend long I sniffed my sweater to conjure him. The following Sunday he called me for the first time, to ask if I wanted to meet him Monday at the Bleecker Street Cinema, to see James Toback's *Fingers*. I said I did.

After the movie we went to the Caffé Via Reggio for cappuccino.

"So, what did you think?" he asked.

"Great. Harvey Keitel is a wonderful actor."

"You didn't think it was a strange movie?"

"Very strange."

"So, you like Harvey Keitel?"

"Oh, a lot."

"Would you rather be with him than me?"

"What?"

"Would you rather be sitting here drinking cappuccino with me or with Harvey Keitel?"

"You."

"You're sure?"

"I'm sure."

"So who would you rather be with than me?"

"No one I can think of."

"Well, think."

"No one. Stop it."

"Donald Sutherland."

"No. Why would you say Donald Sutherland?"

"Warren Beatty?"

"No, not Warren Beatty, either."

"Who?"

"No one!"

"A rock and roller, I'll bet. I'm not a rock and roller. I do not rock and roll. Billy Joel?"

"Stop. Now you're tempting me."

"Are you for real?" he exploded. "You'd rather be with Billy Joel than me? He's not even smart! I have a Ph.D. But he's Italian, excuse me."

"He's not Italian."

"He's not Italian?"

"No."

"What is he?"

"Jewish. And I was kidding, anyway. I'd much rather be with you."

"No. You'd rather be with Billy Joel."

"Who would you rather be with?"

"Me?"

"Yeah. Charlotte Rampling?"

"Too skinny."

"Nastassja Kinski?"

22

"Tits too small."

"Jean Shrimpton."

"Now you're tempting me."

Just then one of the other cappuccino-drinkers got up from his table and wandered over toward us, trying painfully hard to be casual.

The intruder cleared his throat. "I'm really sorry to bother you like this, but"—he held a felt-tipped pen and a napkin toward Coyote—"may I have your autograph, Mr. Hoffman?"

Coyote sat back in his chair and said, "Me? Who? No . . . I'm not him . . . I'm me. We're different."

I was laughing, and the autograph seeker returned to his table looking angry, feeling cheated.

"I think you just lost Mr. Hoffman a fan," I said.

"I thought you said I looked like Woody Allen in these glasses."

Wednesday after class, Coyote had decided that I should begin my exploration of New York's museums, so instead of a movie we went to the Whitney, to see the Calder "Circus" and an Andy Warhol exhibit. After, we had white wine at the museum's café. Coyote told me he hated white wine. Then we went back to his office, on the fourth floor of the academic building, to pick up the book bag he'd left there. On our way back downstairs, on the third-floor landing, he turned to me. We stared at each other while a lone student trudged upward, past us. When the student was out of sight Coyote took me in his arms and kissed me. He tasted like wine and the Juicy Fruit that he'd been chewing to kill the taste of the wine. I could have died then and not felt cheated. My hair, my clothes smelled like him. I pushed my hair in my face as I rode the subway home, so I could smell him.

Friday after class we went to the Central Park Zoo and watched the animals. We sat on a bench opposite the elephants and watched them lumber and drink water for a while. Then Coyote pushed his face into my neck and kissed it and blew in my ear and nibbled my earlobe. He held my head tightly with his hands so I couldn't pull away and so that he could devour my ear.

When we left the zoo, my ear and hair and neck and crotch were very wet. We turned down Fifth Avenue to walk to Bergdorf's, where he was picking up a pair of pants that he'd had altered. We passed a woman handing out leaflets about a walkathon for the ERA. I took one; he refused.

"You believe in that stuff?" he asked.

"Very much," I replied.

He laughed.

"What's so funny?"

"The day you're liberated, Shrimpton, there'll be a parade down Fifth Avenue."

He called every day. Every day there was at least one postcard in my mailbox. We kissed a lot, mostly on benches in Central Park or on deserted landings in the academic building, where his office was located. He started calling me twice a day. More often than not there were two postcards a day in my mailbox. We started seeing each other Tuesdays and Thursdays, between his ten o'clock and my four o'clock class. In Central Park he pinned me up against a tree and ground his hips into mine and sighed. It was almost November and I was sorely neglect-

24

ing my studies. I'd auditioned for nothing. In his office, after a kissing session that made my lips sore and my body tremble, over Styrofoam cups of coffee he said, "I'm not getting any work done."

"Yeah," I said.

"I haven't worked on my book since I met you. I've hardly had time to keep up with my lectures. You know, it takes a lot of time to write a fifty-minute lecture."

"I haven't gotten much work done since we met, either."

"Why can't we work?"

"We're spending too much time together?"

"I think so."

"So, we'll stop seeing each other."

I thought my heart was lying on the floor and he was ready to trample it until it stopped beating. So, where did I expect those crazy kissing matches to go? Coyote treated my heart kindly, though.

"No, that's not the answer."

Suddenly I was in control.

"Well, we've got to do something. I'm supposed to be acting. And studying. And auditioning. And so far, I haven't been. My money's running out fast too."

"Okay. Okay," he said.

We sipped our coffee silently.

"Look," he said. "I need a research assistant."

"Are you asking me to work for you?"

"Twelve hundred dollars for six weeks' work. It's not much, and I know it's not acting . . . but it'll keep you going, and I do need someone."

"It might as well be me, then."

"Is that a yes?"

"Sure."

"It'll be nice working together."

We were headed to the Museum of Modern Art Film Library to begin our first day on the job. We stopped first at the cafeteria in the Victoria Hotel on West Forty-seventh Street for lunch. I ordered the tuna salad plate and Coyote ordered a meatball hero from a handsome young Puerto Rican in a greasy white apron.

Coyote pushed our tray down the metal slide along the counter and poured two coffees in Styrofoam cups from the self-service industrial-size urn.

"This is a hotel for bums," Coyote told me. The Puerto Rican handed us our lunches. "There used to be a lot of famous writers hanging out here. Now, it's just bums." Indeed, a lot of filthy old men were there, some lounging over free coffee refills, some grunting while eating their food from the paper plates, some picking their teeth with their plastic forks.

Murals of southern Italy were painted on the walls of the dining area. Coyote gestured toward them. "I know you like Eye-talian restaurants," he said.

After we ate, as we lingered over free coffee refills and cigarettes, Coyote, who was not comfortable lingering, fidgeted with his cigarette, sat up in his chair, leaned far over the table toward me, and asked, "Why do you keep seeing me?"

I shrugged. What was I supposed to say? I smiled.

"You're fun to be with."

"That's original. And very complimentary."

Because you're my teacher. Because you're my employer. Because you kiss great. Because I love your hips.

"Well, you are," I said. I was getting very nervous and my voice was quivering.

"Do you consider me as just a teacher?"

"No," I said. No, you asshole. I would not spend all my free afternoons with a person I considered just as a teacher. I wouldn't let someone I considered just as a teacher suck on my ear in Central Park.

"Just as an employer?"

"No."

"Then why do you keep seeing me?"

Because you have sexy hips. Because you kiss sexy. Because I'm hoping we'll go to bed together. Because you represent credibility to me. Because I'm enthralled by the romance of this relationship and I want to start having enthralling romances so that I can be a good actress. Because I love you.

My brain short-circuited.

I loved him?

I loved him? How could I love him? Don't define it, Mickey, I told myself. Just say it. I reached across the table and took his hands, each in one of mine, to tell him that I loved him. Our cigarettes were smoking like crazy. A bum belched. My God, I thought. He's so much older, and my teacher, and I work for him, and he's married.

"I . . . think you are a really terrific person."

"That's why you keep seeing me?"

I nodded.

"Okay."

He withdrew his hands from mine and put his cigarette out and was all perpetual motion again. He put on his coat and scarf and shrugged me into my coat and dumped our leftovers in a nearby garbage can and put our tray on top of a stack of other dirty trays and mumbled that we should get to the library. Before I could rethink my response we were sitting in the sterile stillness of the Museum of Modern Art Film Archive.

Two hours passed. Coyote was a streak of colored light, darting from file drawer to archive assistant to file catalog, and back to the table we shared in silence, absorbed in his subject: Howard Hawks. I was trying to be a good research assistant, trying to copy from the many catalogs the lists of articles from books, magazines, newspapers, on Howard Hawks and/or his films. I was really spending two minutes copying letter-by-letter the words that made no sense to me, four minutes kicking myself for not telling Coyote that I loved him, eight minutes trying to figure out what was possessing me to think I loved him, convincing myself there was no way I could love him, too many reasons why I should not love him. Then why did I keep seeing him if I didn't love him?

Coyote slipped a note to me on the back of a Resource Reserve card. "What were you really going to tell me in the Eye-talian restaurant?" the note said. He looked at me and leaned over the table. I looked at him, at all the quiet, studious people around us, and whatever I had to say in response I knew could not be said there, so I shrugged.

Coyote went back to work; nothing had transpired. I gave the Hawks listings another try. Another two hours passed.

Anyway. We'd reached Alice's toadstool and were circling the boat pond toward Hans Christian Andersen. Coyote was quizzing me about my virginity.

"When did you lose it, Shrimpton?" he asked. "How old were you?"

True, we had, in the months we'd known each other, kissed in the corridors of academic buildings, and on benches in Central Park he had held me very tightly and licked my ears. Though we had never spoken it, that we were falling in love, it was true we knew we were. Still, that quiz was as close to real physical intimacy as we'd ever been. I did something very uncharacteristic; I became coy and hid behind my red carnation and giggled.

"Fourteen."

"Fourteen?" Coyote was shocked. "You were fourteen when you did it for the first time?"

"We just wanted to see what all the fuss was about, so we did it. This friend of mine and me. It was pretty awful. I bled all over my white bedspread and it hurt, both of us, and neither of us really enjoyed it. We cried afterwards. I don't know why we did that. Cried, I mean. But at least we got it over with and didn't have to go through the whole mystical, deflowering guilt number when we got older and started doing it for real."

Coyote stared at me for a while before he shut his gaping mouth.

"So how old were you when you lost it?" I said.

"Thirteen. My dad took me to a whore when I was thirteen."

"And you became a man."

We both giggled.

"Did you do it with a lot of women? Over the years, I mean?"

"Just with that hooker, until I was seventeen. And then just with gentiles. Until I met my wife."

PART THREE

December. Nearly Christmas. Work on the Hawks book was progressing rapidly. I'd gotten all the answers right on my final exam for Cinema History One, and Professor Hellerman had written "Good thinking, Ms. Azzi" on top of my paper. Coyote and I had a date to make love.

We hadn't said, specifically, that we were going to make love, but I'd asked Coyote to come to my apartment, which was clean and which I'd filled with fresh cut flowers, and which I hoped he wouldn't think was too much of a hovel. He was bringing a pizza at seven, and I'd bought a bottle of red wine and there were no plans to go to a film, or a restaurant, or museum, or anything. I'd showered and was wearing a white lace teddy under my jeans and sweater and there were clean starched sheets on the sofa bed. I'd left the sofa bed unfolded. The doorbell rang. Suppose he wasn't coming to make love to me? I buzzed to let him in the building and folded up the sofa bed. He knocked at my door.

Coyote drank a glass of wine, quickly, and told me he'd rather have Coke with lots of ice and a lemon. He gobbled a piece of pizza we hadn't bothered to take out of the box, and paced. He commented on how clean my apartment was and, when he was done with the piece of pizza, started unbuttoning his shirt. He removed his shoes and his socks. I went to the bathroom and took off my clothes and put my diaphragm in. I didn't bother to put the teddy back on, embarrassed at the idea of seducing Coyote with lace.

We faced each other: naked.

There was a small patch of gray hair on his chest and a long, thin scar on his right leg that ran from hip bone to mid-thigh.

"Where'd you get the scar?"

"I fell out of a tree when I was a kid. There's a pin in my leg."

I nodded.

"Where'd you get the hips?" he asked.

I glanced down at my hips: lean, but very wide.

"Italian hips," I told him. "Good for having babies."

We met by the kitchenette and kissed. He led me to the sofa and I helped him remove the pillows and open the bed, which we struggled with because it stuck, and we fell on the sheets and kissed again.

He kissed my lips and neck, and moaned, and kissed my cheeks and ears and jerked away and sighed and kissed me again and jerked away again, as if it was all very painful.

Suddenly he stood and told me to get up, and he put on his underwear—blue bikinis—and started to fold away the bed.

"What are you doing?" I asked, naked and hurt and a little shocked.

"I wish you had a Coke." He drank a glass of wine and put on one of his socks.

"What are you doing!"

"I can't do this," he said and tried to put on the other sock but lost his balance and fell on the couch. "Shit," he moaned and curled into a fetal position.

"Are you all right?"

"No, I'm dizzy."

"Oh, for Pete's sake . . ." I went to the bathroom and put on my white terry robe and wrung out a washcloth with cold water.

"Here." I put the washcloth on his forehead. "Better?"

"No," he sighed, and moaned.

"Coyote, what can I do?"

"Nothing."

I knelt by the couch.

"I'm so embarrassed," he said.

"It's okay," I told him. "Just tell me why? Is it me? Is it . . . that you're married? What is it?"

"Charles Bronson."

"What?"

"Charles Bronson wouldn't do this. He'd be able to perform."

"You're not Charles Bronson."

"Of course I'm not. I'm just saying that Charles Bronson would be able to make love to you. Even after building it up like this . . . even after waiting this long."

"Charles Bronson wouldn't have waited this long," I joked, thinking he was joking.

"Exactly," Coyote moaned.

The next day I was waiting for him in his office and when he came in, his clothes were covered with greasy spots.

"What happened?"

"Shelley threw a plate at me."

It was the first time I'd heard his wife's name. That he had another reality, outside of City College and Howard Hawks and me, became very clear.

"By the looks of it, the plate had food on it." I tried to joke and sound noncommittal.

"Two eggs, over, and an English muffin. Buttered. Look, Shrimpton, I don't think I can see you anymore."

"Okay." I picked up my book bag and started to leave his office.

"Okay? That's it?"

I felt like crying and I wanted to get out of his presence before I did because it was going to be one of those cries, I could tell, when you didn't really know why you were crying and the confusion made you absolutely convulse.

"That's it." My back was toward him. "We're pretty much done with the Hawks book, and the course is over. There's no reason to see each other anymore."

"Where should I send the check for the research?"

"To my apartment."

"Okay."

"I hope that . . . nothing will affect my grade. . . ."

"You think I'm pretty low if you think that anything besides your work will affect your grade."

"Yeah, I think you're pretty low."

Three weeks before Christmas. There were parties to go to, New York friends to say goodbye to for a while, family to visit in Pittsburgh, shopping for presents, hometown friends I hadn't seen since summer to spend the holidays with, cards to send. I was immersed in my plans. I spent the time I wasn't immersed in my plans immersed in crying convulsively, filled with confusion. Who was that Coyote, anyway? And where did I get all those memories? We spent three months knowing each other, Coyote and I, three months and one week, and I couldn't remember when I didn't know him.

Going to the cinemabilia on Thirteenth Street to gather material for the Hawks book and ending up buying each other stills of Bogey and Hepburn, and James Dean.

Meeting at P. J. Bernstein's for potato pancakes and applesauce, or at Donnelly's for french fries with vinegar and catsup and a beer.

Rushing to cross Sixty-sixth Street in the rain and running for shelter to a florist shop where he bought me yet another red carnation and we waited for the rain to let up.

Three months and one week was not a major portion of my life, so why did I miss him so much? Why did he feel so integral? And why couldn't I stop crying?

There was a stack of Christmas cards in front of me that I had to finish addressing and get in the mail. The hem of a skirt I wanted to wear to a party needed to be restitched. Shit, how could I go to a party when I couldn't even stop crying? When I couldn't even move.

I couldn't move.

That was ridiculous. Of course I could move. I was not immobilized with grief.

So I got up.

But when I was up I didn't know what to do with myself.

Turn on the TV. Turn on the stereo. Turn off the TV. What record did I want to play. Make some coffee. But filling the kettle with water and waiting for it to whistle and filling a cup with Taster's Choice and Sweet 'N Low was too much fucking trouble.

The phone rang.

"Shrimpton." It was not a greeting; it was a statement.

"Coyote." I responded in the same tone.

"Meet me at the Gotham Book Mart in twenty minutes."

I hung up and ran out of the apartment.

At the Gotham I waited impatiently, pretending to be interested in the books, while Coyote purchased a biography of Arthur Penn.

He looked good. So hard and cool. I wanted to wrap myself in him but I didn't know what he wanted so I controlled myself.

We left the bookshop and he kissed me on the cheek, took my hand, and led me into a jewelry store in the diamond district. In the back of the store was hidden a lunch counter. He ordered bagels and coffee for us and handed me a letter.

"I got this today," he said.

I started to open the letter, assuming he wanted me to read it, but he grabbed it away.

"You don't have to read it. It's from Clyde Palmer."

"Who?"

"Santa Claus."

"Oh, right . . ."

"He told me I'd never be happy until I lifted myself 'out of the dry dust of academia' and started to enjoy 'the juices of life.' What do you think?"

I sat silently.

"Well? Do you think I'm an old fuddy-duddy? Clyde Palmer, who's eighty-one, says he thinks I'm an old man."

"You do suffer from a kind of mental gerontomorphism."

"That's cute, Shrimpton. Cute. Make fun of me. You just don't care, do you? You really don't."

"I wasn't making fun . . ."

"So, what were you doing?"

"I'm sorry. I care."

"How can you tell me that you think I've got an old mind? How can you just tell me you think I'm low and walk out of my office and forget me?"

"You told me you didn't want to see me anymore."

"I lied."

"How was I supposed to know that?" I said that louder than necessary.

"Shhh!" Coyote hissed.

I hissed back at him: "What's going on? Why am I here? Do you like me? Do you want to see me? Are you in the throes of some sort of midlife crisis? Do you need someone to lean on while your marriage falls apart? Do you want me around to juice up your dry academic life? What? Tell me. I'll handle it. Just don't treat me like a frivolity."

Coyote looked at me for a long while.

"I guess you do care," he said.

"Of course I care."

He looked at me and then at the floor and then at the bagel the waitress had just served him.

"I'm too young to have a midlife crisis," he said.

He came to my apartment the next night. That time, instead of pizza he brought cannolis which neither of us ate. That time, I had Coke with lots of ice and lemon which he didn't drink. That time, he made love to me properly. Twice. "Once for this time, and once for last," he said.

He dragged a tree, bigger than he was, down Sixth Avenue, to my apartment.

"I don't see why you need a tree. You're going to Pennsylvania for Christmas."

"I don't need a tree. I want a tree," I told him.

"My grandmother would roll over in her grave if she could see me," he said. But he hummed along to the carols as he placed the bulbs carefully on each branch. He even consented to string popcorn, though he wasn't very good at it and broke a lot of the kernels that he didn't eat.

"It was my first tree," he said afterward.

Then, during our after-sex cigarette before we dressed, he told me he was going to Florida, with his wife, for the holidays.

"I'll miss you," I said.

A puff on my cigarette.

"How long will you be gone?"

"Three weeks."

"That's a long time."

"It seems almost as long as I've known you, Shrimpton. I won't be able to call. Not call much. I will if I can."

"You do that. If you can."

"Are you mad?"

"No." I shook my head. "I'll just miss you and I don't want to think about it. Let's just have a lot of fun before you go."

"I'm not going to die. I will be back."

"I know, I know!" I was out of bed, crushing out one cigarette and lighting another.

"What are you so upset about, then?"

I plopped down on the edge of the bed.

"Coyote, I'm getting used to you, that's all."

He crushed out my cigarette, and rolled me over on the bed and dove, his head between my legs. "Amazing," he muttered.

"Ummm?"

"Fucking amazing."

"What?" I asked.

He rested his chin on my belly so when I looked down I saw a decapitated head between my legs, one that was staring straight up at me.

"You have no vaginal odor," he said.

We both laughed and I pushed his head lower.

While Coyote was getting us an ashtray and I was making instant coffee, he asked me if I planned on ever getting married.

"Come on, I'm only nineteen."

"I didn't ask if you were getting married tomorrow. I asked if you planned on it. You know, eventually."

"Well. Sure. I suppose. Eventually."

"Not to me," he said quickly.

I answered evenly. "No, not to you." It was the first time I'd thought about getting married to him. It was the first time I'd thought about any sort of future with him.

"Well, what about your future?" he asked.

"What about it? I like things the way they are. Don't fuck them up by talking about the future."

"What are you? Some sort of existentialist? You have to talk about the future."

"There isn't any point in it."

"Why?"

"There just isn't. Not with you, anyway."

"Because I'm married."

"Precisely."

"My marriage is a shambles. You know that. Shelley and I hardly see each other. We see our friends on weekends, our families on holidays. We put up a good front. That's it. Everything we do is perfunctory. Even sex."

"Please, I would prefer to delude myself that you have no sex at all."

"You're joking. I can't believe you're joking."

"And what are you doing? Proposing to me?"

"Look," he said, grabbing me by the collar of his shirt, which I was wearing because I was cold, and pushing me up against the wall. "I love you, Shrimpton. It's okay if you don't want to tell me that you love me, but I know you do, and I want you to know that I love you too."

He pushed his face very close to mine and didn't let me go even when I began to cry.

We were walking down Sixth Avenue, to Fifty-seventh Street for a drink downstairs at O'Neal's. I was talking about what I was going to do for money when I came back from Pennsylvania after the first of the year.

"Well, you know I've been auditioning. And there's this rep company. Off Broadway. Good parts. I got offered a job with them. My first role would be Ann in Philip Barry's *Hotel Universe*. It's not like appearing on Broadway, but then, I haven't appeared anywhere yet. And the pay's pretty good. A lot better than you paid me."

"Shelley and I talked about getting a divorce last night."

I looked at him as we walked. I felt the unexpected rise of panic in my chest. I was breaking up his marriage and that meant I'd committed myself to him. But then, I was in love with him. Mixed with the panic I did feel a quiet, intense joy at the prospect of his divorce.

"So, what do you think?" I said finally.

"I think you ought to take the job."

We were sitting on the floor, on a piece of brown shag carpeting, under my Christmas tree, exchanging gifts. It was the last time we'd see each other before he left to spend three weeks in Florida with his wife, and I left to spend three weeks in Pennsylvania with my family, and some old friends.

"What is it?" I shook an oblong package, but there was no sound. "A book?"

It was Tom Robbins's *Even Cowgirls Get the Blues.*

"Ever read any Robbins?" he asked.

"Sure. *Another Roadside Attraction,* and I thought that, Christ, a man who writes like that . . . can think like that, could talk like that . . . could keep me faithful for years!" But Coyote didn't appreciate my comments. "Okay. Here, you open one now."

"No . . ."

"Go on."

He peeled the paper from a thin square package. It was a Jerry Vale album.

"I know how you like Eye-talians," I said.

"Only ones with big tits that smell like garlic and have hair in their armpits."

"I bet Jerry Vale has hair in his armpits."

"Open this one."

In my box was a small porcelain doll dressed in Italian national costume.

41

"She's beautiful," I told him, kissed him, and gave him another present.

He pulled the paper from a tiny Tiffany box. Inside was a thin silver neck chain.

"It's wonderful. Did you really go to Tiffany's?"

I nodded and helped him put it on.

"I wanted to get you something that would last."

He went to the bathroom to look at the chain around his neck in the mirror.

"What are we going to do, Shrimpton?" He asked that as he stood looking at me from the bathroom door, fingering the chain.

"About?"

"Us."

"Oh."

He was seated beside me again, on the floor, and I was lying on my side, twisting a piece of tinsel around my finger. The tree smelled so good, piney and happy and festive.

"I'll call you while I'm away."

"If you can, please."

"I can. I'll make sure I can." He picked needles from the tree. "Damn it, Shrimpton, I hate leaving you."

"I hate you leaving."

"So what are we going to do?"

"I don't suppose there's a whole lot we can do. Not right now, anyway. Unless you want to run away to Panama . . ."

"Get serious."

"Look, Coyote, let's just play this one by ear."

"What does that mean?"

"Ride with the tide, go with the flow."

"I know what it means. What I mean is how can you say it?"

"What else can we do?"

"We can make plans. We can make some decisions. We've got to do something." Coyote paced the floor.

"Coyote, it's not time yet. When it's time, we'll know. For now, just let it ride."

"I'm crazy about you."

"I'm crazy about you too."

"And you're willing to just let it ride?"

"For now, yes."

"Well, I'm not. I can't!" He was pacing furiously. "I have to know what's going on. I'm not the kind of person who 'rides the tide.' I plan things out, and I follow through with my plans. I'm a planner. I can't just sit back and see what happens."

"Look, Coyote. You're going away. I'm going away. Tomorrow. Just for the duration of that time, why can't you play it by ear?"

He turned toward me and threw his hands to the ceiling.

"Because I'm tone-deaf, Shrimpton!"

That night the phone rang before I fell asleep.

"Hello?"

"Panama."

"Coyote?"

"Panama is not such a bad idea."

"You're nuts."

"Just about you."

And in the morning, before I woke up, the phone rang again.

"Hello?"

"Your voice sounds like warm toast in the morning."

"Good morning."

"My plane leaves in three hours. Can you meet me for breakfast?"

"Where?"

"The coffee shop on Sixty-ninth and Lex. In about half an hour?"

The snow was two inches deep and still falling when I rushed outside to find a cab. It was 6:25 A.M.

Coyote was wearing the silver chain and carrying an overnight case which held his razor, his aftershave, some books, and a package of letters I'd given him, one for each day he'd be away, all tied together with a satin ribbon.

We ordered eggs and toast and coffee.

"Shrimp, don't do anything, not until I come back. We'll make plans then."

I nodded.

"Promise."

I didn't know what I was promising, but I said it. "I promise."

Outside in the snow we hailed a Checker, kissed frantically, and waved goodbye. Coyote's mittened hand was waving at me, his nose pressed to the cab's rear window, until the driver turned a corner and we couldn't see each other anymore. I flagged down another cab and went home to pack. My plane was leaving in four hours.

PART FOUR

"Awww! Shit!"
I was sprawled in the
the gutter at the corner of Sixth Avenue and Fourth Street,
my feet, my hands, my ass soaking in the cold slush.

I leaned back on the icy curb and gritted my teeth
against the surprise of the cold and the shooting pain that
started in my tailbone and made its way to the base of my
neck, where it fingered out over the back of my skull.

A bum leaned over me, tilted his head with doglike
curiosity, and asked me for a quarter.

Cold, pain, and now Muscatel breath and intense
body odor irritating my senses, I screamed at him: "Get
the fuck away from me!"

The bum backed away with silent, bold gestures of
offended sensibilities. I climbed back to my feet and shook
my hands, slapped my ass, to get rid of the excess water.

Rain that should have been snow was falling on my
suitcase and dripping into the shopping bags of Christmas
presents I was taking home to my loved ones. The wrapping paper was spotting and running.

I'd gone before, to a girlfriend's, or maybe a boyfriend's, house for a few days, but I'd never gone away so

far, or for almost four months. Still, I'd gone away with the same warning ringing in my ears: "If you leave, don't bother coming back," and the same determination to take the warning seriously this time. Once again, I was coming back. Home for the holidays.

My father picked me up at the Pittsburgh Airport. He was wearing tight jeans and a short brown leather jacket over a thick pink ski sweater. The women in the airport watched him as he walked to me: tall, muscular, a college track star who'd kept his physique, graceful, like an illusion when he moved. Evaristo Azzi: a dark, Italian, almost Arabic-looking man with the surprise of watery blue eyes.

When he saw me at the gate he ran to me and picked me up in his arms and twirled me around. I let my body relax into the spin. I was welcome, and as usual, I didn't even consider that that was just a temporary phenomenon.

In a red '57 T-bird (the one he bought the year I was born), early Sinatra in the tape deck, Dad and I rode to our house in Shadyside in qualified silence. Dad was sober, I was scared, and we were both too determined that the joyous mood of the reunion be preserved: we would not provoke controversy. We would not talk about our last battle: the night he drank too much and raged around my room, destroying my books and records and clothes, complaining about all the money he was pouring into a daughter who wasn't worth it. I smoked, and fucked around, and majored in drama-for-Christ-sake, and I've always thought that what really pissed him off was that I cut back on my hours at the gallery so that I could rehearse and he had to pay someone else a lot more to do my job. He threatened to cut me off that night, and we would not talk about the fact that I took him up on it, and that was why I was in New York, struggling, three years before I had planned to be. We were both too aware that the slightest misplaced sound might provoke the other.

I broke and spoke first.

"How's the gallery?"

Dad took a long drag on his unfiltered Camel and used long, winter-tanned fingers to pick away a stray piece of tobacco from his lip.

"Good. Business is good."

"Well, great."

"I bought a couple more Vasarelys for the house."

"I love Vasarely."

"Yeah, well. You have good taste in art. I drilled that into you if nothing else."

Quick. I reminded myself of my resolve: no controversy.

I answered. "Yeah. Well."

"So. How are you getting by in New York?"

"Fine. I'm doing just fine. I'm . . . I got a part in a play."

"That's nice. That's what you want, right?"

"Right."

Dad nodded.

"Mickey, it's important to me that you are nice to Shelley while you are here."

My father said that, not looking at me, concentrating all his extraneous energy on making a left-hand turn. I should have felt relief that the first point of potential controversy was his, that I was offered the role of magnanimous one.

Shelley was Dad's new girlfriend, an eighteen-year-old art student at Pitt who answered his ad in the *Press* for a gal Friday to help out in the gallery. Boy, was she helping out. Moved right in: not just into the gallery, but out of her dorm and into our house. She shared Dad's bedroom. And that name, Shelley, with Coyote's wife. I'd never met her and I was not favorably disposed. But, I wanted to tell Dad about Coyote and I couldn't think of a way to make him understand the difference between me and Coyote and him and Shelley. And, it was important to Dad that I was nice to her while I was home.

"I promise, Dad."

He looked at me and winked because I was a good daughter.

Frank began to sing "The Girl That I Marry," and Dad and I sang along. " 'Stead of flittin', I'll be sittin', next to her, and she'll purr like a kitten.' "

When we got to the house, he took my bags up to my room and said he had to go to the gallery for the afternoon, but he'd pick me up at seven for dinner. "We're going to Christopher's, your favorite place," he said. "Be ready on time, okay, Mickey?"

When he drove away, I unpacked, put my things into the drawers of my Victorian cottage furniture and stuffed my luggage under my sleigh bed. I thought Coyote must be in Florida by now and I wished he would call.

I found some wrapping paper in the extra room and rewrapped my gifts and put them under the tree. I found Shelley's things all over the house, signs of her living there, and I methodically, absently picked apart a wicker place mat we didn't own before I left for New York, while I drank a cup of tea. Then I went upstairs to take a bath.

The phone rang.

I left big drippy footprints on the floor when I jumped out of my bath and ran to my room.

"Hello?"

"Hi, Shrimpton." Coyote. I threw myself across my bed and hugged the phone.

"Hi."

"Guess where I am?" He was puffing, like he was trying to catch his breath.

"Florida?"

"Yeah, but where?"

"Where?"

"I'm at a marina. In a phone booth. Running. I came out to take a run . . . as soon as we got settled in . . . so I could get away and call you. Except . . . this place is a real retirement haven, and no one runs . . . especially on the beach. So, I'm . . . sort of a . . . tourist attraction."

I laughed into the receiver and clutched it closer to make him seem nearer.

"You have the best laugh. I miss your laugh," he said.

There was a pause as we listened to each other breathe.

"Are you reading your letters?" I asked.

"I'm reading my letters."

"Do you like them?"

"No. They make me miss you more."

"I couldn't miss you more if I tried."

"Try."

Dad held court at the head of the table: sharing a bit of conversation with the maitre d'; seating everyone (Shelley to his left, Neil to his right, me between Neil and

Ginch); greeting friends who stopped by our table with a special mention of Shelley, his "new girlfriend," and me, his "daughter, who's going to be in a play in New York." He didn't know what play I was going to be in and referred questions about that to me. He ordered champagne to celebrate his "two girls."

I looked to Neil, who patted my knee under the table and smiled at me. I understood. It was a paternal pat and a smile that said he was on the alert to monitor Dad's drinking.

Most people were afraid of Neil, the framer at the gallery. He was huge, for one thing. And for another, he was the hairiest creature you could imagine. His two big black eyes and his pug nose, and the curl of one thick, chewy bottom lip were the only things you could see under all the blue-black hair on his face and head. His body was hairy, too: long, thick black fur. He didn't look like Grizzly Adams so much as he looked like Grizzly Adams's bear.

Lastly, Neil was crippled. I knew that what crippled him was a car wreck, long ago, when he was a student at Point Park College, and that was why he wore one normal shoe and one with a three-inch platform. But there were a lot of local legends about Neil, with a fairly macabre one about how he got to be a cripple, and they were all repeated with the tag moral: Stay out of his way, because he's crazy mean.

He was about as crazy mean as I was. But he was strong, and protective, and so the legends kept getting reinforced.

Once, when I was a sophomore, I was at the gallery helping Neil frame some new prints and my boyfriend pulled into the driveway in his new MG Midget. We'd had a fight, my boyfriend and I, and I didn't want to talk to him, so Neil barred him from the gallery. The boyfriend, however, wouldn't go away. He sat outside in his MG, beeping his horn incessantly, shouting for me to come out and talk to him.

"Mick, Babe," Neil had said, "you gotta go out there and talk to him, or he's gotta leave."

"I don't want to talk to him."

"Okay."

Neil limped outside to my boyfriend's car. He stood in front of the MG, dwarfing both boyfriend and car, and I could see from the gallery's front window that he was trying to persuade the boyfriend to leave. Rather bravely, the boyfriend refused. So Neil did this incredible thing: He bent over and grabbed the MG's front bumper, picked it up, turned it around by pivoting it on its rear tires until it faced in the opposite direction, out of the driveway. The boyfriend looked as if he were making a mess in his underwear, and when Neil put the car down and pointed a finger out to the street, the boyfriend scooted out of there like a cockroach when the lights go on. Neil came back into the gallery as if nothing exceptional had happened.

Neil was always doing extraordinary things for me. Except when it came to my father. When it came to my father, Neil patted my knee and smiled. Sometimes I thought I should tell Neil what Dad did, how things really were at home, and Neil would do something about it. Like, maybe he'd kill him. Really kill him. But the thrill of my father being dead always dissipated before I would get up the nerve to talk to Neil, and Dad and I would make up and he would swear it would never happen again, and

51

once more I would love him like I couldn't live without him.

Ginch, on the other hand, was too spaced to give a fuck about anything. Not artificially spaced, you understand. Naturally spaced. So spaced that sometimes when he was sitting and thinking he would get so involved in his thoughts he would forget to swallow and would drool on his jacket. He was a CPA, and my father said Ginch was his best friend, though Neil really was.

And: while Neil had given up dating (after four wives who were all wonderful women I remember as being very good to me), and Dad had, after Mom left, stuck to a series of intense relationships that averaged about eighteen months in length, Ginch had never married and never stopped looking. There had been an incredible number of women in Ginch's life, and no one ever got to know them very well because they were never around more than a few weeks, maybe a month. I was the woman Ginch knew best, and for the last five or six years, Neil had been quietly, if very, present when Ginch grabbed me to tickle me and roll me around on the floor in the back room of the gallery the way he'd been doing since I was a baby. Ginch was ogling every woman in Christopher's and there was a puddle of drool on his lapel.

Then there was Shelley. She was bright and bubbly, with a headful of short red curls and a constant high-pitched giggle; the sort of girl I would never pick for a friend. She kept reaching over and touching my father, his hand, or his shoulder, or his face, while he talked, and then looking up at him and watching to see if what she'd done was all right with him. Sometimes he'd reach back and pat her hand before he removed it. Most of the time he'd ignore her touch, and that seemed to make her happy.

Of course Dad drank too much. He toasted all the way through dinner, a couple of different toasts per course: to me, and my impending success as an actress; to Ginch, the greatest CPA in the world, a man who pays no taxes, and whose clients pay less; to Neil, the meanest son of a bitch in the shadow of the Alleghenys. At one point, when the lobster with linguini arrived, he stood up and ordered everyone in the restaurant to toast the chef.

And he toasted Shelley. He toasted her beauty, and her youth, and her sweet nature. He made a long point about how comforting it was to have a woman with a sweet nature finally in his life. He laughed this disgusting drunk laugh and pressed me to agree that if my mother and I shared one thing, it was that neither of us had a sweet nature.

There were three memories I had of my mother; in all of them she was screaming.

The first one was of her screaming at my father about speaking Italian to me. I was four; her face was bright red and she pounded the refrigerator with her fists before she sank down to the floor and slumped beside it and cried. She shouted that she couldn't even talk to her own kid, and shook her head so violently that she spattered me with tears.

It scared the hell out of me. Not only didn't I know what Dad was doing wrong (didn't everyone speak Italian and reserve their English for those who couldn't understand Italian?), but I couldn't figure out what was wrong with Mom that she didn't speak our language. Worse, I knew that her screaming and crying like that was going to make Dad so mad that it would be days before he'd speak to either of us.

The second memory was from when I was five. We'd all driven to New York City and Dad and I had gone off together to visit some artist in his studio. I saw the artist's paints and wanted to play with them. They let me; I slopped a little paint on a clean canvas, and a lot on me. Dad took off my clothes, so I wouldn't ruin them, and let me paint naked while he talked to the artist. Then, later, Dad and the artist helped me paint. We painted me: bright flowers all over my body, orange and purple and yellow and red. "A living canvas," they called me when every inch of me was covered; I thought I looked beautiful.

Later, when I stood in the hotel bathtub while Mom scrubbed me with a potato brush, I shouted at the top of my lungs because the brush hurt and my beautiful colors were fading away, down the drain. Dad stood at the bathroom door, listening to me, and to Mom screaming about lousy drunks painting a kid with toxic paint.

The last memory (I was six) was coming home from school and hearing her yelling: "How could you! You bastard!" and stuff like that over and over and over, getting louder as I neared the house. Dad left her screaming in the kitchen and took me out on the front porch. He brought a tin of anchovies, our favorite treat, to eat while we talked; I got the heads and he got the tails.

"Do you know your Dali House?"

My Dali House was my favorite thing to play with: a dollhouse with lots of rooms and windows and staircases and furniture (some on the ceiling), and no doors. Dad made it for me when I'd asked for a dollhouse and I played with it every day at the gallery, where we kept it. Yes, I nodded. I knew my Dali House.

"Well," said Dad, and fed me another anchovy head, "do you know how much five hundred dollars is?"

I shook my head.

"It's a lot of money, Mickey. It's how much money that someone paid me so that they could take the Dali House to their house."

"You sold my house?" I asked.

Yes, he said, he had sold it. But, he added, he had gotten so much money for it that we could go to the department store and he would let me pick out any doll-house I wanted. He said he'd take me to the store right then. He said I could even keep the new house in my room at home and I wouldn't have to go to the gallery to play with it. He said I would like having a regular little girls' dollhouse a lot more than I'd ever liked the Dali House. I wasn't sure I believed that last part, but I did know Dad was usually right. We finished the anchovies and went to Sears.

I must have seen Mom after that. I mean, she wouldn't have just left while we were at Sears. I remembered sitting on Judge Harris's lap and telling him that yes, Mom yelled a lot, and sure, it scared me, and that uh-huh, I wanted to stay in my own house with my own Daddy. So, I knew that there were arrangements made about me, and a divorce, and that must have taken time. It was just that I didn't remember seeing her after she threw the fit about the Dali House and we left for Sears.

It was a lot less scary coming home after Mom left. No one would be screaming and making Dad mad, and if you didn't make him mad, he was just fine. I knew, now that Mom was gone, I could make him happy. And I did, too. Most of the time. Every once in a while I'd still get mad and yell back at him, and then he'd hit me, but he was always sorry the next day, and we both knew that it was okay to just forget the incident.

"Sometimes I just have too good a time," was the way he'd apologize, meaning he knew that he'd had a little too much to drink and that had made him unreasonable. He'd scoop me up in his arms then and hug me and take me out to dinner or, if it was a bad incident, to the store to buy new clothes or toys or whatever he'd damaged along with hitting me.

We'd go on picnics in the mountains and hunt for Indian arrowheads. I learned later that Indian arrowheads did not lie around the mountainside like so many fallen leaves, and that when Dad said he was going off to relieve himself he was really going off to scatter the arrowheads he'd bought and brought along with him for me to find.

He'd taught me to dance, me standing on his feet while he whirled me around to the tunes of Frank and Dean Martin.

Every night after dinner we'd spun the globe and whatever country I'd picked with closed eyes, he told me about; or, he read me poetry by everyone from Eugene Field to Lawrence Ferlinghetti; or, we looked up funny long words in the dictionary and I tried to guess what they meant. As I got older I got paid for remembering things like a country's capital city, or the next line to a poem, or how to spell and define a particular word.

Later in the evenings, most evenings, Neil and Ginch and sometimes all their girlfriends or wives came over. Ginch tickled me and wrestled with me. Neil held me and rocked me and maybe told me a story. Dad supervised my washing up and kissed me and tucked me into bed.

───────────

The fight we'd had when I was fourteen was the one incident that we didn't forget.

I'd just lost my virginity, the night before, to a friend in a rather sad experiment, and I was trying to wash the blood out of my white bedspread.

"What happened?" he asked when he saw the stains. I was pulling the bedspread out of the washer and it hadn't come clean. He'd surprised me; it was late on a Saturday morning and I thought he'd already left for the gallery.

"Cutmyselfshaving," I said quickly.

He looked concerned.

"That's an awful lot of blood. Maybe we'd better take you to the emergency room. Let me see it."

"What?"

"The cut."

"NoI'mfine." And then I thought of a better lie: that I'd gotten my period in the middle of the night, in my sleep, and that was what had happened. He insisted on seeing the nonexistent cut on my leg, so I tried the better lie.

"Oh!Youmeanthis!Whathappenedhere!Well,Igotmy periodinthemiddleofthenightinmysleep,andI'msorry." This would usually shut him right up because he hated to talk about things like that—it made him queasy. But that time he just stood there looking at me and I felt my face getting hotter by the second.

"Jesus Christ," he said and grabbed my arm and dragged me off to the doctor.

We wouldn't know for a while if I was pregnant, the doctor said. We'd have to wait and see if I missed my next period, and if so, then I should come back in to be tested. Don't worry, Evaristo, he'd told my father, he'd perform the abortion, if necessary. Also, he'd said to me, if I was going to be sexually active, I'd better tell him so that he could put me on the pill.

My father, who was sitting in front of the doctor's desk, in the chair next to me, grabbed my arm.

"Tell Dr. Clark that you don't plan on being sexually active."

"Idon'tplanonbeingsexuallyactive," I said. Dad released my arm and it throbbed where he'd grabbed it.

Then Dr. Clark explained to my father that once teenagers starts experimenting with sex, it was rather optimistic to believe that they wouldn't continue and it was better to be safe than sorry. I thought my body was going to burst into flame as every drop of blood rushed to the surface.

When we left the doctor's office, Dad dropped me off in front of the house. I wasn't to leave, or to let anybody in. I was grounded.

"For how long?" I asked.

"For forever," he'd said and pushed me out of the car.

Late that night Dad came home. I'd had my light off for a few hours, but I still couldn't fall asleep, so I heard him park the car and come in the front door and go into his study, where I knew he was doing what he always did when he was both drunk and really mad: sitting in the dark, smoking a cigarette, listening to weird, sad Italian opera. Something soprano was drifting upstairs and I tried to let it lull me to sleep.

The aria would have put me out except that, undetected, Dad had come upstairs and kicked my bed and sent it, and me, crashing into the wall.

What he was saying, growling really, about my being

a tramp and that I should take my clothes off so that he could beat some sense into me, was lost on me. I was too concerned, as usual, with remaining as physically unhurt as possible.

First he grabbed me by the back yoke of my nightgown, and sat me up. He was holding the yoke so tightly that the neck of the nightgown was choking me. I gagged, and started to struggle, so he shoved me free and sent me flying across the room into my bureau. I landed on the floor.

"Get up!" He screamed and ran over to kick me, which he did until I was on my feet. The room was dark and my head was spinning and it took me a while to get my bearings and put the rocking chair between us. He lunged over it, screaming all the while, and caught me by the hair. He dragged me around the room and slapped my face and I dug my nails into his hand that was holding my hair. He let go, because I was digging into him hard, and threw me toward the rocking chair, which I tumbled over and took to the floor with me.

I lay on the carpet. He screamed for me to get up. I didn't. The pain in the rest of my body had given way to a whole new pain in the middle of my face. I had never felt such incredible pain.

"Get up!"

I didn't move. It was all I could do to hold my face and try to contain the pain with my hands.

I heard him switch on the light. "Get up, Mickey!" He was still ready to go at it, but when he turned me over and saw all the blood, he just gasped.

"I think I hit it on the arm of the rocking chair," I said when the pain had subsided a little. He filled the ice bag for me to hold on my swollen and bloody nose. Boy, was he sober now.

He sat down at the table. "All right. We'd better get you to the emergency room." His eyes rested on the ice bag I was holding on my face. "You'll tell the doctor that you were getting up to go to the bathroom and you didn't turn a light on, so you tripped over your rocking chair."

"I think we used that one before," I said to him.

"What do you want to tell them?"

"I'm not going to lie."

"Then I won't take you to the hospital," he said. His trump card.

"Fine," I said. Mine.

He sat with me, in the kitchen, in silence, until the dawn broke.

It turned out that I wasn't pregnant. I got my period two weeks later and I never said a word to him because he never asked and I didn't want to provoke him. My nose healed. There was a bump in the middle, and it was a little off-center, but it was not unattractive. Just different from what it had been. He didn't look at me much after that fight, so I'm not sure he really noticed the difference, although he never hit me again. He also forgot I was grounded and I became, gradually, sexually active, with the protection of a diaphragm I got at Planned Parenthood.

Anyway. I lifted my glass in a toast to Shelley-with-the-sweet-nature.

Neil helped my father to his car at the end of the evening and Shelley drove us home after Neil refused to let Dad in the driver's seat.

Early the next morning I heard Dad yell at Shelley

about not letting him drive and, so, offending his dignity. Then he went back to bed and drank the Bloody Marys Shelley had mixed for him and enjoyed his hangover.

Christmas Eve I got a Federal Express Overnight Letter from Florida. It read:

Dear Shrimpton,
If I could choose between a seven-course gourmet meal on the Concorde en route to Paris, and a pizza and Coke in your overheated apartment with you, I would undoubtedly choose the latter. If that's not true love, I don't know what is.

Merry Christmas,
Coyote

Even when Dad got punchy from too much spiked eggnog and practically ordered me to my room so that he and Shelley could open their presents to each other in privacy, I just reread that letter and felt good.

I noted: I was good enough to have this incredible person fall in love with me. I was happy. I was happier than I'd ever been. I was lying in my bed, holding the letter, when I got the feeling that I was floating, suspended above myself, and if I fell, it wouldn't matter because Coyote loved me, and I would be safe. I was working with a net.

I made a few calls and found a party going on among some friends from high school. I changed, and skipped out of the house, through the living room, calling out as I passed Dad and Shelley that I was taking the car. Dad and Shelley looked up from their heated embrace and watched me go.

Christmas Day began with Coyote's call, at six A.M.

"Where the hell have you been? I called you four times last night!"

"I was out. At a party."

"Do you have any idea what I have to go through to get out to call you? For Christ's sake, Mickey."

"I'm sorry."

"I was so worried. Do you know what I've been doing? I've been running along the beach for an hour, till I thought it was late enough to call you. I've just been running and shouting your name."

I tried to picture that.

"Really?"

"I don't think I could've stood to hear that girl tell me one more time that you weren't home yet. I've been up all night. Who is that chick that's been answering the phone?"

"My dad's girlfriend."

"Yeah, well, she's not too nice."

Again. "I'm sorry."

"Who were you out with?"

"Friends."

"Boyfriends?"

"Just friends, Coyote."

"Shrimpton . . . Mickey . . . you can't do this to me. You gotta wait."

"Coyote . . ."

"I'm telling Shelley I want the divorce. Will you wait for me?"

There was an edge of panic in his voice.

"Will you wait?"

"Oh, David." Of course I'd wait.

"Will you?"

"I'll wait."

There was such a long silence on the other end, and a lot of crackling of long-distance lines, I thought I couldn't possibly have heard that conversation correctly.

"Mickey," he said finally. "Baby, I love you. I mean, I really love you."

"I love you."

"I love your laugh, and your smile, and your big eyes, and your hips. I really love your hips."

"I love you."

"And I love that you're Italian, and I love that you're Catholic, and I love that you're an actress, and I don't know if I told you this but I'm real proud that you're going to do that play. Just don't let Hollywood steal you away from me."

"I love you so much."

When we hung up I floated down the hall to my father's room.

"Merry Christmas!" I beat on his door.

"Merry Christmas!" Shelley shouted back.

Shit. Shelley.

Dad came out of his room wrapping his robe around him, kissed the air around my right cheek, and started downstairs. Shelley followed him out of the room and tried to follow him downstairs.

"No." I stopped her.

"Aren't we going down to open the rest of the presents?" she asked.

"Not yet. Not until Dad turns on the tree and makes coffee and puts on Christmas music. He'll call us when he's ready for us."

"Well, why don't we go help him?"

"No, damn it, Shelley, it's our tradition! No one downstairs until he says so!"

It was our tradition Dad started because he hated people around him when he first woke up and he needed time on Christmas morning to prepare for people. Also, the Christmas I was three we were robbed and there were no presents in the morning and Dad needed to make sure it was Christmas downstairs before it could be for him. Before I could decide whether it would be more fun to hold Shelley upstairs against her will, or let her go downstairs to make Dad mad, he called for us.

There were a lot of presents that year, so I thought Shelley must have shopped. Usually all I got was something like a wallet with money in it. Christmases when Dad had a girlfriend, there usually were a lot of presents, and I was at the mercy of the girlfriend's various tastes.

The first present I unwrapped was a robe: a baby-pink flannel robe with snaps all down the front and lots of baby-blue kittens all over it. Now I was sure it was Shelley who'd done the shopping.

"I will, of course, exchange this," I said when I took it out of the box and held it up. Even Dad, who had asked me to be nice to Shelley, laughed when he saw it.

December twenty-sixth. Post-Christmas blues set in, along with a major snowstorm. Traveler's advisories were out and Dad's car was so stuck in the ice I walked the seven blocks to the drugstore for aspirin.

Shelley was worried because Dad wouldn't get out of bed; I told her that Dad never got out of bed the day after Christmas. December twenty-sixth was his day to recover from his Christmas drinking and get a good head up for his New Year's bout. She worried anyway and said that he was complaining about being numb.

"Look, Shelley, I'm hung over too. I'll go get the damn aspirin, but I really don't need to hear how lousy everyone else feels." I shoved my feet into snow boots. "Look, if a David Hellerman calls, tell him where I went, that I'm sorry I wasn't in, and to please call back later. Thank you."

I had to walk very slowly, even in snow boots, because of the ice and the many hills. Still, I fell twice into thick snowbanks made by the snowplows. When I got back, there was an ambulance parked in our driveway. I rushed inside, moving with dangerous speed up the icy steps. There was too much activity there and it put me in a sort of soft-focus, sensory-overloaded trance.

Dad had had a heart attack. I got that information from the paramedics. Shelley was frantic, crying, and she had a death grip on the stretcher that was carrying Dad through the living room, out to the ambulance. She crawled into the back with Dad. I shook my head to clear it.

"Wait," I said. "I have to go with you. The car's stuck and I have to ride with you." I jumped into the ambulance with my paper bag of aspirin. The equipment around Dad beeped; his eyes were closed and he was inhaling oxygen from a mask. Shelley knelt beside him, held his hand, and fretted. Dad looked gray and translucent and dead. Shelley looked worse.

"Has he had heart trouble before?" one paramedic asked.

"What?" Shelley looked up at him.

"A previous heart attack?" another paramedic clarified.

"I don't know," said Shelley, and looked to me. The paramedics looked to me, too, and I nodded.

"Four," I told them.

"Four?" said the first paramedic, and Shelley parroted, "Four?"

"Yeah. Four. He has them around Christmas, but he usually waits till after New Year's," I told them. They looked at me incredulously and I started to come out of my daze.

"I've never seen him have one before," I said. My eyes were starting to tear. "I mean," I continued, "he's always had them while I was in school, and afterwards, when I found out about them, he was already in the hospital, and getting better, so they didn't seem so creepy, like this one seems." I snorted to keep the snot from running down my face. "Are you sure it's a real heart attack? I mean, he just had one last year, and he never has them two years in a row."

I dissolved into my own pain, and when we got to Mercy Hospital a nun took me aside to comfort me.

"God damn it!" I yelled at Sister Mary Hubert. "You have no idea what I'm feeling, so stop trying to make me feel better!" Once, when I was six and had my tonsils out, I kicked a Sister of Mercy when she tried to draw blood from my arm. I wished I were six again, so I could get away with kicking that one.

The problem was, *I* had no idea what I was feeling. It occurred to me, in the ambulance, that if Dad died I would feel enormous relief. So I held on to my tension. From my chair in the waiting room, I willed him to live. I clenched my fists, rocked back and forth, and concentrated on Dad's life. I chanted, "Come on, Dad, come on, Dad," like a cheerleader for the Cardiac Care Unit. Each time a nurse came out of the CCU, I grabbed her and demanded information about my father. How was he?

When could I see him? When I grabbed the doctor by the lapels of his lab coat and ran him up against the wall after he told me that I couldn't see Dad, they sedated me.

Neil was standing by Dad's bed, joking.

"Couldn't wait a few more days, huh, Ev?"

"I guess my timing's off this year," said Dad. Underneath the bravado, I could see that he was terrified, and still awfully white, like the salt part of his salt-and-pepper hair.

"I brought the things you asked for," I said, and hoisted the suitcase I was carrying onto a chair.

"Finally," said Dad. "I feel as though I really should be dying in this." Dad tugged at the hospital gown with the hand that was not encumbered by IVs.

Neil and I waited in the corridor while Shelley helped Dad into a pair of pajamas.

"Did you talk to his doctor?" I asked.

"Yeah."

"Well?"

"Same thing. No more drinking. No more smoking. Relax, not get so angry. Eat regularly. Sleep a little."

"Well"—I thought about the way Dad lived—"if you tell him to eat, he gets angry. And the only time he'll sleep is when he's hung over."

"Yeah."

"So? What are you saying? There's nothing we can do? He's just going to keep having heart attacks?"

"Sometimes I'm grateful for the heart attacks," said Neil. "They're the only things that keep him alive. At least, in here, in the hospital, he lives a little better."

I wished that I could talk to Coyote. If I could talk to Coyote, I might feel a little more powerful against the fickle forces of my father's heart. But there was no way to call him, and I was spending all my days at the hospital. That whole first day I was there, except when I went back to the house to get his pajamas. On all the days that followed, I was at the hospital for all the visiting hours (eight A.M. to eleven A.M.; one P.M. to four P.M.; six P.M. to nine P.M.). Shelley and I were both required to be at the hospital. Neil was excused because someone had to run the gallery, and Ginch was excused because of his practice, but they were both there every evening. When Shelley and I had to leave the hospital, for lunches and dinners, we were required to run errands for Dad or relieve Neil at the gallery.

On the third day I made the mistake of asking for the afternoon off. I had also refused to bring Dad both rum and Camels. Shelley had not asked for any time off and she'd taken care of Dad's contraband needs.

By the fifth day I had gone from the status of loyal, dutiful daughter to being nonexistent. First, Dad showed me Shelley's offerings with a sneer of contempt for my disloyalty. Then he showed in every action (mostly his complete attention to her and his refusal to acknowledge that I was even in the room) that Shelley was now the favored one. It pissed me off.

"If she really cared about you, she wouldn't bring you that stuff. You don't see me or Ginch doing it. And you knew enough not to even ask Neil," I said to him, but he pretended not to hear.

Something ought to have existed to make me feel more powerful against my father's fickle nature.

On the sixth day, while Shelley had gone to renew

his television subscription, something he hadn't even asked me to do, we had the following exchange:

"I'm going to leave if you won't let me take care of you."

Dad had the TV on, staring at it as if I wasn't in the room. I didn't please him by being there but I would displease him if I left. Finally he spoke, in a soft, resigned voice.

"You're just like your mother."

"Dad, why are you pushing me away?"

"Like your mother."

"Is this a test?"

"Did I leave you when your mother left? No, I stuck by you, Mickey."

"I'm sticking by you."

"It's too much for you to even be here with me. No, you want to go running around somewhere. Did I go running around when your mother left? No, I stayed with you."

"You're my father. You're supposed to."

"I didn't have to!" He shouted this and it made both of us jump. Then he calmed again, reached for water, and when I tried to help him, he shoved my hand away. "I stayed and took care of you. Nobody else would, so I had to. That's called honor, Mickey. You ought to acquire some."

That was new. Before, when I threatened to leave we would have a fight that would end with "Go if you want to. Just don't bother coming back." I thought that saying that was just his way of hitting me, since my broken nose had made him fear actually hitting me. I wasn't prepared to deal with this if it went deeper.

"Dad, just say you want me to stay." I said that

hoping that maybe this time we could avoid the real fight and just reconcile. Maybe this time, because he'd said something so hurtful right up front, he'd want to reconcile right away too.

"Baby"—he said the word without affection—"I don't want you to do a damned thing. I didn't want you before you were born, but your mother said she was going to have you anyway, so I married her. Then she ended up not wanting either of us. Funny, huh? I got stuck with you, and I did what I had to do, and now you're nineteen and you can do any fucking thing you want."

I thought about it. There it was, that sense of relief again.

"I guess I'll catch a plane back to New York." He didn't say a word. "I mean, I'm not going to hang around here just to fight with you. I'm not going to stay if you're going to lie there and tell me all this stuff about how you never wanted me."

I said that in the most pathetic voice I could manage. Not that I wasn't feeling pathetic anyway. "Fine," he said.

I took a breath, to give him time to renege. When he didn't say anything, I said, "Fine," too.

I started to leave. Dad plumped a pillow behind his head. "If you leave," he started to say.

I interrupted. "If you say it, Dad, this time I will take you seriously."

"Finally!" He sat up in his bed and threw his arms up in the air. "I knew you weren't thick, just a little slow! Baby, don't come back. Got that?" He laughed with what seemed like the most intense and deliberate joy I'd ever heard, and I left.

Once, right after Mom left, when I was seven, I cried for her. It was right after Dad and I had our first fight. He'd grabbed me by the pink cotton T-shirt I was wearing and yanked me with such force that the T-shirt ripped right off me. It had shocked us both. I'd run to my room, slammed the door, and started to sob. I'd realized that, even if Mom screamed, when she was around Dad fought with her and not me.

He came into my room, and I told him in the nastiest voice I could muster through my tears that I wanted my mother back.

"Oh, Mickey." He gathered me up in his lap and rocked me in my rocking chair. "Baby, I have to tell you, it's just you and me, kid. And, well, maybe you should think of it . . . like your mom's dead. I mean, she's not, but she's not going to be around anymore, so you may as well think of it that way. Just, all gone. I mean, Mickey, if you can't have a mother around, there's no use wanting one."

In other words, as he told me when I was older and had come to him in tears because I hadn't made the cheerleading squad for Immaculate Mary's brother school: "Why make yourself miserable over things you can't change? It's unnecessary. Stop crying."

So I decided not to feel unnecessary feelings for my father. I was dangerously close to feeling them on the plane back to New York, but I made myself close my eyes and sleep.

Back in New York, I unpacked and studied my lines for the play, and bought a space heater because I was colder than I'd ever remembered being. And Coyote called. He was frantic.

71

"Six days you weren't home, Mickey! Where the hell were you? What are you doing in New York—you're supposed to be in Pennsylvania?"

"My father died."

That shut him up.

"Oh, Mickey. I'm sorry."

"It's okay."

"What . . . is there anything I can do?"

"No, I'm fine."

"I'm sorry I couldn't be there with you."

"Look, it's all right. Really. I'm just fine."

"But he was your father. When my father died . . . I just went to pieces."

"Well, I didn't."

"You think you're pretty tough, don't you?"

"Yep."

PART FIVE

Katie said my shaking was a delayed reaction to wrecking the car, so she'd taken over the driving. I rode in the passenger seat, watching my hands tremble. She said it was either a delayed reaction or I just couldn't handle being named Best Actress in a Soap, winning the biggest award given by *Daytime!*, soapdom's number one magazine. She said that if that were the case I probably wouldn't make it through the week ahead, picking up my award and dealing with the attendant publicity. She said this jokingly, but when she looked at me she reached over and took my hand.

"You think you can make it through, kiddo?"

Katie was only a few years older than me, but I loved it when she called me "kiddo."

"I don't know why it's so bad now, Katie."

I slumped in the passenger seat. I didn't know why, but whatever the reasons, there they were: the feelings that were unnecessary to feel, pushing, raw and demanding, and causing me to have to suck for air. Too much air.

"Katie . . ."

She pulled the car over, a tricky feat in any case on

the Pacific Coast Highway, but she did it while she was telling me, with well-modulated calm, to breathe into the Neiman-Marcus bag that she was emptying of my after-noon's purchases.

"It's okay, Mick," she said. She'd gotten the car parked in the Jetty's lot. "You're hyperventilating, that's all. Just breathe into the bag."

I nodded that I understood and sucked into the bag for more carbon dioxide. It was not the hyperventilating that worried me. It was the look of serious concern on Katie's face that upset me more than any of the ditsy things I'd been doing lately.

"You weren't kidding, were you, kiddo?" she said.

No, Katie, I wasn't kidding. I wasn't happy. And the worst part about not being happy was that my life was going so well and I was supposed to be happy. Look how long it took you, my best friend, to be concerned about what appeared to be this terrific life. I fucked everything up real good a while back, and I'm sorry if it seemed like I was whining, but I just couldn't get comfortable with the way things had turned out.

Of course, I didn't say these things to her, because I was still gasping into the Neiman-Marcus bag.

Ben was on the phone when Katie and I arrived at the house. Either Ben was irritated or he was speaking with someone he considered important, because he wouldn't stop the conversation to greet us. He turned his back on us as we entered, lowered his head, and stuck the forefinger of his free hand into his ear to indicate that he was concentrating.

Katie dropped her suitcases on the living room floor and walked out onto the terrace that overlooked the ocean at Malibu, and breathed in deeply. Katie loved the view from this house, the air around the ocean. She was the type of person who derived energy from the water, who could jog barefoot on the beach and enjoy the sweaty, salty, sandy sensation.

I joined Katie on the terrace, but the view and the ocean air couldn't affect me because I wasn't the sort of person easily affected by externals. Also, I had said Coyote's name aloud that afternoon, verbalized it for the first time in a long while, and that was what was affecting me, making me alternately chilly and anxious, warm and light.

Through the glass doors of the terrace I watched Ben on the phone. Ben was a big man. Physically big. He was six foot one, but slouched to six even. He weighed about one ninety-five, but he carried himself like a ton, on large splayed flat feet. Years ago, when I'd first moved in with him, he'd assured me that I'd get over Coyote. In time, he'd said, the pulls toward Coyote would diminish, and it would be as easy to forget him as it was easy to forget anything that was dead.

How could I tell him, after all our years, that Coyote was still not dead?

Ben took the finger out of his ear to munch on a hangnail.

No. The pulls toward Coyote hadn't diminished at all.

Ben hung up the phone and waddled out to join Katie and me on the terrace. He kissed Katie. Me, he handed a copy of *People* magazine, the new one that had just hit the stands, the one in which an interview with me was to appear.

"Page one-oh-four," said Ben, and when I got to that page, Katie said, "That's a great picture!"

It was. I was tanned and wearing a black T-shirt and my hair was blowing around my head. I was looking over my shoulder, smiling at the camera like it was just the two of us in on a delicious secret.

"A guy named Frank Bennett took it one day a few months ago, out on Zuma Beach. I should call him and thank him. . . ."

There were three inserts: one was of me as Lacey Martin, the character I played on *Our Time to Live,* with my TV husband, hunky Jeremy Schaffer, clowning around on the set of the soap; one was the poster that I did wearing a pink one-piece that was slit to my pubic bone; one was of me and Ben (who, it was prominently mentioned in the caption, was both my manager *and* my live-in lover) attending one or another of the parties we constantly attended.

"I'm not entirely happy about this." Ben jammed his finger into the fold of the magazine.

"What? The picture?"

"The whole interview."

"What did they print?" What did I fuck up this time? Ben had been telling me that this interview, short as it was, was for a national, nonsoap magazine, and that therefore it was a very big deal. And now he was saying that he wasn't entirely happy about it. Sometimes, when he got mad, Ben understated things, for emphasis. I found understatement terrifying when it concerned my possible fuck-ups. I could feel my mouth drying out.

"Just read it, Mick. I gotta get my hair cut before the party tonight and Rosalie said she'd squeeze me in if I can get right over there."

"Is that who you were on the phone with?"

"Yeah, why?"

"Never mind."

Ben rushed to leave, grabbing his keys. Katie and I settled on the terrace with the magazine. Ben clomped down the stairs to the garage and I heard his footsteps stop, pivot, and clomp upward. "Mickey," he hollered, "what the hell happened to your car?"

He appeared at the terrace door. "Are you all right, babe?"

"I love you, Clint. I always have. I always will. There is nothing you can say that will change that."

Those are the words that Lacey Martin uses to stop her philandering husband from telling her about his latest infidelity. The actress who plays Lacey on daytime's *Our Time to Live*, Micci Azzi, fixes an adoring look on the actor who plays Clint, Jeremy Schaffer, and holds it for a close-up.

When the director has yelled "CUT!" Micci grabs Jeremy by the lapels and jerks his face close to her own. "Unless, of course, you are going to tell me you've been screwing around again, in which case, you bastard, I will cut your balls off."

"Just another case of you rewriting the script to suit your own inclinations," jokes Jeremy while the rest of the cast and crew break into laughter.

While Micci takes a moment to confer with the director, I use the time to get to know her better through her co-star, Jeremy.

"What can I tell you about Micci? Let's see. You mean aside from the fact of her well-earned reputation as cast clown? She's just a knockout. You know, lots of fun. And very talented."

Soap fans seem to agree with his last adjective. Micci has just been voted Best Actress by the readers of *Daytime!* magazine, the soap fan's bible. It is her first such award after four years of portraying Lacey Martin, daytime's reigning saint.

"I think that the reason I was even considered for the award this year is because Lacey's not such a saint anymore. She's finally getting to do meatier things than just stand in the background and react to a crisis. She's more of a catalyst now. In general, though, it feels good to be building a reputation as someone who's good at my craft. It's nice to be noticed."

And Micci wants to be noticed, preferably by a whole new audience.

"It's not that I don't like playing Lacey. It's just that, even with the changes we're making with the character, there's very little challenge left in the role after four years. Moreover," says Micci, "I'm ready to play someone a little more human. I've brought Lacey through two marriages, three long-term affairs, brain surgery, her husband's murder trial, and a bout with multiple personalities, not to mention all the various and sundry peripheral dramas, all in the course of a few years. Like, one week Lacey has a miscarriage, and the next week her major concern in life is keeping a surprise birthday party a surprise. No human could possibly have the emotional resiliency of a soap character. I'd like the challenge of trying to build a character's emotional response and sustain her emotional mood."

Does this mean she'll be leaving *OTTL*?

"Not in the immediate, foreseeable future. But, sometime, I'd like to go back to New York and work with Katie again."

Micci began her career as an actress in New York, in productions like *Hedda Gabler* and *Hotel Universe*, under the direction of New York University drama instructor Kate Barrows. That was five years ago, and they have been best friends ever since.

"There's not many people you meet who you can stand to be around for an extended period of time," says Micci. "You meet someone you can, and you should hang on for dear life. I guess Katie and I can stand to be around each other longer than we can stand to be around almost anyone else."

Kate has also been a guiding force in Micci's career, encouraging her to model in the ads that got her noticed by the producers of *OTTL*, arranging her audition for the show, and even introducing her to Ben Townsend, her manager and long-time boyfriend. Micci and Ben share "a small house, up in the hills by Malibu."

About Ben, Micci says, "We have a very comfortable relationship."

What about marriage? "The subject never comes up."

It's clear that, while Micci loves talking about her career, she's not too keen on talking about her personal life. This is the information I was able to gather from her: Her parents were divorced when she was very young, and she "sort of lost touch" with her mother. She lived with her father in Pittsburgh, Pennsylvania, where he owns an art gallery and she attended Immaculate Mary Academy, a Catholic girls' high school. Soon after she graduated, she moved to New York to become an actress. She and her father "no longer speak."

The interview went on, but I couldn't.

"We no longer speak!" I smirked. "How could we speak?"

"Did you tell the interviewer that he's dead?"

"No."

"You usually forget to mention that."

"I'll tell you, Katie. Things don't sound half as bad when you say them as they look in print." And then I got a burst of energy and threw the magazine over the terrace railing. It landed in a growth of bushes, cover up, some twenty feet down.

Katie spoke slowly, carefully, like I was a risk. Like I was going to start hyperventilating again, or hit her, or throw myself off the terrace.

"Mickey, please tell me what happened."

"Oh, for Christ's sake . . ."

"For four years you have bitched about your work, and Los Angeles, and Ben. All that time I've been telling you to leave, to come back to New York, to do whatever you had to do to make yourself happy, and you didn't. You said you could handle things. And then you went out and proved you could handle things. What happened that all of a sudden you're out of control and you have to ask me to come out here and help and I come and I find you like this?"

I folded my arms across my chest. It was boiling outside and my fingers were like ice.

"Sometimes," I said, "when you think you've got yourself all settled and secure, something wakes you up

80

and makes you wonder how much you just settled." I got up and walked into the house and pulled out the book that I kept hidden behind another row of books in the bookcase. I went back out on the terrace and placed the book in Katie's lap and sat down.

Katie picked up the book. It was Coyote's latest, the first for him that had reached a popular audience, a critical look at the cinema of John Frankenheimer.

"I found it in a bookstore I was in, a few months ago. Open it."

She did, right to the two-page spread where it said, in the middle of the right-hand page, simply "To M.M.A."

"I sure didn't stick around long enough to expect that," I said and took the book from Katie and opened it to the middle. I sniffed deeply. It smelled like Coyote.

"Pugnacious. Belligerent. Cold." Ben was in the bathroom trimming his beard, reciting a litany of my shortcomings as they would be perceived by those who would read the interview. "Pompous. Arrogant. Unprofessional."

Every pair of black panty hose I pulled out of my panty hose drawer had a run in them.

Ben sat down on the bed to put on his boots and socks, which he always put on before he put on his pants. I found this habit either endearing or irritating, depending on my mood and if he ripped out any hems trying to get a pant leg over a boot heel.

"What do you have to say for yourself, Mickey?" he asked as he pulled on his pants. No ripped hems, but I was in a foul mood.

"What do you want me to say? I fucked up. Are you happy?"

I found a left leg and a right leg that were intact, cut off their opposite legs, and made them a pair of panty hose.

"What's that?" Ben pointed at my legs.

"Who's going to know?" I asked.

"Mickey, we're going to Rod Adelman's party. You think you could've bought a new pair of stockings."

"Well, if I'd realized I didn't have a whole pair, I probably would've." Ben looked at me like he was trying to decide what to do about my panty hose.

Katie knocked at the door. "Can I come in?"

"Sure," I called.

Ben whistled. Katie whirled around like she was Cheryl Tiegs. She looked great in a hot hot-pink taffeta cocktail dress. "I just mixed up something decadent in the blender. Wanna join me for a drink?"

I slipped my basic black number over my head. "On my way. Coming, Ben?"

"In a minute," he said as he went into the walk-in closet. "By the way, Mickey, have you seen my tan cashmere jacket?"

See, Ben was a poor-boy-made-good. Not that I was a rich-girl-made-better, but Ben seemed to think that traces of polyester still lingered on his skin, and he continually had to reinforce his image or he would be found out. Like, he never called his car his car; he called it his Rolls. He never called his watch his watch, he called it his Rolex. He never just described an item of clothing without adding that it was cashmere, or silk, or one hundred percent something.

Most of the time, when he did those things, I just thought that, well, it was good he lived in Los Angeles, because everybody in Los Angeles was pretty verbally ostentatious. But other times, like when he did those things in front of my friends and embarrassed me and made my friends feel obligated to give me looks of commiseration behind his back, I just went off the wall.

Katie shook her head when Ben disappeared from view and shrugged her shoulders as if to ask what-can-you-do-with-him-anyway?

I walked into the closet, pulled the jacket off its hanger, and handed it to him.

"Ben, please don't find a way to announce tonight that you are wearing cashmere, because I'll tell you, if someone doesn't know it's cashmere just by looking at it, they are not the kind of people who care if it's cashmere. Also, it's tacky to use more than one adjective to describe any item of clothing because it makes you seem like a clotheshorse. Also," I said as I left the closet, "I am tired of wondering if people know it's just you, or if they think I'm an asshole too."

Katie poured two tumblers full of frothy pink liquid.

"Ummm! This is good! What did you put in here?"

"Mostly strawberries."

"And rum."

"And vodka."

"God, it's good."

Katie topped the drinks with fresh strawberries, and we stood, leaned on the island in the kitchen to drink them.

"Think you got Ben to behave tonight?"

"I'm sorry you had to hear that."

Katie waved her hand like it was nothing. "I'm onto Ben, remember? I was here the night when we barbecued and he announced the price of the meat to everybody."

"Oh, God, Katie, why do you remind me of those

things? Do you know Jeremy asked me when he was leaving that night if he should give Ben money? I knew he was joking, but . . . I'll never forgive you for introducing me to him."

"I didn't think you'd go out with him, let alone move in with him."

"Do you understand why I'm with him?"

"No. But did you understand why I was married to a fag?"

"No."

Katie picked a strawberry out of her drink and studied it.

"Do you know why strawberries are so sensual?"

"Why?"

"Because they look like the heads of penises." She sucked on her strawberry for a long second before she bared her teeth and bit it in half.

"So," said Katie while she wiped strawberry juice from her chin, "you seem in better spirits since we talked."

"Confession's good for the soul."

"Short-term. What's the solution?"

I poured more of the pink liquid into our glasses.

"Look, Katie, I admit that my lucid moments are fairly rare these days, but when I have them, I know that whatever I do, I can't do something rash. Just on a practical level, I can't go to New York now. I've got the show. Lacey's on trial for murdering her father's wife, for God's sake. I've got to stay at least until she's acquitted. I'll just tough things out."

"It's hard to leave someone. No matter how badly you want to."

"Will you stop doing that?"

"What?"

"Reading my mind."

"Mick, I know that this will sound silly to you, but I'm worried. These things you're doing . . . you must think they're more than just isolated incidents or you wouldn't have called me and begged me to come out here and take care of you."

"You think I'm losing it in a big way, right?"

"Don't act like this is nothing. . . ."

"It isn't nothing!" I screamed back at her. "I know it isn't nothing! I'm the one that's living it, don't forget, and I'm scaring the piss out of myself!" I lowered my voice and forced out my words, kept my eyes open wide so that my tears wouldn't streak my makeup. "Do you know how much I would give to kiss someone that I really want to kiss? Something simple like that has me up all night just imagining it. But I know, when I'm up all those nights, all I have to do is reach over, and Ben's *there*. Maybe he's a jerk sometimes, but he's always *there*. Maybe I don't think I'm madly in love, but what does that mean, anyway? Maybe I'd like to go back and fuck Coyote's brains loose, but what would that get me?"

When I first started going to those parties, I was just the new blonde on some soap opera. I would turn a few heads, but the heads would stay turned only as long as it took them to not recognize me. When I got introduced around, hands would clasp mine, but even as the hands clasped, the eyes would be spinning in their sockets, searching the room for someone more important with whom to make contact.

Possibly because there was rarely anyone more important in the room than himself, Rod Adelman always looked you in the eye when he talked to you. This flattered (as well as intimidated) most people with whom he talked. He was the president of the network that aired my show, and I regarded him as a true Tinseltown treasure.

"Hi, Rod."

"Mickey!" For some reason, Rod had always had a special affinity toward me; he stretched out his arms to welcome me into his home. He held a drink (seltzer) in one hand, and a cigar (unlit) in the other and he embraced me as best he could. If Ben was a poor-boy-made-good, then Rod was a poor-boy-made-great, and he himself could still not believe it. He ushered me into the lavish Spanish-style palace he called home.

"How's my girl?"

"Nervous, Rod."

"You're always nervous. You shouldn't be nervous. You should relax. This is my house—I want you to relax. So, what do you think?"

Unlike Ben, whose origins mortified him, Rod liked acknowledgment that he'd made his dreams come true. "We just redecorated. Not bad, huh?" He swept the hand that held the cigar around to indicate the party scene, one of prime-time soap opulence. He put the arm that held the drink around my shoulder. "Loosen up, Mickey!" He massaged my right shoulder with his thumb.

"Rod, the party's kinda for me, and it's a little hard . . ."

The party was to celebrate the sweep his network's soaps had made in the awards this year. The awards were a real coup for his underdog daytime lineup, proof that his massive shake-up of the daytime department last year had been a success, and he wanted everyone to know. The press was all there.

"You need a drink," said Rod, and swept me off to the bar. I paused to grab Katie's arm and drag her with us.

"Rod, I want you to meet Kate Barrows. Katie, Rod Adelman."

"Good." Rod took Katie's arm in his free hand. "Now I can buy *two* gorgeous girls a drink."

I wasn't the new blonde on some soap anymore. I was one of its stars. I was one of the guests of honor at Rod Adelman's party. A steady stream of well-wishers kept separating me from Ben (who was hustling deals) and Katie, who loved parties and had totally captivated Rod, much to the chagrin of his girlfriend. Jeremy came over to rescue me from a short, dark little man who'd felt no need to introduce himself to me before he launched into a windy appraisal of my virtues.

"Who was that?" I asked.

Jeremy shrugged. "Probably someone important." He was sloshed, which surprised me because I didn't think he drank.

"Nerves," he said.

"You too?" I gulped my third straight vodka.

"Jesus, Mickey, it's not just this party. The movie airs this week."

Yeah. The movie. It was a made-for-television movie and it was truly great. It would probably catapult Jeremy out of the soap for good. It would probably mean that Lacey would soon be a widow or I'd have to get used to calling some other actor Clint. I hugged Jeremy and hoped that Clint would die.

"Just ease up tonight. The movie doesn't air until Thursday."

"Oh, God, don't remind me."

"What?"

"That I'm up against Bill Cosby."

"Can I ask you a serious question?"

"Mickey, I'm really drunk. . . ."

"No, listen, I want to know. How do you—how do you find the time to worry about things like that? Like, the peripheral things? I get all worn out just worrying if the people who see it will like what I do. How can you worry about what the people who don't see what you do will watch? I know people do that all the time out here. Ratings. But I figure, ratings are Rod's worry. That's *his* job. If I worry about them, on top of my own worries, I can't function. Like, I have to delegate some worries and trust other people to worry about them, or I'd . . . I'll just . . . I couldn't do it."

Jeremy hugged my neck and giggled. "You're drunk, too, aren't you, Mick?"

I gulped down another drink.

"You okay?"

"Yup. Why?"

"Just checking."

"Katie, I feel great!"

I did feel great. I was high. And because I was high, I was chatting people up like I was Barbara Walters. I was talking to practically anybody about practically anything. It was so much easier to find interesting things to say to people when all they wanted to talk about was you. The stupid award was setting me free! I was saying "thank you" every other minute.

Someone handed me another drink.

"Thank you." I didn't know who he was, but I hugged him for bringing me a drink.

"Mick." Katie steered me toward a quiet corner. "Maybe you'd better not have that." She tried to take my glass away.

"No!" I whined. "Why?"

"Because you're starting to hug the waiters."

I found this unbearably funny and while I laughed, Katie grabbed my vodka. She left to find a surface on which to get rid of my drink and I grabbed another from a passing tray. I gulped. Scotch. I didn't drink scotch, usually, but that stuff was pretty good. What the hell, I was celebrating; I guzzled the scotch too.

"Adrienne!"

I reached out to hug Rod's girlfriend. Adrienne didn't like to hug too tight, or kiss at all, because she worried it would smear her makeup, so I grabbed her good and gave her a big sloppy kiss on the cheek.

"Adrienne, don't be such a tight-ass," I remembered shouting when she pulled away.

We sat in Rod's powder room, surrounded by Rod's collection of Victorian seashell boxes. I sat on the toilet and Katie sat on the sink.

"Katie . . ." I rested my head on my knees and whined.

Katie fussed around me, trying to get the compress she'd made from a linen guest towel on my forehead. "Look up. Here." She clamped the dripping thing to my face. "Do you have to throw up again?"

I shook my head.

"Do you think you can go out now?"

I shook my head.

"Mickey, honey, we've been in here for twenty minutes. Look. You just lean onto me and we'll go right to the car."

"I can make it to the car on my own. I just don't want to."

"Mickey . . ."

"What's the worst thing I did?"

"You made a scene with Rod's girlfriend."

"What did I say?"

Rod knocked on the door. "All's right in there?"

"All's right, Rod. Thanks," I called.

"Good, good," he muttered.

"What did I say, Katie?"

"Nothing. Don't worry," she replied.

"Katie, I feel like a real shit. Should I?"

"I guess so."

I did have to throw up again. Ben pulled over and I tried to lean out the passenger side window and get as much as I could out onto Wilshire Boulevard.

"Tissue," I commanded.

But neither Katie nor Ben had one, so Ben gave me the tie from around his neck. "That's one hundred percent silk," he said and put his head on the steering wheel and shook it back and forth.

PART SIX

R oy Lichtenstein said: ". . . form is the result of unified seeing." Of course he was talking about his art, life reduced to its simplest and purest lines. However, if I saw my life in a unified way, perhaps I could give it form.

I was hanging out at the Whitney a lot, waiting for rehearsals to begin for *Hotel Universe,* and for Coyote to come home from Florida. Maybe that idea of Roy's could apply: simply and purely, my lines were acting and Coyote. If I used just those two graceful strokes and their accompanying bright colors, my life could make a brilliant piece of art.

I had yet to be exposed to Lee Krasner and his theory concerning the mystery of painting: that even when you intend to paint a blue picture, it sometimes comes out alizarin.

Coyote just kept telling me to hang on, he'd be back in New York soon. He called at least three times a day to tell me that, and every day there were at least two postcards in my mailbox. They said things like: "Darling, I haven't stopped thinking about you for a minute," and

"Baby, I miss your face," and finally, "My plane arrives JFK, 6 January. I can be at O'Neal's at ten P.M. Can you?"

Of course I could! Of course I could! Of course I knew Coyote never expected a regret to that invitation.

Seven-thirty A.M., 6 January, Epiphany: two and a half hours before my first rehearsal; fourteen and a half hours before Coyote came home. I was sitting at my kitchen table wrapped in my robe, drinking my second cup of coffee, trying to contain my fear, my joy, and decide what to wear.

I opted for black wool tights, purple cowboy boots, my denim miniskirt, and a big bulky-knit sweater that contained all the colors of a midnight rainbow.

Then I sat down to reread *Hotel Universe,* and all my lines that I already knew by heart, because there was nothing else to do and I had to do something.

I've got to say, Kate Barrows scared me when we first met, at the auditions for the company a month earlier. And at the first rehearsal, the imposing blonde in the spotless white wool jumpsuit who sat on the edge of the stage, her legs wrapped in fine, cream-colored leather boots and dangling into the orchestra pit, intimidated me no less. And it wasn't just her looks (which were absurdly perfect), nor her attitude (one of innately casual confidence), nor her knowledge (which seemed limitless). It was the whole package that was Kate Barrows, which, while it didn't inspire envy, was singularly enviable.

We, the actors, assembled in the first few rows of the theater. When Katie saw that we were all there, she stopped her conversation with the stage manager, who sat in the theater directly facing her, and began.

"I'm Kate Barrows. In case any of you don't remember, I'm the director. Being director means that I have ultimate responsibility for this company. It means that it's my ass on the line. In order to meet my responsibilities, and protect my ass, I need your full cooperation. The only reason I will accept from any of you for not giving me your full cooperation is death. Your death."

She paused a moment, to let us assess our devotion. One of the other actors laughed out loud, and it made Katie smile. Then she passed out thick blue notebooks and Xeroxed copies of the play.

"In these notebooks," she continued, "you'll find a brief biography of Philip Barry. For those of you who are illiterate, he wrote this play." There was also a complete listing of Barry's plays; Katie approached directing the way she approached her theater history classes at NYU. "If you can't find these plays in the libraries or bookstores, you aren't looking. However, I do have them in my office, so, rather than not read them, ask me to lend you a copy."

She took in a gulp of air and squared her shoulders. "Philip Barry wrote two sorts of plays. He's known for the first sort, the sophisticated social comedies, like *The Philadelphia Story*. Light pieces, they're often overburdened by their own cleverness. And very worldly.

"For example, in *Paris Bound*, Barry proposes that too much importance is placed on marital fidelity. According to the author, a couple has no right to break up their marriage, and ruin the happiness of their children, just because one of them slipped into somebody else's sheets and now the other's pride is hurt.

"Personally, I think Barry's a little too obvious with these plays. Too manipulative.

93

"But the second group of plays, the imaginative plays, are Barry at his best. This is where he shines! *Hotel Universe* is one of the most important dramas in the genre and, I believe, Mr. Barry's most distinguished work."

Here Katie grew passionate, standing and striding around the stage as she made her point, her passion humanizing her immensely in my eyes. I alternately leaned forward in my seat, eager to catch her every word, and slunk low in my chair, afraid I'd disappoint her passion with my amateur attempt at Ann, the main character.

"In *Hotel Universe*, Mr. Barry abandoned social comedy and tried to communicate his knowledge of what it means to be alive, his vision of what life can be. There is magic in this play. A beauty that is so pure it's unreal. This play, if it's done right, has the power to engage an audience's emotions as very few plays can." Katie, you could tell, was pumped for this opportunity.

"The characters in this play are restless, obsessive, seeking to relieve their present sufferings by reliving their pasts. Suicide, death: these are constantly recurring themes, but this play is about hope. Life continuing."

Here Katie sat again on the edge of the apron. "The characters Barry created are patterned after those rebellious young people of the post–World War One period. Distrustful of permanency, desperate for purpose, your characters have not yet found an abiding home for themselves.

"In order for you to better understand them, I've given you a list of books and articles, concerning the period around 1929, the south of France, the city of Toulon. Please read them. Again, I will make copies available to you if you are unable to locate them."

Additionally, in our notebooks, were rehearsal schedules and a performance schedule and the dates and times we were expected to be available for costume fittings.

Katie brushed her hair back from her face with one long-fingered hand.

"In the play, your characters wear evening clothes, appropriate to their time, so you'll all want to make a trip to the theater's wardrobe closet when we're done here and find some suitable rehearsal clothes.

"I expect you all off book by Friday. And I'll expect, from now on, you'll arrive a half hour before any sched- uled rehearsal to warm up. Today we'll have our first read-through and tomorrow I'll start giving you your block- ing. Any questions?"

Questions? It seemed to me that Kate Barrows had covered everything quite clearly and the fact that every one of us was overwhelmed by her was no excuse for not understanding her.

"Let's get up on stage then and warm up," said Katie.

She took us through a series of physical and vocal exercises, pairing us off with each of the other actors for any given exercise, so that we might begin to know each other.

I found myself face to face for a mirror exercise with my lover in the play, Pat Farley, played by a slight but sturdy-looking redhead named Jamie Miller. The mirror exercise, with one person gesturing and the other aping the first person's movements, was designed to promote trust between actors. Jamie was making it difficult for me to follow his movements by jerking his limbs, or turning too quickly.

"You're missing the point of this exercise," I said finally, frustrated.

"I don't think so," he replied. "I'm not sure Ann is supposed to trust Pat."

When it was my turn to lead Jamie, we moved together in almost perfect unison.

"Question," I said to Jamie when rehearsal was over and I'd found out he'd worked with Katie before. "Is she always so . . . intense about details when she directs?"

Jamie laughed. "I worked with her when she directed some episodes of *Our Time to Live*, that soap opera—you know it?"

"Vaguely," I replied.

"It taped in New York then. I guess, oh, a year or so ago, it moved to L.A. Anyway, I was supposed to do a character for three days. A sailor. And when she found out I'd never sailed before, she arranged for me to crew for one of her friends the weekend before we taped. Yeah, I'd say she's always fairly intense."

I was at O'Neal's at nine-thirty, sitting at a back table in the dark downstairs room, alone, waiting, hoping that every time someone entered it was Coyote coming in. By 10:10 I'd had three kirs and had worked myself up into an almost unbearable state of anticipation. That was when he walked in.

Something kept me in my seat: the way he entered the bar, slowly, and sauntered to my table as if it were just another meeting and not a reunion-at-long-last.

"Hi, Shrimpton," he said and sat down. His voice had lost its urgent edge, and his body looked resigned too. He stared at me.

"What's wrong?" I felt like I was walking on the San Andreas Fault.

"I told you I was married" was what he said, as if that should explain everything.

"Yeah. So. What does that mean?"

"It means Shelley knows I'm here. She knows why I'm here. The night we get back from vacation, ten o'clock, and I've got to run out . . . I told her I want the divorce and she's really hurt."

"Look," I said, partially, and practically speaking, unable to understand this new attitude after three weeks of passionately professed love, "so, now she knows. . . ." He had to tell her sometime, didn't he?

"You don't understand. . . ."

"If you're going to tell me that . . . if you're going to dump me, I better tell you that I don't want to be dumped."

Coyote blinked his eyes and broke into a grin.

"I missed you, Shrimp."

"Yeah, I missed you too. Now explain all this shit you're handing me."

He ordered a kir from the waiter who'd come to the table, and breathed in deeply, as if he were steeling himself for pain. I was the one who should have had the bullet to bite.

"Shelley," he said, "told me that if I left her she would hire the best attorneys in the country to make sure that I would never see the kids again."

Kids?

"Kids?" I said. "You never mentioned kids."

"Two. Jane and Maggie."

"Jane and Maggie."

"And if I leave, Shelley says I'll never see them again."

"Your two kids . . ."

"Right, two. Look, I know that she won't be able to

97

carry out a threat like that. I know fathers have rights. I'll just—Mickey, are you listening to me?"

I nodded.

"I'll just need a little more time than I thought. I just need more time to make sure that things are . . . handled, you know, the way that they should be handled."

"I think," I said and got up from the table, "that if you have a girlfriend, Shelley's got a stronger case against you."

I left O'Neal's.

"What was that all about?"

It was 10:45. Coyote had followed me home and was storming around my apartment.

"Shock. I think I'm in a little shock. Kids, Coyote?"

"I told you I was married! Didn't you just assume I had kids too?"

"No."

"Well, that's not my fault."

"What?"

"Well, okay, maybe I should have just told you."

"Yeah. Maybe. That might have been nice."

"So, you want out now that you know I have kids?"

"It's not that. . . ."

"What is it?"

"Are there any more major bombshells you've got hidden from me?"

"Well, that's certainly a trusting attitude."

"Give me something to trust."

The kids. Two. Jane and Maggie.

Time. Because of the kids, Coyote would need more time.

He was going to tell Shelley that he wanted the divorce that they'd already talked about and that meant (didn't it?) that we would be together. That he was coming home to me. That we would leave O'Neal's together and go back to my apartment together and begin our life together.

But he had kids and that was going to complicate the situation. He couldn't just leave them, could he? Of course he could, if he didn't have Shelley to pacify. God, she must have really been in love with him, which was understandable. Or, she must have been desperate to keep a husband. Why would a woman want a husband who obviously wanted someone else?

I pointed out, as I caught his rage and stalked around the apartment, that putting kids in the middle of a divorce decision was probably the sickest thing anybody could do.

So, I asked, how much time was he going to need?

He shrugged solemnly to indicate his understanding of how much time he would need, and he left my apartment without making love to me, with me screaming after him that he could take all the goddammed time he wanted because I didn't want someone I couldn't trust in my life.

"I think Ann's in love with Pat. Very much in love. But she felt obligated to follow her father to Toulon and help him recover from his illness. She feels isolated there— she is isolated there—and she's overjoyed that her friends, and Pat, have come to visit."

Katie and I were sitting in a little café in the West Village where we were going over the play, line by line, developing a history for Ann, an understanding of Ann, that would give meaning to her every word.

"The visit," I continued, "isn't everything Ann wanted it to be, though. Her friends are all wrapped up in their sorrow—the death of some boy they met in Antibes. And Pat—he's still wrapped up in this guilt for leaving another girl and causing her to kill herself.

"Ann feels useful, taking care of her father. And she loves him, so she doesn't resent that her place is with him. But she's lovely and bright and she knows that she's fading away at that house with him. Pat's her escape, and she's his, and he won't have her."

"Well," said Katie, "I think that that's a good start. . . ."

"I think Ann's awfully weak. She's willing to settle for someone who doesn't want her."

"Well," said Katie again. "That's an interesting way to look at her."

My respect for Katie was growing in direct proportion to my enthusiasm for this process she was taking me through. When we were done for the afternoon there were four empty iced-espresso cups sitting in front of each of us, and my big blue notebook was half filled with insights into Ann.

"Kate, I've never worked so hard in my life. It feels so good." I hugged her with my whole heart, and I guess I expected her to, kindly, disdain my exuberance.

Instead, she said, "You're very talented, Michele," and hugged me back.

We met at McAnn's or O'Grady's, one of those Irish dives that seem to be on every corner in Manhattan. He sat me at a table, and sat across from me to speak.

"My mother lives in Florida. Sarasota. She lives with a nurse who takes care of her because she's just about as senile as anyone could be. She doesn't recognize me half the time and she has no idea who Jane or Maggie are. My father," he continued as he handed me a Xeroxed copy of an obituary, "was a highly respected surgeon in Michigan. I was very close to him." He paused to let me read the praise-laden article, then added, "He died seven years ago. To give you an indication of the kind of relationship I have with my wife, when he died she refused to go to the funeral. She doesn't like funerals. So."

We ordered Budweisers from the waitress.

"Jane is eight. She's in third grade at Dalton. That's one of the best schools in the city. My dad left me some money. Not a lot. I take care of my mother and send my kids to good schools. Maggie. She's four, in preschool. Jane is beautiful and serious. Maggie looks like me and is so happy she practically floats everywhere she goes."

Coyote poured his beer: left the glass flat on the table, picked up the bottle, and tipped it almost upside down so the liquid sloshed and foamed into the glass. He slurped at the suds that were bubbling out, over the rim.

"I"—he licked off his foam moustache—"am an only child. Now you know everything."

"Except," I said, "how anyone can act like that around beer."

"Are we friends again, Shrimpton?"

George Segal said, "If I'm going to come anywhere close to the essence of experience, I'll suppress extraneous detail."

I knew everything about Coyote then, so we went back to my apartment to make love. Passion. And hysteria.

"Make yourself come," he said. He was on top of me, moving slowly, supporting himself on the full stretch of his arms. He watched intently while I made circles around the place where our two bodies met.

"Say it," he'd asked when we were in bed for only the second time and he'd wanted to know what made me really hot.

"Circles," I'd replied.

"Circles?"

"Around, you know . . ."

"Around . . . ?"

I'd sighed, grossly shy and completely unable to say the word that would clarify things. No one had ever asked me, especially when I was totally naked and he had his head in my crotch, what made me really hot.

"Should I make circles around this?" he'd asked and looped his tongue around and around my clitoris.

"Yes." I'd bucked closer to his mouth.

"Say it," he'd insisted.

"I can't," I'd mumbled. I couldn't say it; I could just feel it.

"Say it, Shrimp."

"I can't." But please don't stop.

"Why not?" He'd held my hips to the bed and lifted his mouth away from them.

"God!" I'd cried. "Because I can't pronounce it, that's why!"

"Darling," he'd said, truly astonished that I'd never heard anyone say the word before. "It's clitoris." And he'd gone back to looping his tongue around it.

When I'd exploded into the fluid, concentric rings of orgasm, he moved on top of me and pushed inside.

"Now show me. Show me how you make yourself come."

That first time I was mortified that he, somehow, knew I'd ever masturbated. But he'd guided my hand downward and helped me begin to make circles around the thing whose name I could now pronounce. When I came, the concentric rings of my orgasm grew very wide, as wide as I'd ever dreamed they could go, closing around and capturing him as he moved inside of me. I'd gripped my legs tightly around him and pulled him deeper.

"Well," he'd said when my legs had fallen, lifeless limbs, from around his body, "did you come?" He was joking, but I couldn't speak.

So when he asked me to make myself come, I slipped my fingers into the moistness between us and began to make circles. I gripped my legs around his waist to pull him deeper. I felt the undulating circles that emanated from inside my hips begin to move outward.

And then I felt Coyote pick me up and move into an upright, a kneeling position on the bed.

"Oh, God!" I had to use my legs and arms to grasp him, had to hold so tightly to stay attached to him that I couldn't move at all, had to surrender to his furious movement. And I learned why he sometimes liked to lie still while I curled on top of him and moved: that surrendering your power to your lover could widen the circles even more.

I was clinging to him, attached to him like some absurd parasite, my head bent back to receive his afterglow kisses on my neck, when I made the mistake of glancing in the full-length mirror on the back of the bathroom door. There we were, reflected in total: one skinny brown man supporting a pale, substantially riper woman. I began to laugh.

"What?" Coyote said.

"Look." I nodded my head in the direction of the mirror.

"What's so funny?"

"You look like you could break!" I hooted and slid down his body, hit the bed.

Coyote studied his body profile in the mirror.

"I'm not that little," he said.

"Then I'm that big!" I was rolling over and burying my laughter in a pillow.

"Oh, so you think I'm skinny?" He picked up another pillow and hit me with it.

"Scrawny is more the word for it." I rolled over, ducked his next shot. "Emaciated," I taunted him.

"Oh, yeah?" The pillow thudded over my head.

"Poster-child, relief-fund material!" I gasped and grabbed a free pillow and let him have it across the back.

"Ohhhh!" he sighed and fell across the bed in a diagonal. "That hurt, Shrimpton!"

When I stopped beating him, concerned for an odd second that he wasn't joking, he leaped and pinned me to the bed and began to tickle me unmercifully.

"No fair!" I screamed and laughed and tried to struggle away.

"You? And who are you that you shouldn't be failed some time?"

"Christ," said Jamie, which was not his next line.

"Mick"—Katie used her hand to indicate a downward trend—"a little less angry. Remember, you love him. I think Ann's more frustrated here, shocked maybe, than truly mad." She paused. "Don't you think so?"

"Yeah, sure." I nodded.

"Let's go on." Katie pointed at Jamie.

"I don't know, Ann. I've often wondered." Jamie moved toward what would be the terrace wall once the set was built and looked out over it, to the almost-finished backdrop of the lighthouse.

"You want to talk about it?" Katie came to the dressing room where I was the last one still changing back to my street clothes. "I mean, the reason you've been playing Ann like the last bitch on earth?"

I slipped my sweater over my head.

"Because Ann's a sap, and I'm trying to play her a little stronger," I said.

"Oh, yeah?" said Katie, like she would never believe me.

"He's wonderful, Katie!"

I'd finished dressing and we were sitting in the dressing room, sharing a Coke. "He's driving me crazy too. See, he's married."

"Oh, Mickey . . ."

"No, Katie, I know what you're thinking, but it's not like that. He's leaving his wife."

"Mickey . . . I'm married. And I fool around. Kiddo, I've been telling men I'm going to leave my husband for years."

"Yeah, but he really is, Katie. He'd leave her even if I wasn't in the picture, so I know he's really leaving. It's just that I don't know when, and I guess I'm taking that out on a lot of people I shouldn't."

"Set a time limit. If he doesn't leave his wife by the date you set, you walk. Tell him that. Please. Limit the problem."

She patted my hand, and what I felt was that Katie was telling me to do something for my own good.

That was when Coyote, all smiles and charm, walked in.

"Coyote, this is Kate Barrows. Katie, David Hellerman."

"Hi." Katie shook his hand.

"Hi." Coyote shook her hand. "You ready to go, Shrimp?"

"Sure," I said. "Where?"

"The Right Bank. We haven't gone out and had champagne to celebrate your getting this part yet. Would you like to come, Kate?"

At the Right Bank, Coyote ordered champagne and spilled it all over himself when he popped the cork, which he had insisted he was capable of doing.

I mopped him up and Katie took the bottle from him and poured. There was something irresistible about the way Coyote was inept; I could tell Katie was warming to him.

"June," said Coyote when we got back to my apartment.

"June?"

"Look, not that I wouldn't have bought you champagne anyway, Shrimpton, but you must think I'm nuts if you think I'm going to have your idol, Kate Barrows, against me. I know what you two were talking about when I walked in. I heard what she said. And she's right. So. June, okay? By June I'll be out of my house."

I ran to him and hugged him. "Okay," I said. "June."

That night I made a calendar, counted the days until Coyote was out of his house, backward from 138. I marked each day with the number of days I would have to wait.

When I slept, I dreamt of dead animals.

I came into my apartment, which in my dream state had grown enough rooms to house not only me but Coyote, his two daughters, and a menagerie of animals.

The first thing I saw when I walked in was a tankful of dead neons. They were shining and crowding the surface water of the tank for space.

Then I saw a huge black metal and Plexiglas cage full of husky angora guinea pigs, curled up and still, balls of fur.

Then I saw a perfect white kitten on her side, on the kitchen floor. Her head lay pathetically close to an empty food bowl painted on its side with her name, FLUFFY.

Oh, my God . . . the panic was rising in my chest . . . I'd forgotten to feed the animals. I began to run through the apartment, stretching my arms out to revive the animals, but the floors stretched, too, and kept the animals from my reach. The panic grew. I discovered a dead golden Labrador puppy in the corner of the living room.

"Please," I cried, "wake up!"

There was a dachshund on its long back, its feet curled like a dead roach, lying on the couch.

I'd starved my animals. I'd starved my animals to death! I tried to remember the last time that I'd fed them, when I had an even more horrible thought.

Had I fed Coyote's girls?

I raced to their room, following an ever-stretching hallway, until, breathless, I reached their door.

They were in their beds, still.

Sleeping, I told myself. Just sleeping.

"Maggie." I shook the little one but she didn't move. "Jane." I grabbed the older one and tried to make her limp body sit up.

"Oh, God!" I slapped their sweet, faceless faces. "Please, get up." I'd starved Coyote's girls! They were dead. . . . I sank to the floor and howled. I howled so loudly that I woke myself up.

The next morning Coyote came to my apartment early, to take me to rehearsal, ride with me on the subway.

"In June," he said when we were seated side by side on the Number 6, "we won't have to rush to grab a little bit of time together. We'll be together all the time." I was bundled in a big down coat, clutching on to his arm for warmth, for comfort.

"I had a bad dream last night, Coyote."

The trains grew loud and Coyote put his hands on either side of my head, over my ears, to block the roar of the subway.

"What did you dream?"

"That I starved Maggie and Jane to death."

"Mickey, my girls will not let you starve them. They'll let you know if they're hungry."

"I'm not sure that was the whole point of the dream."

"Sweetie, I'm not going to make you take responsibility for my kids. You'll help me, and you'll see how easy it is. I'm a great father."

I snuggled into his shoulder and let him hug me. I caught my reflection in a sooty subway window, looking up at him, to adore him. He kissed my nose, and said that it was like a little piece of ice.

All I had to do was trust Coyote. He'd be my net.

And so, Coyote and I entered into our best period.

He bought me a red carnation every day, coming to my apartment to exchange it for the one he bought me the day before.

There was the night we locked ourselves into the editing room at City College and watched *Letter from an Unknown Woman* with Joan Fontaine and *The Big Sleep* with Bogey and Bacall on the Moviola and ate peanuts and kissed until our lips were raw. When we left, I took a subway to the Village and he took a bus home and I cried because he hadn't touched my body and I ached for him. He'd called later that night and whispered into the phone that I was a terrific kisser.

There was the day we spent on the Lower East Side. To Umberto's in Little Italy to eat calamari and drink coffee soda and see where a gangster had been murdered. To the tourist shop filled with statues of the Infant of Prague and steamed milk makers, where Coyote bought me a T-shirt with the Italian flag on it. To a little café with exposed brick walls for cappuccino and babas au rhum. Walking past a furniture store filled with gold lamps and red velvet sofas and joking about Italian-style interior decor, on our way to Chinatown, ripe with the smell of dead fish, pressed ducks hanging from the shop windows. Taking pictures of the huge brightly colored murals painted on the sides of the buildings and poking each other, jabbing at our mutual incompetence when we realized we had black-and-white film in the camera. Eating egg rolls and drinking strong drinks from ceramic glasses where flesh-colored nudes in grass skirts stood still mid-dance on blue backgrounds. To Katz's Deli, which, he claimed, had the best kosher food in the city. Eating chopped chicken liver and drinking Dr. Brown's celery tonic. Finally rolling back uptown on the subway, stuffed and giddy, to the Astor Place stop, where he dropped me off, let three of his trains home pass while he kissed me goodbye.

There was the freezing day we spent on the Staten Island ferry, taking pictures of lower Manhattan and the Statue of Liberty, drinking lots of beer and hugging each other to keep warm.

I'd go to his lectures and marvel at his brilliance. He'd come to my rehearsals and marvel at mine.

We'd work together in my apartment, he on his Hawks book while seated at my kitchen table, and me on my role in the play while curled up on the couch. Every once in a while, in the easy silence of our work, I'd feel him looking at me. I'd look back at him and he would smile at me, and wink, before he went back to his book.

The only part I didn't like about my life then was the sad time, late in the evenings, when he would go home to be a perfunctory husband and pacify his wife so that she would be fair with him about the kids.

When I'd shut the door behind him, I would go to my calendar and mark off another day without him that was over.

Besides the reading I had to do for Katie, for my role, there came from Coyote a subtle reading list: books he bought, brought to my apartment, and left there. He never gave them as gifts, and they were never praised as "must" reading. They—the books by Philip Roth and John Cheever and E. L. Doctorow and Joseph Heller and David Hellerman—were never, in fact, even mentioned. They just stayed, and became a part of Coyote that was always in my apartment. Eventually I picked them up and read them, always late at night, always after Coyote left for the evening.

Opening night.

I sat at my dressing table in the theater, looking at my reflection. I knew my lines; I knew my blocking; I knew the most intimate details of my character's life. I knew I looked incredible in the filmy blue dress the costume designer had made from scratch, especially for me. I was ready to go on. The stage manager poked her head in the door and called, "Half hour."

I'd heard all actors got butterflies before they went on stage and that the great ones could channel that nervous tension, change it to energy for their performance. I was amazingly calm.

The other actors and actresses chattered incessantly. Jamie stood in a corner doing breathing exercises. The stage manager came back in to call "Twenty minutes," and to deliver a full bouquet of red carnations to me. The card read: "Bon Voyage! Coyote"—referring to this, my maiden voyage on the New York stage.

Katie came back to the dressing room.

"Okay, people," she said. She looked stunning in a full-length, dark-gray cape. "You are all, thanks to my brilliant casting and your own hard work, more than prepared to go on that stage. So, I want you to relax! And think about this." She moved into the room and rested her hand on Jamie's shoulder because he was the most fretful. "One of the strongest criticisms ever leveled at your playwright is that his people are unconventionally conventional. They escape one cliché, only to fall into another. They believe that they are being genuine, but in reality they've only established more elaborate artifices for themselves."

"What the hell kind of thing is that to say to us now," moaned the actress who was playing Lily Malone.

"Think about it," said Katie and kissed us all for luck. When she kissed me, she held my face and winked. "Break a leg!" she called and swept out of the dressing room.

That was when the nerves hit me.

The stage manager called, "Places," and I stumbled out to the wings, concentrating on channeling the energy of the butterflies into a more useful energy.

In my head, I heard Katie's voice. "Skim over it. Don't fall into any of the traps. What I was trying to tell you, Mick, is that you know your character well enough now to just go out there and play her right on the surface." I heard Katie telling me this, but, of course, she was out front, seated next to the husband she'd mentioned having.

I walked out, onto the set, guided by the glow of reflective tape. The chair I'd sat in for weeks in rehearsal was suddenly comfortable. The lights came up and I was Ann, so much Ann that my lines tumbled out of me without a thought. For a few odd moments during the course of the play I could actually see myself on stage, moving with Ann's grace, speaking with Ann's voice, feeling her love and despair.

"That's the way to do it," said Katie to me after the show.

Back in my apartment, after the opening-night party at Katie's elaborate East Side place, Coyote cuddled me in the sofa bed.

"Was I really good?" I asked him for the hundredth time.

"You were really *fabulous*," he assured me again. "Even I didn't expect you to be that good."

"Really?" I prodded.

"You're fishing," said Coyote and smiled at me as he cut off my line to compliments.

The next day there was a short write-up in the *Post* about *Hotel Universe*. They praised the costumes, the set, Katie, Jamie, and me, as "capturing the ethereal mood of the play perfectly," and me, specifically, as "lovely to watch, almost too at home on the stage." They ran a picture of me in my blue dress next to the article. Coyote presented it to me behind the glass of an antique wooden frame, and hung it, my first review, on the wall of my bathroom.

I was making instant coffee, was wearing Coyote's yellow button-down. Coyote lay in bed, naked, watching me.

"You know," he said, "there's one thing you do when we make love that really, *really* drives me wild."

"Oh, yeah?" I sat next to him on the bed, Indian-style, and handed him his cup. "What?"

"Oh, no," he said, "I'm not telling you. . . ."

"Why? What . . . tell me what it is."

"No. If I tell you, then I'll always wonder if you're doing it naturally, or just because you know I like it."

"Oh. Well. If you don't tell me, I may, just naturally, never do it again."

"That's a chance I'll have to take." Coyote sipped his coffee.

We were to have one more blissful month, Coyote and I. He was nearly finished with the Hawks book; I performed in the play and, because of Katie's insistence and incredible contacts in the "industry," modeled for magazines: a perfume ad, a cigarette ad, and a couple of fashion layouts.

Coyote and I would lie on my pulled-out bed and look at photos of me taken for various magazines and giggle like kids.

"You look soooo chic," he'd chide me, but I knew he was proud of those pictures, even if we both agreed they were silly.

We went to plays, to a matinee of *A Chorus Line,* where we scrunched low in our balcony seats and hummed along. We went to museums, to the Museum of Natural History where I posed ferociously next to the ferocious cave bear for Coyote's camera. We went to the movies, to cinemas all over the city where we would see yet another foreign movie. Once, coming out of a screening, he pushed his face into my hair.

"What perfume are you wearing?" he asked.

"Chanel Nineteen," I replied.

"Very high test," he approved and kept leaning over to kiss my neck, and smell it, as we walked down the street.

We explored every nook and cranny of New York, from the Cloisters to the Bowery and, most notably, the piers on the Lower West Side.

There, on a rainy March afternoon, we sat and watched the water, nuzzling each other and letting the rain drizzle on us. We walked and held hands and stopped every few feet to eat each other up with kisses.

When it really began to pour we found a small Cath-

114

olic church, dedicated to some unknown saint, and ducked inside to keep dry.

Inside the church, statues of saints stood behind rows of lighted candles. A small, highly ethnic woman, probably Italian, knelt before one of the statues and prayed. Dim light flickered in through the stained-glass windows in dark reds and blues. It smelled like fresh incense. Coyote was intrigued by all of it.

"Light a candle. . . ."

"What?"

"Show me how you light a candle."

I shrugged and dug for change in my pocket, dropped it in the container for Saint Jude. I picked up a long wooden matchstick, lit it from an already burning candle, and touched it to a fresh wick. I replaced the matchstick in its holder and dropped to my knees for a prayer.

I didn't pray often. When I did, I stuck to the formula prayers, like the *Our Father* or the *Hail, Mary*, because if I prayed personally (like Protestants pray, my dad once joked about it), then I had to think about things I really didn't want to think about. Like my dad. And that was a dead issue.

Even just reciting an *Our Father* made me a little misty, so that when I stood up and said to Coyote, "Well, that's how you light a candle," I had to wipe my eyes.

He held my hand.

"You're the sweetest woman in New York," he said.

But that was before he noticed the casket in the front of the middle aisle of the church. It was an open casket, and some old dead man was lying in there.

"Oh, shit," said Coyote, and grabbed my hand and led me back out into the rain.

He spat on the ground, and kept spitting between his questions.

"Did you know that that guy was there? Do all Catholics have open caskets, just lying in the church? Just *there* for anyone to wander in and see? Gross, gross, gross!"

"No, Coyote, it must be some weird branch of the church. I've only seen open caskets in the funeral home. They're usually shut by the time they get to the church. . . ."

But he kept spitting, and making loud hawking noises to emphasize his disgust.

"I don't know what you're so grossed-out about," I said finally. "It was just a dead guy."

Then the bliss ended.

We filed into the City College auditorium to attend a tutorial performance. The tutorial project, a series of slides projected onto a large screen, their changing choreographed to original electronic music, was touted as the best student work to come out of City College in years. A few days before the screening, the young musician/photographer had asked Coyote personally to be sure to attend.

"I flunked him once, when he was a freshman," said Coyote, "but he said he wanted me there because he has 'always respected' me. I don't know, Shrimp. I feel obligated to be there now."

"I don't mind going," I said.

It seemed like the entire faculty of the school was there, along with a large portion of the student body. Coyote and I talked to an art instructor, an old friend of his who knew about us and, what was more, approved.

When the lights began to dim, I scooted into a seat between Coyote and the art instructor.

"Oh, God," was Coyote's reaction, and he crushed my hand with his grip.

The art instructor said, "I can't believe it. . . ." and she gripped my other hand.

I stared straight ahead.

There, on the large screen, in front of the majority of the institution, were Coyote and I, no mistaking us. We strolled hand in hand, gazed at each other, lapped at each other's faces. For thirty minutes we watched David and Mickey parade on the piers of the Lower West Side, the slides blinking on and off to the moans of the synthesizer music. The show ended with us ducking into the Catholic church: long freeze and slow fade.

When the lights came on, Coyote grabbed my hand and we slunk out of the auditorium, to the corner coffee shop.

"Why, do you think, he'd do it?"

"I don't know." Coyote stirred his coffee and slopped it on his place mat.

"Because you flunked him once, do you think?"

"Probably, Mickey. That's probably why, yeah."

"Jesus," I said, "I feel so sleazy. Like I was fucking in Macy's window . . ."

Coyote just shook his head.

"This is going to hurt you, isn't it? I mean, Shelley can use this against you, can't she?"

"Of course she can. If she finds out." He wouldn't look at me, just at the coffee in his cup. "This whole thing . . . it's really hard on me. I'm afraid . . . I don't want to hurt my kids."

"I know that. . . ."

"I'm leaving them as it is. . . . I get to be a weekend father. You make sure I know I'm leaving, too, don't you . . . that goddammed calendar you keep."

"Don't blame this on me. I didn't tell that kid to follow us and take those pictures."

"You just don't care how hard this is on me. You don't realize how much I've got to give up to be with you. And now this. Thank God I've got tenure."

I went home and tore up the calendar.

While I was sitting on the couch, staring into the wastebasket full of ripped calendar sheets, Coyote called.

He told me not to worry, that he'd gotten the pictures from the photographer/musician. That he'd found out from the kid's photography instructor that those weren't the pictures originally intended for the tutorial, and the kid just snuck them in at the last minute, just replaced all three carrousels.

He called back later to tell me that he never spent any time with his kids anymore because he was spending so much time with me.

Then he called to tell me he'd decided to take "the family" to Vermont for the weekend, and he'd call me when he got back to New York.

When I'd waked up that morning, everything had been fine. Then, all of a sudden, Coyote was in Vermont with "the family" for the weekend. I put on my makeup and my costume for the performance that night.

What was I feeling?

Anger.

Mostly anger.

How dare he?

How dare he blame me for taking time away from his kids, and then run off to Vermont and leave me to sit and stew? He'd pursued our relationship. He'd fallen in love with me. By the time I'd found out anything about the goddammed kids, it was too late to do anything about me falling in love with him.

My eyes were tearing so much that I had to reapply my makeup twice, and my eyes were getting awfully red and were starting to puff up.

When the other actors wanted to know why I was so upset, and was there anything they could do to help, I wasn't ready to talk. By the time the stage manager came in to call "Fifteen minutes" and Katie came backstage to give us that evening's pep talk ("Performing in the live theater is an adventure, and no two audiences ever see the same adventure"), there was no time left to talk.

I gave the sappiest performance of the entire run of *Hotel Universe* that night, speaking my lines over the urge to cry and a raging battle to suppress those tears. There was no Ann that night, and the other actors certainly found being on stage with me an adventure.

Katie wouldn't say "I told you so," even though I gave her the opportunity. The first thing she said to me, in fact, had nothing to do with my problem.

"Don't ever, *ever* let something that's happening in your personal life affect what you do on that stage." She was a little pissed at me for making such an ass of myself. "That is completely unprofessional, Mickey. People are paying their good money to see you, and they couldn't give a crap that your lover's giving you a hard time."

When I apologized, and promised that it would never

happen again, *ever*, she dropped the subject and addressed the real problem.

"I knew this wasn't going to be as painless as you seemed to think, kiddo." She handed me a jar of cold cream and I slathered it on my face. "David's charming. I understand totally what you see in him, and it's clear that he adores you. . . ."

"But . . ." I said and wiped the cold cream off my face, past tears, filled with a hollow determination not to face another loss, to convince myself that I didn't deserve another death.

"I've been married for four years," Katie said. "For the past two and a half years I've been alternating between fighting to keep my marriage together, and fucking around to maintain my sanity. I love my husband very much, Mickey, and it's very hard to leave him even though he's gay."

"What?"

"He's gay. He told me outright about a year and a half ago."

"Oh, Katie . . ."

"I want to leave him. He wants to leave me. It's really the only thing we can do. And yet, neither of us can do it."

"For Christ's sake, Katie, you pack a bag, and you leave."

"It's not that painless, Mick. I love Bradley. We have a home together. Not just an apartment with furniture in it. We've got a home. And a history. And we cared enough about each other to get married in the first place, so, you know . . . We have more of a reason to split up than most people, and no kids to keep us together, but we both still want it to work so very much. . . ."

"Oh, Jesus . . ." I shook my head, mopped with half a heart at the remaining cold cream on my face, held Katie in my arms while she sobbed.

"I like it better when things are more black-and-white, Katie," I said.

After Saturday night's performance Jamie persuaded me to go out for drinks with the rest of the cast, and Jamie and I ended up at a rock and roll club together at three in the morning, drinking Sambuca and dancing.

It wasn't a black-and-white thing to do because I'd promised Coyote that I wouldn't go out rocking and rolling anymore, and because I was vaguely attracted to Jamie after all those performances in which I'd loved him.

Jamie and I danced around the floor, mimicking Chuck Berry moves when the D.J. put on "Maybellene." I moved with that dry, sticky feeling you get from a liqueur drunk. Jamie kissed me.

"I can't do this," I told him when our lips parted, and I backed away.

I gathered up my things from our table and went home.

Sunday morning, while I was nursing my headache, Coyote rang my buzzer.

"Where were you? Last night, where were you?" He sat behind my kitchen table like a judge, mad because he hadn't been able to get hold of me and had cut the weekend in Vermont short to come home and find out where I'd been Saturday night.

"Where were *you!*" I shouted.

"In Vermont! You know that!" he shouted back.

"With 'the family.' Well, I was out with a friend."

"A boyfriend?"

"You got it."

"Oh, wonderful, Shrimpton . . ."

"You son of a bitch! You can just take off for Vermont and expect me to sit around and wait for you? Last night I wasn't sure I *had* a lover anymore, and you expect me to be a hermit in this apartment, sitting around, pining away for *you!* I was *mad,* you bastard, and yeah, I went out on a date!"

"*You* were mad? *You* were mad? Shelley smashed one of our friend's Baccarat wineglasses over their mantel when they told us about the latest divorce in our circle of friends. Then she told them that she and I would soon be the latest news. I'm breaking up my family, spent an entire weekend explaining to these people that, yes, I thought a divorce was the best thing for us, and *you* were mad?"

"Don't blame me! You were the one who took off and left me hanging. I'm not forcing you to do anything. You're the one who suggested the divorce. I never asked you for this, said 'Hey, asshole, you want me, that's the price.' You do whatever you want to do. I'm not even sure I want you anymore!"

"What?"

"I don't need this! I don't need to hurt this much. I hate feeling sleazy, like I felt at that tutorial performance. I hate feeling guilty, like I'm depriving you of your precious little girls. I hate being so in love with you that I don't even want to kiss anyone else, that I can't kiss anyone else and like it. If you think that you can just take off any time you want to, to punish me because you fell in love with me, you can just leave now. Just leave now so that I can start getting over you."

122

He gathered me in his arms and I pressed my face next to his. I would rather hurt forever than have him leave.

"You didn't sleep with this guy, did you?" he asked.

"No!" I batted him away. "Did you sleep with Shelley?"

"Not recently," he said.

"Jesus!" I exploded, stomped around the living room trying to put as much space as possible between him and me, but there was nothing to do in the end but fall on the couch and cry.

He knelt beside me.

"I love you, Shrimpton." He stroked my hair.

"I love you too," I whimpered.

He bent over me and kissed my salty face, my eyes, and my forehead and my cheeks. I turned my face toward him to kiss him back and he pulled me onto the floor. We undressed each other and I crawled on top of him.

He held my hips tightly with each of his hands and moved me slowly at first, then faster, then, finally, frantically, slamming me down on top of his body, on top of him, putting me in my place.

"Never do this with anyone else," he growled.

"No," I cried softly.

"Say it! Say it!" He was shouting.

"I'll never do this with anyone else," I promised him and came in circles that just rolled over me.

When I rolled off of him there were black-and-blue fingermarks on my hips.

PART SEVEN

The spring was when the fighting began in earnest; I didn't trust him to leave and he didn't trust me to wait. The spring was when the six A.M. phone calls started.

"Are you alone?"

"Of course I'm alone!" I would scream that, or I would say it delicately, reassuringly, depending on my mood, how much I thought about the fact that he was certainly not alone.

The bottom line was that I couldn't believe it was so difficult for him to leave his kids. My mom did it easily enough, didn't she?

But then, Katie was having a difficult time leaving her husband, and, besides not having any kids to keep them together, he was gay.

I was beginning to think that maybe people didn't just pick up and leave. After all, didn't it take me years to pick up and leave my father? And didn't I leave only because he really shoved?

It was getting too complicated. The only thing that was black-and-white was that I wanted Coyote and he wanted me and there were a lot of gray areas we would have to go through to get each other.

The first fight of the season was over Coyote redecorating his apartment. Or, rather, his wife redecorating their apartment.

"Why are you redecorating if you're leaving?" I screamed. We were in a hardware store and he was buying cans of light-blue glossy paint for the master bath.

"She's going to stay in the apartment, Mickey. That's where Shelley and my kids are going to live. Don't you think I owe it to them to help paint before I go?"

"No."

Honestly? No. Painting an apartment is an investment in that apartment, and whatever you may want to believe, Coyote, your investment there is over. Painting it now just digs you in deeper. Makes it harder to leave.

"You're not going to leave, are you?" I asked.

"Yes. Yes. I'm going to leave. But I'm going to paint the bathroom while I'm still there." He paid for his purchases. "Do you want to help me?" he asked.

He walked out of the hardware store, holding his paint supplies, and tried to hail a cab. I stood beside him, holding two cans of his paint, and tried to feel that the situation was comprehensible. Did I want to help?

A cab slowed and pulled in to the curb.

"So," he said, "are you coming home with me or what?"

Coyote's apartment was large, and lived-in. It had started out as a tasteful, eclectic mixture of sleek modern pieces and only the most interesting of antiques. Somewhere along the line Coyote's library had overrun the shelf space and spilled to the floor. The Italian leather sofa showed

126

the wear and tear of too many years with kids, and small children's clothes and toys dotted the furniture tops and floors. Sunshine streamed in the picture windows, and a forest of plants thrived in every room.

The two things that intrigued me most were, first, the eight-by-ten glossy on top of the chest in the foyer: a studio portrait of the three Hellerman ladies.

The picture showed an unsmiling eight-year-old, a dark girl with huge, solemn brown eyes, a wide mouth with dark-cherry lips, and hair that was long and thick and smooth. Jane was a little girl who would grow up to be what people would call a "haunting beauty."

Next to Jane was a four-year-old, Maggie, the antithesis of Jane. She had short auburn curls, small pale features, and was wearing a smile that seemed to encompass her whole little body. A child who, you could imagine, had a husky laugh and a healthy disdain for anything that didn't provoke it.

Behind them both was Shelley. She had her arm around Jane, and she was holding Maggie's hand. Jane got her features from Shelley; Maggie got her coloring from her. Shelley's expression was one of someone who has always been well cared-for. Her frame was slight, but she looked solid and dependable. And pretty.

The other object that caught me was a large carved wooden mezuza hanging diagonally on the wall just inside the front door. Less than a religious object I knew, because a mezuza was to hang outside the door, this one was more a piece of art. Still, as my lighted candle in the Catholic church had intrigued Coyote, this mezuza intrigued me. And it made me sad. Here was a tangible object of a background and tradition that Coyote and Shelley shared. And, more than just the implication of a mutual heritage, that damn mezuza made me feel like an outsider unable to laugh at their in-jokes

The girls were in school.

Shelley was on a four-day antique hunt in upstate New York.

Coyote and I sanded and spackled and slapped two coats of paint on the bathroom walls.

I had a photo session in the early morning. I was to pose in a red-white-and-blue costume (actually a red-and-white striped skintight bodysuit, and blue-dyed hair high-lighted with glittering silver star-shaped barrettes) for the July cover of a cable television monthly.

In the afternoon I had a first read-through for Katie's next production, *Hedda Gabler,* in which I would play Thea.

In the evening, I was to go to Coyote's place again. Shelley was still on her antique hunt, and if I arrived after nine, the kids would be in bed. We could have a nice quiet evening together, Coyote said, drinking wine and watching *All the President's Men* on cable, and fucking. When I got to his building I was to breeze in past the doorman as if I lived there, and go directly to his apartment. He didn't want the doorman to know he was having company, and besides, the intercom buzzer was loud and might wake the kids, who were not sound sleepers.

Except the doorman was onto me.

"Where you going, Mizz?" he said with his heavy Spanish accent. His name tag read JOHN.

Oh, God.

"Seventeen C."

He picked up the intercom phone. "Your name, Mizz?"

Ummmm.

"Michele."

"Yez, hello. Mizz Michele here to see you," he said into the receiver. "Yez, I tell her. Okay. Bye." He hung up. "Please, you have a seat. He's come down to get you."

I sat on the edge of a large marble planter in the lobby and waited, with a quick pulse, the twenty minutes it took for Coyote to show his face.

"What took you so long?" I whispered as he led me to the elevators.

"Christ, Shrimpton, I told you not to have the door-man call. Maggie woke up and I had to get her back to sleep."

"Sorry," I said, "but John seemed to know I didn't live here. What did you want me to do? Make a run for it?"

The elevator doors opened.

"Just get in." He motioned. "I don't want the kids to wake up and not be able to find me."

And whose law is it that says the worst will happen, always with the worst possible timing?

The elevator stopped and the doors remained closed. The light indicated that we were on the seventh floor. Coyote pushed the button to seventeen again. Nothing. Then he pressed DOOR OPEN. Nothing.

"Come on," he said, and hit the door with his fist. The elevator lurched downward a good four inches and the doors started trembling and making noises like they wanted to open.

"Shit!" Coyote grabbed the double doors with his

hands and tried to pry them open, like an ape intent on escape from a cage. The doors remained closed and I went for the DOOR OPEN button. Nothing.

The elevator was now buzzing, low and furious, like an incensed bee.

"Shrimpton, what's going on?" Coyote turned to me. His face was drained of color.

"I don't know. It's your building!" I accused him.

"Fuck!" said Coyote, and looked around the elevator like there was maybe something interesting to see.

"We're stuck," I said.

"No shit?" he shouted.

"So, what do we do?" I shouted back.

"I don't know!" he screamed.

Three maintenance men worked on the elevator for half an hour and when they finally got the doors open we saw that we'd been stuck halfway between six and seven, and we crawled out on six with the help of the maintenance men and a ladder.

Coyote was not for trusting the other elevator, so we ran up the eleven flights of stairs to his apartment. He was noticeably relieved when he found his kids still in their beds, asleep, and after a glass of wine he was calm enough to let me peek in on them while they slept, my first meeting with Jane and Maggie.

The lean Jane lay like the sleeping princess in fairy tales. Chubby Maggie was curled up like a monkey in her blankets and smiled in her sleep when Coyote bent over and kissed her.

Even after we'd polished off the wine (and given up on *All the President's Men*), Coyote still wasn't calm enough to fuck. And then, because Jane and Maggie would wonder who I was when they woke up in the morning, I had to leave.

It was after midnight. I looked up from the cab's rear window and spotted Coyote on his seventeenth-floor terrace, waving to me.

"Thea," I said to Katie, who was every bit as meticulous about *Hedda Gabler* as she had been about *Hotel Universe*, "is the original flower child."

"How do you mean, Mick?"

The costumer who'd made me the beautiful blue dress to wear as Ann was pinning me into the stricter, more sensible clothes of a century earlier for the dowdier Thea.

"I hate this costume," I said. "It's so . . . *brown*." The costumer shrugged and we both looked to Katie.

"Thea is plain, Mickey," Katie explained once again. "She's downtrodden."

"I think we see her differently . . ." I replied.

"Thea's beauty is, well, okay, her *hair*. But more inside of her. After all, she's been married for many years to an older man, and he only asked her to marry him because he wanted a cheaper nanny for the kids he'd had by his first wife. Mickey, Thea is not well-dressed."

"I wish I were playing Hedda," I said. There was a fabulous red velvet gown hanging on the door which belonged to Hedda.

"Mick, let's get back to this flower-child thing."

"Okay. Okay. Look, Thea just believes. She believes in love. She believes Lövborg will stop drinking for her sake, for the sake of their 'child,' that book he wrote. She believes she can leave her husband, run away with Lövborg, and survive the scandal. She believes in the great

.mind of her great man. She just . . . believes in love, in the best sense of the word. You know, like that sex is pure, a cosmic union of two like souls. . . . Sex is never sweaty for Thea, you know?"

"So, you think that she and Lövborg have a sexual relationship?"

"I think that's a given."

"I'm not so sure about that. . . ."

"Oh, come on, Katie. You think people in nineteenth-century Norway didn't fuck around?"

"I'm not sure Thea did."

"Well, you're the director. . . ."

"No, Mick, she's your character."

"Okay, then, let's talk about this costume. I see Thea in something in pale green. . . ."

"Brown, Mickey. Stop bugging me about the costume."

Coyote and I were supposed to meet at his place again that night, but there was a hushed and urgent message on my machine that Shelley had come home a day early from her trip. Instead, he said, he would come down to my apartment that night after his last class. He didn't say what time he would be there, and when he buzzed to be let in, Katie and I were still having dinner.

"I'm sorry about tonight," he apologized to me.

I got up to broil another hamburger for him. "It's okay."

"You're mad?" he ventured.

"No," I said.

I wasn't mad. I felt cheap. Not sleazy like the day of the tutorial performance, and not hurt like most of the other times. Cheap, because, as Katie had said when I was bitching about our plans being ruined by Shelley coming home a day early, I *was* "the other woman."

"It's what you have to expect when you're the other woman," was exactly what she'd said.

I'd gotten mad when she said that, and we were having a difficult dinner because of it, so I didn't want to provoke a fight with Coyote. I didn't want to increase the tension. But Coyote prodded me.

"Tell me what the problem is, Mickey," he said.

"Please, just back off."

"No! Shrimp, you can't be mad at me for this. Shelley just . . . she just decided to come home. There was nothing I could do about it."

"There is something you could do. You could stop putting me in a position where I feel cheap! You could leave. . . ."

"In June, I told you."

"So, I can just feel cheap until June, then?" I was stooped in front of the oven, turning his burger, crying.

"Shrimp . . . " He started to come toward me.

"You know what I think?" I said this before he got close enough to touch me. "I think that, whatever your reasons are, only a mediocre person would make someone he loved feel cheap."

"Mediocre?" he asked.

Katie was bending over her plate, pretending not to hear anything. When Coyote stormed out of the apartment she said, "Mick, I didn't mean it that way. I didn't mean for it to upset you, and get you and David into a fight. I don't . . . I . . . it was a stupid thing to say."

"It sure was," I said.

He was frazzled. He called because of the fight and he couldn't sleep and he wanted to make up. I wanted to keep fighting. It was four A.M.

"Our relationship is not cheap," he said. "How can love be cheap?"

When he said that I was reminded of the time the cat had kittens. One of Neil's wives had found a very pregnant stray out behind the gallery, in labor, and she brought her inside, placed her in a deep box full of shredded newspaper to have the kittens.

I was eleven; the cat was screaming, howling. Neil and the wife were taking turns rubbing the cat's stomach to help her. Dad was watching. I was sitting out front, listening to the cat's agony, scared to death. They were all calling me, urging me to come help, to at least watch.

"Is it gross?" I'd called back, sincere about wanting to know which parts of the cat were not intact.

Dad stuck his head out into the gallery. "It is not gross," he snarled at me. "How can birth be gross?"

That was the first time Dad had alluded to anything sexual in front of me and *that* was gross. Just like what Coyote said was cheap.

And repulsive.

I responded to the repulsion.

"I don't want to see you anymore." I shivered.

We were both silent.

"Did you mean that, Shrimpton?" Coyote asked after a few minutes.

And, after a few minutes, I answered. "Of course I didn't mean it."

But, however much I didn't mean it, however much I desperately wanted to see him, or vice versa, we had begun the fight season's playoffs. They lasted during the whole of the rehearsal period for *Hedda Gabler,* and culminated in "Black Sunday."

We fought because I made him ride the Ferris wheel with me at a spring festival in the Village and when it broke and we got stuck at the top I rocked the seat to taunt him because he was afraid of heights and it made him nauseous.

We fought because of the transit strike. The morning I had an early modeling job uptown, an hour's walk away, he surprised me by showing up on his bike to chauffeur me to my job in Maggie's baby seat. The ride was a delight, with the early-morning rush-hour crowd applauding our ingenuity and cheering us on. But when we got to the photographer's studio, Coyote's back tire was flat and it made him late for class.

We fought when he took me along as a guest when he sat on a panel at the New York Film Festival. We met an old friend of his there, an Amazon of a fellow panelist, who had to bend over from the waist to kiss him hello, and I laughed out loud.

We fought because when we were in his office at City College, and I was logging grades as he corrected mid-terms, and we started to kiss and decided to just screw on his couch, I wouldn't get completely undressed because I was paranoid about being discovered by a janitor with a master key.

We fought because when we went a week without fighting he sent me a bouquet of red carnations with a card that read "A whole week with no misunderstandings. Isn't that a new North American record?" and his attitude pissed me off.

And then I got sick. There was a flu going around and I caught it, along with Shelley and Jane and Maggie.

Coyote spent four days running between the Village and the Upper West Side, taking us all to the doctor's, getting prescriptions filled, buying orange juice and making hot tea and pumping it into everyone.

On the fourth day when Katie called, as she did every day, to see if I needed anything, I said yes. Please bring me some ginger ale. Coyote had provided for my every need, but he wasn't due back at my place until late that morning, and I wanted the soda.

Katie was sitting on the edge of my bed and I was drinking the ginger ale when Coyote walked in. It was eleven A.M. and already Coyote's second trip to my place that day. He looked beat.

"Did you go out?" he demanded when he saw the ginger ale on my counter, while he measured my medicine into a tablespoon.

"No, Katie brought it," I told him.

"I could have brought you ginger ale," he said and shoved the spoonful of medicine in my mouth.

"I don't mind." Katie shrugged. "You must be exhausted from trying to take care of everyone who's sick right now. Anyway, you look tired." She smiled at him.

"I'm perfectly capable of taking care of Mickey myself, Kate," he said and walked to the kitchen sink, where he rinsed off my medicine spoon.

Katie just stared at his back.

When he turned around to face us he said, "I'm under a lot of pressure. Thank you, Kate, for helping out."

"Sure, David. No problem," she said.

"No more fights?"

"No more fights."

"I can't take the pressure."

"Me neither."

We lay in the bed at his apartment. Luxury: Shelley had taken Jane and Maggie and gone off for a weekend at her mother's, and Coyote and I were going to spend our first full night together.

I ran my hand through the sparse patch of gray hair on his chest.

"I love having time to enjoy you," I said and brushed my face across his chest hair.

It was a cold night in late April and when we crawled under the covers to sleep, skin to skin and spoon-style, Coyote wrapped his arms around me and cuddled me close to keep me warm.

"We can sleep like this every night when we're together," I thought out loud.

"Every night." Coyote squeezed me to him.

A gunshot on Coyote's terrace woke me. I thought I was going to open my eyes and see that I was in the arms of a corpse, Shelley standing over us, and me her next victim.

But when I opened my eyes all I could see was the digital clock that blinked 3:47 in luminescent numbers. I started to turn over; Coyote gripped my body and held me in place.

"Did you hear that?" I whispered in my smallest voice.

"Yeah," he answered back in his.

"What is it?"

"I don't know."

"Well, get up and see."

"If we just lie here, they'll think we didn't hear it. They'll think we're still asleep."

"They who?"

"They whoever fired the gun. Now shut up."

"But it sounds like whoever is in this apartment."

"Shhhh."

We lay in bed, wide awake, still and silent in the dark, under the covers. We heard four more shots, and then it was dawn.

Coyote lifted his head to look around. When he saw that there was no one else but me in the room he crept out of bed. He started to put on running shorts and running shoes and a City College T-shirt.

"Don't take the time to get dressed. Just go see what the hell happened."

"I'm not going out there to investigate gunshots naked!"

He opened the door to the bedroom slowly and peered out before he ventured down the hall. I sat up in bed, and then decided to get dressed in case Coyote needed me, or we had to make a run for it. My heart was audible and I fumbled with my clothes, but I was dressed when he walked back into the bedroom, smiling and jaunty, carrying the tops of some seltzer bottles.

"They were stored on the terrace, and I guess it got so cold last night they just exploded," he explained.

"What?" I said. "You mean we lay in bed, terrified, for over two hours because of some seltzer bottles?"

"Yeah." Coyote laughed.

I picked up my sweater and hit him with it.

"You asshole."

"Come on." He was still laughing. "No more fights, remember?"

"No more fights?" I hit him again. "I just spent the night with a jerk. Someone who let me spend two hours in terror because he doesn't have the goddammed guts to protect me from fucking seltzer bottles! Jesus Christ." I hit him one more time before I left his apartment in disgust.

There was a cab right on the corner and I jumped in. "Sheridan Square," I told the cabbie.

When the cab pulled up to my corner I jumped out and walked the half a block to my apartment. When I turned to close my apartment door behind me, there was Coyote, leaning in the doorway, drenched in sweat and panting to save his life.

"That cab . . ." he struggled, "made every green light."

"Did you run all the way down here?"

"Yeah." He gasped for air.

"So fast?"

He nodded and coughed. Then he looked at me like he didn't know whether to try a grin on me or not.

"Oh, David . . ." I reached out to him and he fell into my arms and then we started to laugh about the seltzer bottles, and me hitting him with my sweater, and that cab gunning it down Broadway, and every other stupid fight we'd had over the last few months.

He called later that day, Sunday, to tell me that the kids were home safely, and he loved me, and he couldn't wait until we were together. It was the only time in our history that we got gooey with each other.

"I love you so much." Kiss, kiss, kiss.

"Oh, I love you so much too." Sloppy-sounding smooch.

"You are everything I've ever dreamed of." Long sigh.

That sort of thing.

"Look, Shelley's out now," he said, "and I can't leave the kids alone. But as soon as she gets back, I'm going to come down there and hug you until your ribs crack."

"I can't wait." I laughed into the receiver and gave him one more kiss, kiss, kiss before we hung up.

But he didn't come. I waited hours. From noon till one. Then till two. Three. Four. When was Shelley coming home? Five. It was an unspoken rule that I never call him when I knew Shelley was going to be there. I wasn't sure if she was going to be there or not. Six. So why didn't he call me? Seven. Eight. I was getting sick to my stomach because I knew something was wrong. Coyote always showed when he said he'd show.

"Hello?"

I pounced on the phone when it finally rang.

"Mickey?"

"Coyote! Darling, I thought you were coming down here, that you'd call. Where are you?"

"At home."

He sounded like a wreck.

"Is everything all right? Are Jane and Maggie okay?"

"Yeah, they're fine. Listen, Mickey, Shelley wasn't out when we talked before. I thought she was, but she was on the extension. Listening to us. We've been fighting."

"Oh, sweetheart . . ."

"Listen to me. It's over. You and me, we're over. The kids heard us going at it, and they're in their rooms in tears. Shelley told me she'd never trust me again, never, no

140

matter how good a husband, how good a father I was. No matter what I did. And Maggie wants to know if she can still trust me. I'm sorry. I didn't mean to hurt you. But . . . this just has to stop."

"Coyote!"

"No. Mickey, that's it. Bye."

And that was it: Black Sunday.

I replaced the receiver in the cradle. I was about to pick it up and dial Katie's number—I didn't know what to do but I knew that I couldn't be alone—when the phone rang again.

"Coyote?"

"No, Katie."

"Katie!"

"Mick, can I come over?"

"I wish you would."

"I'll be there in fifteen minutes."

Fifteen minutes to fill before Katie would get there.

You can do it, Mick.

I talked to myself like that, in the second person, my strong self giving my weak self a pep talk until Katie buzzed. It never occurred to me that she might have something on her mind.

Katie arrived with a full bottle of Jack Daniel's in her purse. She looked awful.

"What's wrong?" This was said in unison. I guess I looked as bad as she did.

"You first," said in unison again and we both managed a small smile.

That smile took it all out of me. I began to cry.

"Coyote's not leaving his wife. We broke up. I'm pretty sure it's for good."

She nodded and sniffed back her own tears.

"Bradley and I decided to see a lawyer on Monday. We know we have to do it, so we just decided to get the divorce over with."

"Oh, Katie . . ."

"Oh, Mickey . . ."

We started to laugh because we sounded like an old, sappy movie. Then we cried, and then we laughed. Then we hugged each other and cried some more.

"Drown your sorrows?" Katie held up the bottle of Jack Daniel's.

"Sounds good to me."

PART EIGHT

The misery of being without him was worse than the misery of being with him.

At least when I was with him there were some highs in my life. Those incredible highs.

The night *Hedda Gabler* opened there was a bouquet of red carnations on my dressing table. The card read: "What can I tell you, Shrimp? You can lead a coyote to water but it takes a lot to get him to drink."

"Is he here?"

"I'll look. Get into your costume."

I pulled on my brown skirt and my beige shirt and buttoned myself into the tight brown jacket with the elaborate darker-brown trim while Katie went to peek at the audience.

"Well, is he here?" I jumped her when she came back in.

"He's here," Katie reported.

"Where?"

"Sixth row. Three seats in from the left."

"Oh, God!"

"Mickey." Katie held me by the shoulders. "Remember, the audience doesn't care if your lover's giving you a hard time. They came here to see *Hedda Gabler.*"

"Yeah, I remember."

But how could Katie expect me to not remember, also, that Coyote was in the audience? It had been only two days since we broke up, but they'd been two days of ridiculously insistent tears and an absurd inability to get comfortable in my body. I'd spent most of those two days unable to get out of bed, tossing and turning, trying to find an escape from the emptiness in sleep. Now Coyote was there, and Katie honestly expected me to forget it?

The play, not short to begin with, took so damn long to get through that night, that when Hedda shot herself I kissed Gretchen (who played Hedda, and had no idea what provoked my action). I ran on stage for curtain calls and searched the audience for Coyote, but I couldn't find him.

"Hi, Shrimpton," he said. He stood in the doorway of the dressing room.

I turned around. I had been just about to cry because I thought he'd gone home without speaking to me. "Hi, Coyote." He looked tired, and pale, and it seemed the lines on his face had deepened dramatically.

"That was . . ."—he swallowed—"a good show."

I nodded acknowledgment. "Thanks for the flowers."

He shrugged like they were no big deal.

So what did we do now? I wanted to walk over to him and wrap myself around his fragile-looking body. He looked like he wanted me to do that, too. But we stood apart, each trapped by our suspicion that the gesture would be unwelcome to the other.

"I wish I didn't love you," he said.

144

"Well. Huh?" There was no earthly reply to a statement like that.

"I am . . ." He was as deeply disturbed as I'd ever seen him. "I am just not going to be good at this, Mickey. At leaving. But"—he struggled—"I don't want to be without you. If you think you can handle it. You know. If you think you can deal with me until I get through the initial craziness, I'll leave." There was a tear dripping slowly from each of his eyes, the only two tears of Coyote's I'd ever see. He used his hands to wipe away the evidence of any emotion, and flatly stated the challenge. "I want us back together. Do you?"

I nodded.

He smiled and made a tentative move toward me. I smiled and made a tentative move toward him. We approached each other warily, like seasoned boxers, worthy opponents, but we were finally locked in an embrace.

"When, Coyote?" I asked him while I held his body and pressed my cheek to his.

"I told you. June. I've only got a week left."

"You think you can do it?"

"I have to, don't I?"

I sighed. "Yeah," I told him.

"So," he said, "do you want to come apartment hunting with me?"

The criteria were these: The apartment must be (at least) a one-bedroom; it must be close to either Dalton or his old apartment, so he would be close to Jane and Maggie; it must not be too expensive because, anticipating child support and/or alimony, he wasn't going to be able to afford much.

The first day we looked at nine apartments and he hated them all.

"I'm definitely not taking the one with that loft thing that calls itself a bedroom," he said when we sat down to talk about it.

"No one expects you to." We were in my apartment and I was making instant coffee.

"You know, every one of those places costs twice as much as the place I'm in now, that beautiful four-bedroom in a great building."

"What about the one on Seventy-fifth Street? That was pretty nice."

"It was a six-flight walk-up, and the neighborhood was not exactly conducive to after-dark strolls, if you get my drift."

"Okay. How about the one on Seventy-second Street? It had two bedrooms and it was real reasonable."

"The one on Seventy-second? Mickey, do you have a nasal problem? Did you not notice the odor in the first-floor hallway?"

"All right, Coyote. Which one did you like?"

"None of them. Christ, Mickey, they're dives. My girls will think that's all I can afford."

"That is all you can afford." I put his coffee in front of him. "Okay, look. I'm making decent money, with the modeling. Why don't you let me help out?"

He snorted at me like that was something he'd do over my dead body, so I dropped the subject.

"Sweetie, then what you saw today is the best you're going to get for your money."

"Christ." He paced around the kitchen table and sipped his coffee. "If I take the one on Seventy-second

Street, Maggie and Jane could have their own room when they visit me."

"There you go!"

"Okay." He picked up the phone to call the broker. "Get your shoes on, Mick. We'll probably have to rush right up there and sign the lease. We don't want someone else grabbing that palace."

"You sure you don't want to talk to Shelley first, tell her what you're doing?"

"I want to make sure I have a place to go when she throws me out."

"She's not throwing you out. You're leaving."

"Whatever. Get your shoes on."

"I know where you can get a deal on nose plugs," I said when we were in the cab, on our way to the real estate agency.

"Oh, that's a riot, Shrimp."

We didn't make love all week. We hardly even saw each other.

I stayed in the Seventy-second Street apartment all day to paint and scrub and wait for deliveries: a couch; two twin beds for Jane and Maggie; a double for Coyote and me. He went out: to lecture to his classes, to have the utilities turned on, to pick up phones at The Phone Store, to buy things like the beds, and sheets and towels and dishes.

In the evenings he worked on the apartment while I played Thea. By the time the play was over each night he would have already gone back to his wife and kids.

On May 31 I had an all-day shoot for a department store catalog and I was glad that I did. That was the day Coyote had a lunch date with Shelley to tell her about the apartment. I threw myself into the shoot, and finally the art director told me to just stand still and let him dress me, to shut up and quit telling him what to do. "Je-sus, Mickey." He twitched his head. "I'm sorry, but you're making me nuts!"

After the shoot I picked up fresh pasta and pesto for dinner (but no wine—that seemed too celebratory and I thought it might offend Coyote, who'd been acting pretty defeated lately) and went to the Seventy-second Street place.

He was in the kitchen making the salad, ripping romaine, when I walked in.

"So, how'd it go?" I asked.

He shrugged. "Okay, I guess."

Some of his things, his clothes and his books and a galley proof of the Hawks book, were in the living room.

"She's going to send the rest of my stuff." He nodded in the direction of his things. "She doesn't want me back in the apartment." He dumped the lettuce into a wooden bowl. "She made me give her my keys. Why don't you put the water on for the pasta? You don't want to be late for the show."

Later that night, when I got home from the theater and we'd crawled in bed together, he rolled over, into the smallest vertical space he could possibly fit, as far away from me as he could get. I got up and went to the living room to cry.

I'd been feeling cool and light, more than happy that he'd finally made this major move in the direction of our life together. I'd also been anxious, hopeful that once he talked to Shelley, released himself from the secret of his new apartment, and his decision, he'd be relieved. I'd been banking on the talk with Shelley to clear the air and let him start acting like he loved me again.

Okay, Mick, I told myself, you just gotta be strong. He warned you that he was going to be bad at this, that he was going to act a little crazy in the beginning. You thought that meant he'd want to fight, didn't you? That, you could handle. It's this no-energy zombie that's getting you down.

Well, kiddo, he's still gotta talk to Jane and Maggie, and he's still got things to work out with the lawyers, and, brace yourself, I think things are probably going to get worse before they get better.

I went to Katie's after the performance the next night because Coyote wanted to take the girls to his apartment for the night and I didn't want to be alone to worry about how it was going.

"It's just a few people, Mick," Katie said.

"Christ, Katie, I don't feel like going to a party. I want it to be just us two, alone with our misery."

"Well, I don't want to be miserable. I want to be around people. Besides, I already invited them."

I was getting back into my civilian clothes after the show and Katie was freshening her makeup in my mirror.

"How are you holding up?" I asked.

Katie shrugged and blotted her lipstick. "Great. Divorce is a whole lot of fun."

"You saw the lawyer?"

"Yeah. The worst. It was abundantly clear, while we were there and trying to figure out a property settlement, just how much Bradley and I love each other. It was 'No, no, *you* take that, you like it so much,' and 'No, no, please, *you* have that, you'll need it more than I will.' He kept insisting that I take the apartment, but I'm moving out. I don't want it. Too many memories. Good memories. Then he has to go and tell me that I can stay as long as I want to, take my time finding a new place. I wish this were a messy divorce—I think that might be easier to deal with."

"Is Bradley going to be there tonight?"

"No. He's spending the night with a friend, if you know what I mean."

"Yeah."

"How're you holding up?"

"I'm hanging in there, Katie. I gave myself a nice little pep talk last night; I do a mean imitation of you. I mean, I love him, Katie, so there's nothing I can do but hang in there."

There were five people at Katie's that night: Katie, of course, and me, Jamie (my lover from *Hotel Universe* who'd come to see the show), a friend of Jamie's, and Ben Townsend.

"So." I sat next to Ben, determined, because Katie said I was acting like a wet blanket, to have a good time. "What do you do?"

"I manage celebrities."

"Oh."

"I was a CPA, but I gave that up. I find managing people to be much more lucrative."

"Really?"

"You know, you're really good. I could probably do something for you. We should talk."

"Right." Why did I sit down here? Not only was he coming on like he was Mr. Hollywood, but he was a former CPA, and, because of Ginch, I had a bad feeling about CPAs in general.

"I just flew in from L.A." He smiled at me.

"No kidding?"

"Yeah. I get back to New York fairly often. Business. You know."

"Sure do." I fought for a new subject. "So, how do you know Katie?"

"Oh, I manage some of the actors on *Our Time to Live*. I met her through them. She's a great girl, isn't she?"

"Great girl." New subject. "That's a nice chain you're wearing."

"This?" He fingered the chain around his neck. "Pure gold," he informed me. "My last wife got it for me."

"Oh, you're married."

"Nope, not anymore."

Ben had been married three times, he told me. First to a woman who "didn't want to move with me." She held him back, he said, wouldn't work with him to achieve his potential. She'd just wanted to be a housewife and have kids; they'd had one kid together before he left. Second came his longest marriage, to a Playboy bunny. She was never in the magazine; she just worked in a club. He left her when he realized she was a gold digger, had married him only to move her career along. Last came a two-week marriage to a stewardess.

"Two weeks?" I was fascinated. Even Neil had always managed to stay married for longer than two weeks.

"Yeah, it was a mistake right from the start. But, we all make mistakes."

"Yeah. But don't you at least regret yours?"

He shrugged. "Who's got time?"

"Not even your kid? I mean, don't you feel guilty about leaving your kid?"

"Guilt is a pretty useless emotion, Mickey."

Now that I could key into. Maybe I wouldn't have suffered so much with my father if he'd been able to pick up and leave me like Mom did. Maybe Coyote wouldn't be suffering so much if he'd just realize how useless it was.

Katie and I emptied ashtrays and gathered up empty beer bottles and washed glasses after everyone had left.

"You sure had a long talk with the Los Angeleno tonight," she said while she polished the glass circles from her coffee table.

"Yeah, I guess I did. You know, on certain things, Ben and I, we really think alike."

"Don't," said Katie, "spread that around."

"So, do you want to talk about it?"

When I got to Coyote's place the next morning, Coyote, who was usually up before the sun was up, was still lying in bed, the covers pulled up to his chin.

"When Shelley told the girls, yesterday," he began, "she sat them down, told them she had something very grown-up to tell them and she wanted to discuss it with them in a grown-up way, so please act grown-up. You know what Jane said? She said, 'If you're going to tell us Daddy's dead, please don't tell us.' I guess that was the most grown-up thing she could think of. Isn't that funny?" But he didn't laugh.

"When I brought them here, you know, to show them this place"—he looked around him—"such as it is, Maggie got very excited. She likes the whole idea. It's an adventure for her, I guess. She said she was going to tell everyone at school that she had two houses. Jane, on the other hand, is not speaking to me. The only thing she said all night long was: 'The hallway smells funny.' See, I told you there was something rank out there.''

He threw the covers back. "Well, anyway. I gotta take a shower." He got out of bed and walked to the bathroom, stooped over like someone had just punched him in the stomach, and shuffling like an old man.

I latched on to songs.

Carole King's songs, I found, were even better music-to-be-bummed-out-to than Bread's. But I tried not to listen to her too often.

Billy Joel singing "Just the Way You Are" helped me remember that there existed a Coyote I wouldn't change for anything in the world.

Best, Deborah Harry singing "The Tide Is High" made me feel her determination to wait her situation out, and gave me a positive sign that patience had a chance of winning.

Even so, there were times I just blew it. Like the day Coyote went to see his lawyer. I'd hoped that having a visitation schedule might cheer him up a little, because, after that initial visit, Shelley had been fairly nasty about him seeing the kids at all.

"I get them Saturdays from noon until Sundays at noon. That's it."

"Yeah, but that's not final. I mean, once you go to court, I'm sure you'll be awarded more time."

"Awarded more time . . ." He rolled the phrase around. "Awarded more time. What the hell does that mean, *awarded more time*?"

153

"I didn't make up the term, Coyote. It's just what they call it."

"I'm thinking about going for dual custody."

"Well. You've got the room here. Why not?"

"That doesn't bother you?"

"Why should it bother me, darling? They're your kids. If it'll make you happy to have them here half the time, I . . . I just want you to be happy."

"You'll be stepmother to kids who are only—what? —ten years younger than you. You think you can handle it?"

I shrugged. "My dad's girlfriend is a year younger than I am."

"Was."

"Was what?"

"Your dad died. She *was* a year younger than you. I assume she's not his girlfriend any longer."

"Right. Anyway, Coyote, that's not the point."

We went into the kitchen to make dinner, and everything I did annoyed him.

I peeled a cucumber: "You don't fucking peel cucumbers, Shrimpton."

"*I* peel cucumbers. I don't want to eat the skin."

"That's the most nutritious part! Okay, okay, tell you what—you peel *your* half."

I didn't peel the chicken: "You don't cook chicken with the skin on it!"

"*I* do. The skin's my favorite part."

"It's also the fattiest. Take the skin off *my* pieces."

When we were cleaning up, I put the wooden salad bowl in the dishwasher and I thought he was going to have apoplexy.

154

"I never did things like this before!" I yelled at him. "What's the big goddammed deal?"

"What do you mean you 'never did things like this before'?"

"I never cooked before. Hamburgers, maybe, but I never made meals before. I don't know how to act around this shit."

"How can someone who is so bright not know that you don't put wood in a dishwasher?"

"Because we ate out a lot when I was growing up. Sorry, my dad wasn't a great cook."

"Oh, you're just going to be great for the girls, aren't you? You have the most fabulous maternal instincts."

I should have given him time to take that back. Or I should have realized that he was upset about things far removed from my ability to cook, and was just releasing some steam. Or I should have just left the room.

At any rate, I shouldn't have done what I did, which was shout: "They already have a goddammed mother," and throw the salad bowl at him.

It hit him on the side of the head.

"Shrimpton." He couldn't believe I'd done that.

"I'll tell you something, Coyote: You better get back to normal soon, because I can't take much more of this. You mope around here like you're at death's door, and I know you have every right to hurt, but you don't seem to understand that this is a happy time for me. I love you, and I'm going to get to have you in my life, and that makes me happy. I'm tired as shit of not fucking you. Fucking you? Who am I kidding? You don't even hold me anymore. You're cold and aloof and you're really depressing. This fight is the most fun I've had with you in weeks.

I'm not asking you to be attractive all the time, but some of the time it would be nice."

I was paraphrasing Thomas McGuane with that last line, and I didn't realize I'd done it until it was done.

"Can't you write your own material, Shrimpton?" He laughed and rubbed his head.

I sighed. "Did I hurt you?"

"There's going to be a bump."

"I'm sorry."

"No, I learned something tonight. Not only are you beautiful, and bright, but you could probably beat the shit out of me."

"I was serious about what I said, Coyote. I can't take much more of this."

"Shrimp, I'm . . . I know I've been a pain lately. I'm sorry if I've been . . . aloof, or whatever. It's just, Mick, I lived in a certain world for almost twelve years, and suddenly I'm . . . in a new world. I know that's a lousy metaphor, but it's . . . I'm having trouble functioning in my new world."

He moved close to me and put his arms around me.

"I'm having such a hard time functioning that, you know, I'm not even sure I can fuck you." He laughed and shook me like he wanted me to laugh too. "I'll get better, I promise."

So, he tried. Not to fuck me—he was serious about that part. But he did lighten up a little, and he did hold me at night. It was a strange feeling, because he was holding me out of duty and not desire, but at least he was trying, and I didn't want to fault him, and perhaps send him back a square or two. "Keep moving forward" was my credo, and it seemed like that was what we were doing.

The show, the modeling jobs Katie got for me, and Katie, kept me going.

Especially Katie.

We spent a lot of time together: Coyote spent every weekend with his kids, and Bradley had practically moved in with his lover. While we were marginally miserable most of the time, we did our best to keep each other's spirits up, and the things that seemed to get us up the highest were (no pun intended) marijuana and rock and roll. Coyote highly disapproved of both, but he tried to be as tolerant of me as I was being of him, and didn't pick any fights about my pastimes.

Katie and I saw every rock and roll concert we could get tickets for, and with Katie's contacts there wasn't much we missed. We'd smoke a joint between us before we left, and take along two or three to smoke during the concert itself. By the time the concert would be over we'd be drenched in sweat from dancing in the aisles, and our faces would be sore from cracking each other up. Just like everybody did in high school.

The time Coyote and I had together was spent mostly nursing him through a series of, I thought, psychosomatic illnesses he developed in lieu of taking his frustration out on me. But when I told him this theory he lifted his shirt and pointed to the raw, tomato-red rash on his stomach and said, "Does this look psychosomatic?"

Coyote and I had our first breakthrough at the same time Katie arranged for my "big break."

The last performance of *Hedda* was scheduled for Saturday night, and Coyote decided that it would be all right to bring Jane and Maggie to see the show. "Look," he'd said, "no one can fault a father for taking his kids to see a play." (Even if they could fault one for having a mistress, I thought.)

"It's kind of a silly show for kids their age," I said.

"I'm not taking them to see the show, I'm taking them to see you in the show, Mickey. Don't be dense."

Turned out they liked it.

Maggie, especially, had been fascinated with the idea that there were people just talking in their living room and letting all those people watch. (It was her first straight drama.)

I was sitting in Katie's living room, gloating about my good reviews from Coyote's kids, when Katie told me her good news.

She'd arranged an audition for me for *Our Time to Live*.

"The soap opera?"

She nodded furiously, waiting for my gratitude.

"Do you really think that that's the sort of thing I ought to do?"

She was visibly flattened by this attitude.

"What do you mean, is this 'the sort of thing' you ought to do?"

"Well, it just . . . it just seems that actresses who do soap operas end up doing soap operas for the rest of their careers."

"Oh, for Christ's sake, Mickey." She rolled her eyes. "*If* you get the part, you'll have nationwide exposure, and you'll make fabulous money."

"I'm making fabulous money now," I countered.

"Yeah, but you're modeling, not acting." That shut me up. "If you don't get the part, you'll have met a lot of new people in the industry who will remember you, besides getting the experience of an on-tape audition and a free trip to Los Angeles. Come on.'' She smiled. ''You've never even been to Los Angeles.''

''I have to go to Los Angeles?''

''Jesus Christ, Mickey, you're an actress—at some point you *have* to go to Los Angeles.''

''A soap opera?'' said Coyote with obvious disgust. ''Los Angeles?'' Coyote, apparently, had been to Los Angeles. ''Well,'' he said and shrugged, ''chances are you won't get the part anyway.''

''Thanks for the huge fucking vote of confidence.'' I kneed him in the ass while he stood at the counter making dinner (now his sole responsibility), but it was a gentle blow and we both laughed, having already decided that, get the part or not, there was no way I was moving to Los Angeles.

Coyote decided that it was time I met Jane and Maggie, face to face and wide-awake.

''You think?'' I was more wary than he was because things were going so well between us and I didn't want anything to set us back.

''It's been almost two months that Shelley and I have been separated. If I don't start seeing someone soon, that could work against me, if you get my drift.''

What the hell? I decided to chance it. ''If you don't fuck me soon I really will get your drift.''

The only problem I had with the way he made love to me that night was that he didn't just swoop down on me and carry me away, but took time to turn off the broiler so that the lamb chops wouldn't burn.

———

We opted for a simple day: a picnic in the park would give me time to get to know the girls, and provide the distraction of the zoo if things went badly. Also, I had to leave for Los Angeles on Sunday and we figured Saturday would be strenuous enough without stretching it into a long drive and/or major physical exertions.

Despite Coyote's being overanxious and my being grossly intimidated by the two little girls, things didn't go badly.

Jane stared at me, looked me up and down, and seemed to check my every feature, my every item of clothing twice. Then she smiled up at me and said, "I've seen you before."

Right, I was about to tell her. *Hedda Gabler.*

"In a magazine. You were all red-white-and-blue."

"Right." I nodded. "That was me."

"And you were the girl with the hair in that play! Where's your hair?" That was Maggie.

"Well, most of it was a fall. A wig," I explained.

"Your name's real funny," Maggie continued.

"Mickey?" I asked her.

"No!" She said this like: hey-don't-be-so-stupid. "Ozzie!" And she let go with a great big husky laugh, delighted by my name. "I'm gonna call you Oz, like in Dorothy," she said.

"Fine by me." I was relaxing a good deal. By the time we were finished eating our picnic, Maggie and I were dancing around the grass to the tunes from Coyote's transistor. Eventually the ever-composed Jane joined in. Coyote claimed his bad leg and sat out, but I could tell by the expression on his face that he felt relaxed and relieved, and part of something.

I spent the night in my own apartment (a girlfriend was okay, but a lover was pushing it) and spent Sunday morning packing. I stopped by Coyote's place before I headed for the airport.

"Hello?" I poked my head in the door.

"In here," I heard Coyote's weakest voice coming from the bedroom. I sincerely hoped he was deathly sick, because if he wasn't, that voice meant he was depressed and I was in too good a mood to deal with it.

I found him sitting in the chair by his bed playing with a Smurf that Maggie had left behind.

"What's your problem?" I sat down on the bed. Be a good girlfriend. Hear him out. This was a rough time for him.

"Maggie wants to know when her mom and I will be divorced, and when that happens can she go and live with Oz?"

"She asked you that?" I smiled.

"No," Coyote said. "She asked Shelley."

"Hey, look." I shook my head. "You know, I'm sorry your kid likes me."

"God, I miss them!" He shouted and bent over, held his face in his hands. He was crying but he was damned if I was going to see something like that again. "You can't imagine how much Maggie saying that hurt Shelley!" He'd wiped his face and was looking at me again. "You don't care how many people you hurt, do you? Let me tell you something: Shelley and I may have had a bad marriage, but she is a good mother. She's a great mother! And I won't have her hurt like that. I can't let you see the kids anymore until Shelley says it's okay. That's it. Period."

And then, as was my habit when attacked, I said something to hurt back. Something incredibly stupid that I wished I could pull back in my mouth the moment it was out.

"Hey, fine. No skin off my teeth."

Coyote sat back in his chair and looked at me like I was the Wicked Witch of the West. "Good God," he said. "I can't believe I gave up my whole family to get you. What a prize."

"Don't blame me for this. I didn't do anything but make that kid happy! I didn't do anything but love you. I will not be held responsible for breaking up your family."

"Who else is responsible? Tell me. Tell me."

"You said you were going to get a divorce the summer before I even met you."

"Yeah, but we wouldn't have. We wouldn't have if I hadn't met you!"

I couldn't think of anything to do but throw myself on the bed and cry. Buckets. I sobbed so hard that the bed began to shake. Coyote let me lie like that for a good ten minutes before he came over and put his hand on my shoulder.

"You okay?"

"No, I'm not okay, asshole." I jerked his hand away.

"Shrimp . . ."

"Shut up!" I bellowed this, and stood up. "That's it. I've had it. I've taken all I can take. I don't want to be in this relationship anymore. I don't want to be responsible for you doing one fucking thing ever again. Go home, Coyote. Go home. Go home. Go home. Go home and be in your miserable little marriage with your precious little kids. I hereby give you back to your family."

I grabbed my suitcase and hit the door. Coyote was on my heels, shouting "Wait a minute, Mickey" in a conciliatory voice. I acknowledged him, on the second-

162

floor landing, long enough to throw him his keys. Then I grabbed a cab for JFK.

"L.A. is limousines, and hotels with room service, and heat. Heat! My God, the heat. There is no moisture in the air here," I said.

"What you call 'moisture' is just humidity by another name, and most people hate humidity."

"God, grant me humidity any day. I've been here for an hour and a half and my skin is dehydrating already. This is supposed to be healthy?"

Katie was cracking up on the other end of the line. I called her as soon as I got checked into my hotel and had smoked the half a joint I found in my pack of cigarettes. I was incredibly high and that was the only reason I wasn't still crying. That, and having cried for six hours on the plane. I was cried out.

"So, really, what do you think of Los Angeles now that you've been there for an hour and a half?"

"Laid back. Laid back. No question. So laid back that if we're all lucky, it'll just lay back and die."

"Yeah. Yeah. Hey, Mick, you really don't sound so good. Are you sure you're all right?"

So I told Katie all about the fight with Coyote.

"It's the last one, Katie. I'm really not able to deal with him anymore."

"I think that's a good decision, Mickey."

"I plan on being a basket case for a while, though."

"Join the club."

"We'll just have to take care of each other."

"Isn't that what we've been doing?" Then Katie got practical again. "Have you been crying?"

"Yes."

"Do me a favor: Put some cucumber slices on your eyes and take a nap. If you don't it's going to look like 'Invasion of the Bug People' when you do your test tomorrow. You know how your eyes get when you cry."

"Katie, I'm in a hotel in a place called Century City and I have no idea where Century City is, but it doesn't look like it has a grocery store. Where am I going to get a cucumber?"

"Call room service, idiot."

Room service was only too happy to comply with my request for a sliced cucumber, and I looked wonderful for my audition the next day. But I didn't feel so hot. I'd finished the joint the night before and I had no more artificial stimulants with me. I didn't think I should call room service for that one, so I dialed Coyote's number. He wasn't home and I went to my audition feeling like I wanted to die.

The audition itself, after I'd met everyone connected with the process—like the director and the casting director and the producer and Jeremy Schaffer, who was gorgeous and whom I would be playing opposite if I got the part—was over in ten minutes.

Jeremy and I stood on the set and everyone else retreated to a little room to watch us on little screens.

"So, you're my would-be co-star," said Jeremy.

For some reason, his comment humiliated me. "Actually, I'm a wouldn't-be, but I've got a friend who thinks it's a good idea."

The disembodied voice of the director shouted, "We're ready. Action."

I had lunch with an agent ("I don't want an agent in Los Angeles, Katie. I want an agent in New York." "It won't hurt you to meet her, Mickey. Her agency does have an office in New York too."), and when my driver finally got me back to my hotel I raced to my room to call Coyote.

Well, he was probably in class anyway.

I dialed Katie's number, but I got her answering machine: "Hi, this is Kate Barrows, and you've called at a time when I just can't answer the phone. If you'd like to leave a message for either Bradley or myself, you'll have thirty seconds to do so at the tone. Thanks for calling."

"Kate Barrows, this is Mickey Azzi, and I just want you to know I fucked up my audition by alienating my would-be co-star and acting like a complete drag because I am so goddammed depressed. I had lunch with your agent friend and I alienated her, too, but she deserved it because she suggested I change the spelling of my name to M-I-C-C-I. *Mee-chi* she wants me to be—can you believe that shit? Also, just so you know, I am not able to deal with this depression over Coyote and I am going back to him as soon as I can, if he'll . . ."

The machine cut me off and I called back.

"If he'll have me," I said at the sound of the second tone, "but I can't get hold of him and I'm scared to death he took me seriously and went back to his wife. God, that sounds gross. I still hate Los Angeles, but I love you. Bye." I hung up before the machine got the chance.

Why didn't I schedule my flight back to New York for the day of the audition? I wasn't leaving until the next morning and I had a whole evening to kill. I should have been nicer to the people I met that day, and maybe I wouldn't have been sitting alone in a room in Century

City wondering where I was, and why Coyote was not home *again*.

I was soaking in the bathtub wondering how painful drowning was when Ben called. Did I want to have dinner? You bet!

He picked me up in his Rolls, which, he informed me, was a Silver Cloud, whatever that was.

"You've never heard of a Silver Cloud?" He was incredulous. "Everyone knows what a Rolls-Royce Silver Cloud is."

I shrugged. "Cars don't interest me. I have this incredible capacity to go deaf when people talk about things that don't interest me."

"A challenge!" said Ben. "Always up for a good challenge."

"Sure you are. That's why you're living in L.A."

He took me to a restaurant called Adriano's, where the owner knew him by name, and which belied its elegant atmosphere and fabulous food by being located in a shopping plaza.

"Yeah, I manage Jeremy Schaffer," Ben informed me when I mentioned that was who I'd auditioned with.

"Yeah, well, don't mention me to him."

"Why?"

"Because he probably thinks I'm the most hostile bitch he's ever met, that's why."

Ben nodded like he understood how Jeremy could think that.

"Look, Ben, I'm sorry." I put down my fork and swallowed so that I could talk to him. "I'm really not that bad. I'm just . . . I broke up with my boyfriend and I decided that I didn't want to break up with him and now I

166

can't get hold of him to tell him so. Rash decisions. I'm good at rash decisions. But you brought me here, to a really lovely place, and I think you're sweet for that and I'm lousy company, so why don't you take me back to my hotel and we'll call it a date?"

"No," said Ben, "I don't think you're lousy company. . . ."

"I give you one shot at getting off the hook. Take it or you're stuck with me for the evening."

"Tell me about your boyfriend."

"Oh, wow. Where do I begin?"

"If you think you've got to give it another try, give it another try. It sounds pretty hopeless to me."

Ben and I were still in Adriano's. I was drinking my third or fourth glass of Amaretto and he was keeping up with Sambuca.

"I have to give it another try. I love him. I feel like dying right now."

"Right now, sure. But give it a little time and that feeling will subside."

"Ben, you don't understand. If you truly love someone, the feelings don't subside. I truly love Coyote."

"How old are you?"

"Almost twenty."

"Oh, for God's sake, you're still measuring your age in 'almosts.' Believe me, you'll get over this Coyote, and you'll be free to love again. Sooner than you think. Maybe even me." He winked at me and took my hand.

"Don't bet on it," I said. But I let his hand remain on mine.

At midnight we were cruising Sunset in Hollywood. Ben was pointing out the sights and singing, displaying a sweet voice and an incredible memory for the lyrics to old television theme songs: *Mr. Ed* and *The Beverly Hillbillies* and *Car 54, Where Are You?* The only one I knew all the words to was *Felix The Cat,* so we did a duet.

"You really have a good voice," I told him.

He nodded. "I should. I sang my way through college."

"With a rock band?"

"Madrigal group."

"Seriously?"

"Seriously."

When I got back to my apartment the light on my machine was flashing. I dropped my luggage, rewound the tape, punched LISTEN, and prayed I would hear Coyote's voice.

Instead, what I heard were one message from Katie ("Mickey, this is Katie. I got your message and I will still love you even if you alienated the whole town. I will think you're an asshole, but I will still love you. Why aren't you home yet? I'm getting worried. Call as soon as you get in."); a dozen or so hang-ups; and exactly twenty-three messages from Shelley. Dad's Shelley.

What the hell did she want?

I dialed Coyote's number. Still no answer. I dialed Katie's number and got her machine. "If you're so fucking worried about why I'm not home yet, why aren't you there waiting for my call?" I said and hung up. Then I dialed my old number in Pennsylvania and hoped that Dad wouldn't pick up, because I really didn't want to talk to him. I was interested in a reconciliation with Coyote, not him.

"Shelley, this is Mickey. What was so damned urgent?"

"Mickey! I've been trying to reach you for days. Where were you?"

"Los Angeles. What did you want?"

"Your dad died on Sunday and the funeral's tomorrow. I thought you'd want to know."

"My dad died?"

"This is probably not the best time to ask you this" —Katie was helping me unpack and repack in time to catch the next flight to Pittsburgh—"but, I thought your dad died over Christmas."

"He didn't."

"You lied about your dad being dead?"

"Uh-huh."

I was gathering up a load of clothes to toss in the washer.

"Will you come with me to the basement? I hate it down there when I'm alone."

"Mickey, will you please stop being so frenetic. Talk to me. Your dad just died, for Christ's sake."

"He didn't just die. He's been dead for two days."

"What are you feeling? I can't tell."

"You? The mind reader?"

I raced back up the stairs to my apartment and tried Coyote's number once more.

"Do you think I should try him at his wife's place? Just in case he's there?"

"I think you should calm down."

I emptied my toilet bag and refilled all the little

plastic bottles with the appropriate liquids from my medicine chest.

"Mickey." Katie followed me into the bathroom. "Why don't I make us some tea, and we can just sit down and talk."

"Because I have to catch a plane in two hours to go to my father's funeral, which I almost missed because I went to that stupid audition. I mean, come on, what would people think if I missed my own father's funeral? The clothes are probably ready for the dryer. Will you come with me while I do that?"

"I'll do it myself. You stay here and do whatever it is you want to do."

"Thank you."

I tried Coyote's place innumerable times, and then I tried Coyote's wife's place, but no one was there either, and I was rather grateful for that.

"Will you order me a cab, and I'll finish folding the clothes?"

Katie put a bra back on the pile of laundry. "I will if you promise to tell me what's going on in your head. I'm getting worried about you, kiddo. What are you feeling?"

"You really want to know what I'm feeling, Katie? Okay. Relief. I'm feeling relief. Will you please call me a cab now?"

Katie rode with me to the airport.

"I do believe you," Katie was saying. "It's just that most people don't feel relieved when their father dies."

"You didn't know my father," I told her.

"Okay. Look. Whatever you say. If you want me to buy it, I'll buy it."

"I don't want you to buy anything. My father died,

170

that's all, and I'm not incredibly upset about it. How can I explain this? There are some feelings that are not necessary to feel. Like remorse about leaving a parent who's treated you like shit, and calling him dead. Guilt is a useless emotion. Now he's really dead, and I still don't think it's necessary to feel remorse. I'll just go home, put in my appearance, and then the matter will really be laid to rest, pun intended. What I honestly feel is relief."

God, it was getting hard to breathe.

Katie emptied her purse and slapped it over my face.

"Do you hyperventilate often when you feel relief?" she asked.

Neil picked me up at the airport. I was still frenetic.

"Was it a heart attack?" I asked.

Neil nodded.

"I figured. Look, Neil, I've never planned a funeral before. I'll need your help."

"Well," said Neil, "I don't know that there's a lot left to do. Shelley's got most of it under control."

He came into the house with me, carrying my bag. "Shelley," he called. "I'm here with Mickey."

"I'll be down in a minute."

She came down the stairs wearing a robe and holding a tissue to her nose, which was swollen and Rudolph-red from crying. Boy, and I thought bug eyes were a problem. Her grief impressed me, because I couldn't come anywhere near it.

I was also impressed by the way she quietly made a pot of coffee and sat down with Neil and me at the kitchen table to talk about the funeral.

"He's wearing his dark-blue suit. The one that's almost black. And a plain white shirt and a striped tie. I

171

found some pocket handkerchiefs, the silk kind, in his closet, but I didn't put one on him because I never saw him wear one." She dabbed at her eyes, which were like faucets. "Also, he's wearing his watch. You should tell the mortician if you want that removed before they bury him. His casket is rosewood, and it's very pretty. I think you'll like it. Neil's going to do the eulogy, and I decided to have a Catholic ceremony even though Ev would probably laugh at that. But I want one. I hope all this stuff is okay with you. . . ."

"Hey"—I shrugged—"I wasn't around. Somebody had to do it."

"Well," said Shelley, "I'm exhausted. I'm just going to go up to bed and go to sleep. Just make yourself . . . well, you know, it's your house."

"Is that the same girl I met over Christmas?" I asked Neil when she'd gone.

"She's taking this really hard."

"Grief suits her."

The funeral home was empty except for Neil and Ginch and Shelley and me. I'd asked for a private viewing before the service, and the mortician and his wife were standing by, ready to seal the casket and load it in the hearse.

Shelley was kneeling on the cushion by the coffin, rubbing Dad's hand with the tip of one finger. Ginch was drooling on his lapel, watching the mortician's wife. Neil was standing behind me, like a bodyguard, while I sat in a chair and got my last glimpse of my father's earthly body.

"You think he could stop for one day," I said.

"Who?"

"Ginch." I nodded my head to indicate the mortician's wife.

Shelley stood up and came over to me. "I'll leave you
alone with him," she said. Then she called for Ginch to
escort her to the car, and he finally shut his mouth and
swallowed.

Neil started to follow them out the door.

"Neil." I shook my head. "I don't want to be alone
in here."

He stopped and turned to stay. I approached the
casket.

Well. He looked natural enough. Except that you
could tell his lips were stitched together. His hair was the
way he always wore it. Neil told me that Shelley had
come down to view the body before anyone else saw
him, and had redone it because it wasn't just right. Well,
she had done a good job.

I thought about how handsome Dad was. How no
one would ever again be impressed by the way he moved.
And how much we had had together in between the times
we fought and hated each other. I thought about the
expression on his face when I was little and would find
an arrowhead he'd planted, and that brought me close to
tears. Then I thought about the way he laughed when he
told me not to come back after our last fight, and that
dried the tears up.

I reached out to touch his hand, but I quickly drew
back; his hand was freezing cold.

Well, what did you expect, Mickey? He's dead.

I stared at him a while, trying to decide whether to
cry or not. I finally decided that the bad times we'd gone
through outweighed the good ones, and I signaled Neil
that I was ready to leave.

Neil was concerned about me.

After the funeral we went together to the house, to sit in the kitchen and drink coffee, to give me time to pack up my things, to wait until it was time to go to the airport so I could catch my plane back to New York.

"I'm really fine, Neil. Please don't worry so much."

"I'm worried, Mickey, because he's dead, and you're still mad at him." Neil handed me a cup of coffee: half coffee, half cream, and three cubes of sugar, like he used to fix it for me when I was a kid. "I know you two fought, had that big fight over Christmas. You know he loved you very much."

"You really expect me to believe that after that last blowup we had? Like he cared if I ever came home again."

"Okay. You want a little misery? I don't think he wanted to love you. I think it's fair to say he never learned how to deal with you. Or how he felt about taking care of you after your mom left. But he worried about you, and he cared for you, and he did the best he could. And he did hope you'd come home again."

"Neil, do me a favor. I've got all this . . . this stuff with my dad in perspective. Don't try to make me feel things that I've already felt, and dealt with, and have under control."

PART NINE

I was dreaming, lately, about being late.

I presumed the dreams were due to *OTTL*, and the ungodly hour they expected me at the studio every weekday morning. And, of course, there was the general problem I had getting out of bed at all since I'd started on the soap: Ben had to drag me bodily out of the sack and shake me awake.

"Shake, shake, shake those sleepies away," he'd say while he wildly rotated my shoulders.

Lately, however, the dreams had progressed to action: I got out of bed and began to actually get ready for work, in my sleep. Lately, I'd been taking sleep-baths.

The alarm would go off and Ben would reach over to drag me out of bed, to start shaking me, and I wouldn't be in bed. I would be in a full tub of warm bubbly water, still dressed in whatever I'd worn to bed the night before, soundly asleep.

This had been going on for about a month, every day, and Ben thought it was very funny. It was the main reason I had insisted Katie come to Los Angeles.

"Mickey." Katie was leaning over me, rubbing my arm.

I felt around me, was relieved to find that I was still in bed and that Katie hadn't caught me in the tub. Then I felt the pain.

"I can't get out of bed."

It was probably the hangover, the best hangover I ever had: headache, body aches, nausea, the works.

I lay in bed, on my stomach. I was still wearing my makeshift panty hose and makeup from the night before. My mouth was open and my face was resting in a puddle of drool. I thought about Ginch and laughed and it made my head feel as if it were going to burst open.

Katie turned me over, propped me up, and handed me two aspirin, a vitamin C tablet, and a can of Coke.

I reached my hand to the other side of the bed.

"Where's Ben?"

"Downstairs. On the couch."

I nodded. I vaguely remembered kicking him out of the bedroom the night before, but I couldn't remember why.

"What time is it?" I put the pills in my mouth and sipped the Coke. Nothing like Coke to clear the hangover fog from your head and clean the hangover scum from your mouth.

"Nine," said Katie.

"I can't get out of bed."

It was probably the late night. Ben and I did go to a lot of parties, but because of my early-morning calls for *OTTL*, we never stayed out quite that late.

"Come on, Mick. It's a beautiful Sunday."

"It's raining."

"Just get up and shower. You'll feel better."

"I don't want to feel better."

"How about some breakfast?"

"Please"—I dragged the word out to an emphatic eight syllables—"no food."

Katie was pulling the pillows out from under my head and ripping the covers off the bed.

"Jesus Christ, Katie." I grabbed for the pillows, the comforter. I shoved her out of the way and rolled myself up in a ball, clutching at the sheets.

"Come on, kiddo." Katie was tickling my exposed ribs with a single finger and being so damned cheerful I wanted to hit her.

"I can't get out of bed!" I screamed at her and I thought the wedge that had been threatening my head had finally split it open.

I felt Katie's cool hands on my back, rubbing my shoulders, making soothing circles at the base of my neck. There was nothing like a good friend rubbing the base of your neck when you had a hangover to make you feel loved. I started to cry.

"Hey, it's okay, kiddo. It's my fault. I should have realized how bad you felt. I should've realized you have to be gentle when you drag a drunk out of bed."

"Stop," I said, "you're making me laugh." And the laughter was making the pain in my head profoundly worse.

First, I peed. Then I brushed my teeth. Hard. Until the gums bled. Then I flossed and gargled furiously with Scope. I used a cotton ball and Vaseline to remove my smeared black makeup from the night before. I turned the shower on, as hot as I could stand it, and got in.

I scrubbed mercilessly: my body with a loofah, and my face with a Buf-Puf, my knees and elbows and heels with a Dr. Scholl's callous remover. I lathered my hair, once, twice; then I rubbed in a conditioner and let it condition while I shaved all the excess hair off my body. Then I stood under the nozzle, turned off the hot water, and let ice water rinse me clean and cold. Even if you couldn't get anything else in your life clean and in order, you could scrub your body until it shone.

Katie came in with a tray: hot coffee and orange juice and toast and eggs.

"Feel better?"

"A little." I poured a cup of the coffee and took a sip. I gagged on it, then swallowed, and waited for the caffeine to jolt me awake.

"Is Ben up yet?"

"Yeah."

"Is he mad?"

"I think so."

I rubbed vitamin E cream on my face, wrapped my old white terry robe around me, grabbed a towel to dry my hair, and my cup of coffee, and went down to the living room to see him.

"Hi."

Ben was sitting on the couch in his red silk briefs, rubbing the sleep out of his eyes. His hair was matted and stuck out from his head in a halo of spikes, like a little boy's. He looked up at me when I spoke.

"I hear you're mad," I said, and sat beside him, smoothed back his tufts of hair.

"Don't you think I have a reason to be mad?"

"Aw, Ben, what'd I really do?"

"You made a mess out of my car, for one thing. Ruined one of my ties. You made an ass out of yourself at Rod's. You threw up all over his bathroom."

"Katie cleaned that up."

"Oh, before that? You ran around kissing everyone, telling them how wonderful they are, telling them how wonderful you are, spilling your drinks. You cornered Rod's girlfriend and physically attacked her."

"I what?"

"You grabbed her and started kissing her, and you know how Adrienne hates that. . . . Then you went into your hate-L.A. routine, lingered on the part about how you hate L.A. women, the kind who 'hug with their asses stuck out and who, though they are well over the age of eighteen, still refer to their fathers in adult conversation as Daddy.' Fortunately, Rod thought it was all very funny. Until you started to cry, and slapped your hand over your mouth and ran for the bathroom. Only Jeremy was in there. You screamed for him to put his 'pecker' back in his pants because you had to 'puke.' "

"I don't remember that."

"I'm sure you'll be able to read about it sometime today. Mickey," he said, "what's wrong? What are you doing? I mean, you've never been the easiest person to live with, but now . . ."

"Don't start on me."

"Mickey, something's wrong. You threw me out of bed last night, so I know something's wrong."

January is monsoon season in Los Angeles. Katie and I took a walk on the beach: a rainy beach to fit my mood. Katie loved it, made designs in the soppy sand with her toes as we walked.

"I developed a crush on one of the *OTTL* cameramen because he cracked his Juicy Fruit while we spoke. Also, I had the embarrassing experience of a public (and almost instantaneous) orgasm at Trumps when I smelled the bartender's Antaeus," I said.

Katie laughed.

"If you think that stuff's good, you ought to be around me when I get a whiff of coconut."

Juicy Fruit, Antaeus, and coconut: Coyote. His smells.

"A few years ago, I bought Ben a bottle of Antaeus to replace that wimpy Lagerfeld he wears, and he wore it, and I realized what a shoddy specimen he was next to Coyote. That's when I started hating him."

"Oh, Mick," said Katie, "how can you hate Ben?"

"You know why I hate him most?"

"No, why?"

So I explained it to her.

Once in a lifetime, if you were very, very lucky, someone came along with whom you could share an unabashed adoration, fight with and still love, and never, ever get tired of fucking. I had been lucky once. And now I had Ben.

Diddle was the worst word in the English language. Diddle: to move from side to side by jerks; to shake; to let your fingers ramble in random assault. *Diddle* was the best word I could think of to describe what Ben did when he clamped his hand over my vulva every other night or so: an indication that he was ready to fool around. *Fool around.* Another apropos description.

Eyes closed, on his back, concentrating furiously (so furiously that, at times, his eyes would squint), Ben would diddle me.

With his free hand he would diddle himself. My job was to lick, in a precisely timed circular motion, his fat pink penis. I had gotten the timing, the motion, and even the moisture level down to an exact science, because variation caused Ben to have a sharp loss of concentration, and that caused immediate deflation.

When we'd reached that semi-soft state, that point of erection when penetration is not impossible, merely implausible, he would maneuver his 195-pound bulk on top of me, complain that I was dry, drip a thick rivulet of spittle on his fingers, transfer the spittle to my vaginal lips, and lunge.

Then he would pump. Pump, puff, pump: clasp me so tightly that I would gasp for air (and he would mistake my inability to breathe for pleasure), and sweat. Sex as, purely, a bodily function. Function. Ben, pumping away, searching not for pleasure but for relief.

The first time, I presumed it was the strain of adjusting to a new partner, and thought that, if things didn't improve, I'd suggest sex therapy. But when it was all over and he'd shot his load, he crawled off of me and downward to plant a big wet kiss on my pubic bush (the closest Ben would ever get to oral sex, I would learn).

"You were great," he'd said.

"Really?"

"Really the best, baby."

I'd felt sorry for him.

As we progressed in our sexual life, I'd tried a few variations in position, displayed a frantic, if imagined, passion, and, God help me, bought Saran-wrap underwear. I was met with ever more deflation as those ploys seemed to interfere with the thoughts Ben needed to think to make himself work.

Then came the day I suggested anal sex as a diverting titillation and Ben suggested *I* see a sex therapist.

I contented myself after that with my own fantasies. If I was careful about keeping my hands under Ben's shoulders when he was on top of me, I could manage to keep my lungs from collapsing, and a satisfactory climax. The worst part was worrying that, hey, if it was good enough for Ben, why wasn't it good enough for me? I'd had my one lucky shot and I'd blown it, and so I had to deal with reality. Why wasn't the reality good enough? At least I was getting it regularly, if not well.

"Yeah, so," said Katie and shrugged. "I always figured Ben to be pretty lukewarm in the sack."

"You know what I fantasize about? Coyote. Or I can't get off."

"I saw that coming."

"Oh, shit, Katie."

"Mickey, if it's that bad, why don't you just leave Ben?"

"I don't know. I guess I can't stand the thought of losing anyone else."

By that time we were soaked through from the rain, and freezing.

"Christ," said Ben when we got home, as he handed us a pile of towels. "You're going to get pneumonia."

"Aw, Ben, I'll be fine." I toweled myself off and coughed.

"This is really irresponsible, Mickey." He shook his head. "And you have to shoot early tomorrow. I thought you'd know better, Kate."

Katie looked up from drying her hair and Ben left the room.

"I can't take your car." I dismissed Ben's suggestion immediately.

"Why not?"

"Because if I wreck it, you'll kill me."

"I'll drive." Katie settled it. "Besides, I'm anxious to see all my old *OTTL* buddies."

"See? Okay. Great. I'll have my secretary take your car to the shop tomorrow and pick you up a loaner."

Ben was making us hot tea with Drambuie. Katie and I were curled up on kitchen chairs, wrapped in Indian blankets. He called me "Sitting Bull" and served me. I reached out from under the warmth to clasp the cup. He kissed the top of my head.

"What would you do if I didn't take care of you?" he said, and meant it.

That night, in our big bed, I curled around Ben's warm bulk. He snuggled me and whistled me to sleep with the theme from *Leave It to Beaver*.

Apparently what had happened was that I'd taken a sleep-bath. Apparently, I'd slipped under the water in my sleep and not noticed. I woke, lying on the floor next to the tub, with my face in a puddle of vomit and Katie, because it had been she who'd administered the mouth-to-mouth, leaning over me.

"You okay?"

Ben had already called an ambulance, and when it got there he and Katie insisted I go to the hospital.

"I'm perfectly all right," I protested as we rode. "I don't need a doctor."

"No, you need a shrink," said Katie under her breath.

"Don't be overdramatic about this," I admonished her in the waiting room while Ben filled out my insurance papers.

"Overdramatic? Jesus Christ, Mickey, you almost fucking drowned! You were almost good and goddammed dead!" She was yelling this loudly and people were looking.

"Will you not shout, please?" I whispered.

"I'm sorry." Katie rubbed her eyes. "It's six A.M. I'm never at my best at this hour."

"Do you think it has something to do with your father?"

"Oh, please."

The doctor had pronounced me physically fit and able to work, so we'd gone back to the house, changed, and were on our way to the studio in Ben's now-spotless Rolls, Katie at the wheel.

"No, seriously, Mickey. I mean that, do you think it has something to do with your father that you're so fatally attracted to someone who's so wrong for you?"

"Fatally attracted?"

"You almost drowned yourself over this thing about Coyote."

"I almost drowned myself because I'm having dreams that I'm late for something and I try to get ready for it in my sleep."

"Tell me about your dreams."

"A little armchair analysis, Dr. Barrows? I'd always thought your doctorate was in theater education?"

"Just tell me."

"Okay. A typical dream: I'm doing something pleasant, and all of a sudden I realize I shouldn't be doing it because I'm supposed to be somewhere else. I never know where else I'm supposed to be, but it's never where I am, in the dream.

"Anyway, before I can go and get ready to make this appointment, the situation gets dangerous."

"Like?"

"Like I'm taking a walk in the woods and suddenly it's full of South American guerrillas trying to shoot me."

"Go on."

"So, before I can get out of there, one of the guerrillas spots me, and starts shooting. I try to run, or hide, and
when I realize that that's useless, I stop and lie very still,
and close my eyes, and try not to hear, on the theory that
if I don't know when 'it's' coming, 'it' won't hurt as
much."

"Then?"

"Then, after I've been lying there for a while, I realize 'it's' not coming, so I open my eyes and I'm in my
bedroom, in bed, and I still have to get to that appointment. That's when I get up and take my sleep-bath."

"Is it always a walk in the woods?"

"No. Sometimes I'm mountain climbing. And it's Nazis
that're chasing me, but I don't think those are the parts of
the dreams that would be considered significant."

Katie shook her head. "I don't know, Mick."

"What?"

"What it means, but it's more complicated than you've
let on."

"Katie, it's just a dream."

"Mick, what are you going to do?"

I shrugged.

"I would hope now that you've almost killed yourself, you would decide that it was time to take some
action."

"You're being overdramatic again."

"You're being an asshole."

"It was an accident. It wasn't intentional."

"Still, it did happen. If Ben's alarm hadn't gone off
when it did, he would have found you a little too late,
and at this very moment I would be writing your eulogy
instead of driving you to work."

"You would've written something nice?"

"I don't believe you!" Katie pounded the steering wheel. "Wake up! You can't pretend that the bad things never happened anymore, Mickey, because it's starting to catch up with you!" She hit the steering wheel with both hands and the car swerved onto the shoulder.

"Watch the fucking road"—I grabbed the wheel and jerked the car back into our lane—"or we'll both be dead."

"Mickey." She grabbed my hand and squeezed it. "Please. What are you going to do? You can't stay in this situation."

"I'm in this situation because of you."

"Oh, blame me."

"You never did like my being with Coyote." I pulled my hand free from hers. "Christ. You never did understand." I said this knowing how well Katie understood, and stared out the window for the rest of the trip.

PART TEN

Of course, when I got back to New York after the funeral, all that was on my mind was to locate Coyote.

I called his place, his wife's place, and at both places the phone just kept ringing. I took to calling all night long and still there was no answer. I couldn't even go to his apartment on Seventy-second Street to check things out, because I'd thrown the keys back at him the day I left for Los Angeles.

Coyote had just disappeared.

I called Information and found out that both numbers were still listed, and that brought me great comfort.

I went to auditions. I never got any parts because I went looking like shit, and acting worse, and with a real bad attitude.

There was the modeling thing, but even that was starting to taper off because I showed up at all the bookings with bug eyes from crying and I didn't care.

Katie came to my apartment almost every night and I'd listen to her whine about her divorce when she wasn't listening to me whine about Coyote. Some afternoons I'd go out apartment hunting with her, but that depressed the piss out of me because I'd done it so recently with Coyote. Eventually even Katie got fed up with me.

I'd been out on a shoot all morning, at a beach on Long Island. The shoot was for a cosmetics company hot to hype its "natural-looking" foundation and I was to ride a gorgeous chestnut horse along the tide line (as if, hey, don't we all wear foundation when we're riding horses on the beach?) while the photographer snapped away.

Unfortunately, the horse was not in a good mood that morning, and our sixth or seventh time down the beach, he bolted. The art director came running to pick me up, and when the trainer caught up with the horse he noticed blood on its gums and yelled at me for pulling in too tightly on the reins.

"I thought you said you could ride," he snipped, hand on hip, the only fag cowboy I'd ever met.

"I can ride," I said. "I can't bust broncos." Typically, I exaggerated all out of proportion, but my ankle was sprained, and it hurt.

"I refuse to let her back on this horse." The trainer simped and posed for the photographer.

"Oh, shove it up your ass," I said and limped to my rented car to go home.

"Okay," said Katie when I told her what had happened, "what you need is to get something new in your life. You need to get Coyote off your mind, stop thinking about him. Begin again. How about a new apartment? You could certainly afford a nicer place."

"Oh, God, no more apartment hunting."

"Well, okay. How about a vacation? Why don't you take a vacation, and just get the hell out of the city for a while?"

"Because I don't need to be alone right now. Katie, what I need is to find out where Coyote is."

I dialed the two places of Coyote's potential residence, and Katie tolerated it. Barely. One day, in the middle of one more vain attempt to reach him, my call-waiting signal started beeping.

"Yes, hello?" I jumped on the phone, still expecting it to be Coyote every time the phone rang.

It was the producer of *Our Time to Live*.

"Oh, hi." I was very disappointed. It could have been God himself on that phone and I wouldn't have cared unless he had news about Coyote.

The producer was calling to offer me the part of Lacey Martin.

Katie had been quick to guess who was on the phone and bop me on the head and scowl when I started to turn the part down.

"Tell him you want to think about it over the weekend," she mouthed.

"But I don't," I mouthed back.

"Tell him anyway," she growled.

"I'd like to think about it over the weekend," I said. And then, when I hung up the phone, to Katie: "Coyote and I already decided that if I got the part, I wouldn't take it."

"You think that's still valid?"

"I think that you keep judging *my* relationship with Coyote based on the lies *you* told all the men about leaving your husband."

"Mick, it could be the something new you need in your life. A new city. A new job. New challenge."

"Please."

"I think you should think about it."
"No, you think I should do it."

The bottom line was that if I took the part on the soap, I admitted that Coyote and I were over and I didn't want to admit that. I didn't believe it. There was something wrong, Coyote was lost somewhere out of my reach, but I knew that I was still with him. He was thinking about me, and loving me, and wanting our unit. Wherever he was, he was trying to heal the hurt of my leaving him as I had the last time we saw each other. I'd stormed out of his apartment and wouldn't turn back to him when he called. I'd let him down, and like a real coyote he was off in seclusion, healing.

Despite Katie's encouragement to take the part and move to Los Angeles, and all her protestations that if Coyote really wanted me he'd have called already (it had been a month), I hung on to him with white knuckles.

What finally got me was fall.

Katie had rousted me out of bed and we'd rented bikes and were riding them around Central Park and I had to stop. I had to stop and sit because I was too numb to pedal.

I could smell the fall in the air. Could feel the air turning sharp and crisp. Could remember all too vividly walking in the park with Coyote and feeling the autumn sunshine and holding a red carnation he'd bought for me.

My face grew into a monstrous mask of grief and I gasped and grunted, willed it to be the previous fall, when Coyote and I were just beginning to be in love and there was something inside of me still alive, and before I had made so many mistakes.

I wouldn't live through the fall without Coyote and no one in the world should ever have to feel the kind of pain I was feeling.

On Monday, after I'd tried Coyote's homes one last time and felt the hollow ringing of the unanswered phones, I called California and accepted the part of Lacey Martin.

Katie brought champagne to celebrate and I started to pack.

The news traveled fast.

The agent I'd met in L.A. called to offer to represent me. Jeremy Schaffer called to tell me he was looking forward to working with me. And Ben called to offer to help me get settled in his city.

Specifically, there was an extra room in his house where I could stay until I found a suitable apartment, and an extra car that I could drive until I bought one of my own. He didn't want me to feel, he joked, like a refugee.

And I didn't want to be alone.

So I told him that I thought his offer was very generous. He told me that I needn't worry about his not being "cool." "In other words, Mickey, I'm a gentleman unless you say different." I told him I'd love to stay with him for a while.

A day later a Federal Express package arrived, stuffed with photos of Ben's Malibu house labeled KITCHEN and MY ROOM and YOUR ROOM and HOT TUB ROOM and so on.

For two more days I did what Katie told me to do. I packed. And I celebrated. And I bought a bunch of new clothes and luggage for the trip west. And I stopped calling Coyote and I focused all my energy on my new life. I acted strong, and tough, and excited. And then I broke down, the day before I was supposed to leave.

I couldn't shake the feeling that I was leaving something important undone, and I knew very well that it was Coyote. I willed him to be dead, but he wouldn't die. I worried that he would try to call me and I would have gone to California and my phone would be disconnected and he wouldn't be able to reach me and he'd hurt as much as I was hurting now.

So I called him, and on the fourth ring at his wife's place, he picked up.

"Where've you been?"

"Florida."

"With the family, I suppose?"

"Trying to put my marriage back together."

Oh.

"I'm going to Los Angeles."

"Shelley thinks you've already gone somewhere."

"No. I'm moving to Los Angeles. I got the part in the soap and I took it."

"I'll be right there."

He was tanner than usual, and his hair was longer. When he came in he hugged me like he was dying and I inhaled deeply his different scents, his fall crisp smell.

"Why'd you go back?"

"Mickey, I didn't think we were going to be together. If we're not going to be together, there's no reason for me to leave Shelley. You didn't call."

"I tried. About a day later, I tried calling. You sure went back in a hurry."

"I waited almost a week. Where were *you*?"

"Pennsylvania. Pennsylvania, my father died."

"I thought he died over Christmas."

"Not really."

"Mickey, I'm . . . I'm sorry I wasn't there for you."

"Me too."

"I don't understand what's going on here."

I opened a bottle of red wine that Katie'd given me and explained about my father, told Coyote everything. About the fights, and the broken nose, and the "If you leave, don't come back." I explained that I'd had to go back for the funeral, and now Dad was really and truly dead.

He held me again and I breathed in more of him. He kissed my neck and cheeks and almost my mouth. I think the packing crates caught his eye.

"Well, Shrimp." He straightened up. "It was good of you to call. Before you left, you know. Before you took off for Oz."

"Yeah. Well. It was good of you to come down to see me. Before I left."

What did I do now? Just let him leave? Just let us blow it because both of us were too mad to say the right thing? Too proud?

"So, you gave up the apartment?" I asked.

He shook his head. "Not yet."

"But things are all worked out though. Between you and Shelley."

"Not yet."

I nodded. "The kids, though—they're happy you're home."

"Yeah."

Then Coyote reached over to me, and kissed my mouth.

"I'm sorry," he said, and meant he was sorry for everything.

"I'm sorry," I said, and meant the same thing.

Then we made love.

I made coffee and he lay in bed and strummed an air guitar while Joni Mitchell sang his theme song.

"Shrimp," he said when the song ended and we were curled up in the bed with the coffee, "you aren't really going to Los Angeles, are you?"

I sipped my coffee.

"The only reason I was going to Los Angeles was to start a new life without you. But I'd opt for my old life any time."

"Complications, and complaints, and me being an asshole and everything?"

"Everything."

We were back together again. I lay in his arms and let the fall breeze from an open window blow over me and I smelled the fall and I ran my face over the stubble on his chest, where the patch of gray hair I loved was growing back after he'd shaved it, in anger at me, one day in Florida.

Happiness.

Coyote got up and went to the bathroom and when he came out he started to get dressed.

"Where are you going? To Seventy-second Street? We can just stay here tonight."

"Shrimp," he said, like don't-be-thick, "I'm going to my wife's place."

"I don't believe what I'm hearing."

"You expect me to leave Shelley, just like that?"

"I sure don't expect to start from scratch here."

"Shelley's very motivated to work our marriage out, now. I can't just call her and tell her to forget it."

"I can't do this. I can't go through this again."

"Don't be overdramatic. It's embarrassing."

I could feel my face flushing and turning red and I could feel, physically, all sense and rationality and sanity fleeing my body.

"How dare you? How dare you make me so happy, and make love to me, and you knew. You knew you were going to leave me again."

"Shrimp, I have to talk to Shelley about this. I will talk to her tomorrow. I promise."

"You're not leaving this apartment."

"Shrimp."

"Because if you walk out that door you can just kiss me off."

"Jesus, Shrimp."

We went back and forth like that for a while, and Coyote checked his watch constantly. Couldn't stay out too late. When he tried to hold me, I shoved him away. When he left the apartment, I followed him, and we continued to fight on the street.

"Don't be so fucking insecure," he shouted at me. "Would you just let me do what I think is the decent thing?"

"The decent thing? What about being decent to me for once, for Christ's sake?"

A cab pulled up.

"I'll call you in the morning."

"Don't bother. I'll be in California," I screamed.

"Shrimp, you're not going to California. I'll call you

early." He got in the cab and shut the door. "I love you," he said and blew me a kiss because I would not accept one on my flesh.

I stood in the middle of the street, clenched fists and wild eyes, with no place to put my anger. "If you love me, why don't you prove it sometime?" I shouted that after the cab as it turned the corner. I stood for a moment, to collect myself, and then beat it back to my apartment to call Katie.

The next morning.

Katie made us breakfast and helped me with the last of my packing.

"Are you sure you want to do this?" was all she said about the incident last night. "Are you sure you want to go now?"

"I have to, Katie. He makes me crazy."

He called. Early, like he said he would.

"You know what the cab driver I had last night said? He said, 'God, she's so beautiful . . . ! He said that about you, Mick, and I was so glad that you were back in my life. Not that that's the only reason I love you, of course. . . ." He paused and sort of laughed.

"Make it quick, will you, David? I have to catch a plane."

"Oh, Christ. You're not still going?"

"In about half an hour, and I still have to take a shower."

"Because I left last night?"

"I told you not to go."

"I had to."

"Well, now I have to go."

"You're just angry."

"I'm fed up. I'm fed fucking up!" I shouted that.

"Don't shout. Don't fight. I already talked to Shelley."

"I'll bet."

"Mick . . ."

"Coyote, I have to go."

"Don't hang up." He sounded frantic and that made me feel so good that it was sick. "I'll come down. I'm here alone with the kids, so I'll be there as soon as Shelley gets home."

"I told you I'm leaving in half an hour."

When I finally hung up on him, I told Katie not to answer the phone, because it would just be him calling back. I got in the shower.

It was hard. Showering. Standing in the shower with the water running over me, and crying too. Washing the last of Coyote, his scents and his stickiness, off of my body. But I scrubbed myself clean and told myself that it was better for Coyote to be dead than for me to cry like that for too long.

I dressed and Katie signed the landlord's sublet papers for my apartment. The phone was ringing constantly. If he really did want me back, I thought, he'd be doing more than just calling. He'd be at my apartment. But he wasn't, so I thought I was doing the right thing. Katie was sad about taking my apartment. "Not only is it really a dive, but it means that I'm really getting divorced," she said.

"It's only temporary," I reminded her. But she was so upset, she thought I meant the divorce.

At the airport, Katie told me that she was going to go into therapy, to help her deal with the divorce, and she thought that maybe therapy would be a good thing for me, too, but I laughed at the suggestion and told her that I could tough things out all right. I told her that I'd call often. I told her that I would miss her. She told me that even though she thought the move was going to be good for me, she would miss me too. We cried and hugged until the last call to board came over the lounge loudspeaker. We kissed goodbye at the gate and I boarded the plane: flew a twitching, pitching 747 through a tornado of turbulence, to Oz.

Ben met me at the gate at the other end. I fell into his arms because his face was familiar and I needed some relief because I hadn't cried on the flight. I'd decided that I just was not going to cry anymore. Period.

Over the next few weeks Ben taught me how to use a Thomas Brothers Guide (the map bible of L.A.), and he showed me where the grocery store and the dry cleaner were, and helped me pick out my first California car. He threw me a Welcome to Los Angeles party, with a cake that had I LOVE L.A. written on it like the "I Love NY" slogan. With the heart and everything. When I couldn't decide whether to sign with the agent or what, and it was getting imperative that I sign with someone, Ben offered to take care of those things for me, manage me. It seemed like a good idea, and a great relief, so I said yes.

I was fairly blunt about still being in mourning over the death of my former lover and Ben patiently insisted that in time I was going to like my life again. He tried to make me like my life. He took me sailing to Catalina on weekends because I told him one of my favorite things about New York was the Staten Island ferry. He drove me to Tahoe to see the season's first snowfall. He came home every night to take me to dinner because I couldn't cook and so I wouldn't have to eat alone. He tried to get me to fall in love with him, but he didn't know what he was up against. Still, his consistency touched me in a vital place.

It was easier to believe Ben than not believe him. It was so easy, in fact, that Ben and I never talked about becoming lovers, or making a life together, or me moving in with him permanently. I just stayed.

PART ELEVEN

I couldn't sleep, so I prowled around the house, made a cup of tea and sat outside, on the terrace, to watch the coyotes who'd come down from the hills to use our pool as a watering hole.

The coyotes had scared me at first: their night prowls on our property, and their howling. Ben had offered to shoot them for me with the gun he kept under his side of the bed, but I found that idea even scarier. Over the years I'd come to enjoy their proximity, the chill and pause given to me each night when I'd watch them come and lap at the chlorinated water.

Katie heard me prowling that night, and came downstairs. I made her a cup of tea and we sat together on the terrace.

"Can't sleep again?"

"No. But, I'm glad. After all these years of not being able to wake up, I see insomnia as a positive development."

Ben made a point of telling me how awful I looked. "You look like a bum" was exactly what he said.

I was wearing jeans, and a white Hanes T-shirt, and a

sweater that was too big because it had once belonged to him, and tennis shoes and no makeup. But even Ben, my arbiter of Los Angeles standards, couldn't get me to change that day, because I was going back to New York and in New York they let you dress any way you wanted to.

Ben didn't want me to go and showed his displeasure and disapproval by letting me drag all my own luggage down to the garage. Katie was already down there, struggling to put the top up on my car (back from the body shop in just five days), so that we wouldn't get drenched in yet another January downpour on our way to the airport.

"Are you sure about this?" Ben asked. He'd been asking me if I "was sure" all week.

"Have your secretary arrange to bring my car back from the airport. I'll leave the parking ticket in the glove compartment. I'll send for anything else I need."

What he was really pissed off about was my walking out on the soap. I'd done what I thought was the decent thing: I'd stayed until my character's main story line was resolved, until Lacey was acquitted of killing her stepmother. Jesus, *OTTL*'s producer was more sympathetic. When I told him I had an emergency out of town, he said he could get another actress to play the role, temporarily, by Monday, and was there anything else he could do? Ben was sure I'd never work again if I walked out, but I'd been a good girl for four years on that show and I deserved to be indulged. The producer told me he'd thought I needed a vacation for a while, but would I please hurry back?

Rod told me the same thing. We were sitting in his studio office and he said, "We'll miss you, so you'll hurry back to us?" If Rod hadn't meant that, it would have been easier to follow Ben's advice and "keep my hand to myself." As it was, I just blurted out that I wasn't sure I wanted to come back. At least not permanently.

Rod nodded. He told me to make sure I got my ass back to Los Angeles when he needed me, and we would work out something on the permanent level.

"Rod, please, I'm trying not to be a jerk about this."

He smiled and ushered me out of his office, the hand holding his unlit cigar around my waist.

Moreover, Ben didn't seem to notice the change coming over me, that I was managing to handle even the peripheral things graciously. I'd gone to Jeremy's house, to his party, to watch his movie air, and I hadn't gotten the least bit drunk or foolish. I'd attended the *Daytime!* awards ceremony and made a quiet, dignified thank-you speech, smiled the whole time, and hadn't said one thing that could be interpreted as belligerent or pugnacious. I wasn't being rash and I wasn't waking up in the bathtub.

When Ben had asked me if I "was sure," I knew it was his bulky, bland way of asking for an explanation. I told him that I had to go back to New York because I was not in love with him. I was in love with Coyote.

"What?" His jaw had dropped. "Why?" he'd wanted to know.

But the only thing I could think of that would clarify my feelings was William Faulkner's: "Between grief or nothing, I would choose grief." And I couldn't tell him that.

I almost giggled. I never giggled, but something unreal, impossible, and impossibly wonderful was about to happen, and it was causing me to giggle. It was inappropriate, however, to giggle around Ben, so I tempered myself.

Ben and I faced each other in the garage.

"I'll miss you," he said.

Sure you will, I thought. How could he miss me? The fact that he was surprised that I wanted to leave Los Angeles, and the soap, and him, was a good indication that he had no idea who I was. But I knew that I could very well miss him. Miss how easy he had made my life, and miss holding onto his bulk when I was alone in bed at night. I looked into his face and saw that he was alone and confused. And sad. It crossed my mind to blank it out: to forget that look on his face; that it would be easier if I simply didn't allow myself to be moved by Ben, or the time we'd spent together. But, as Katie had said, if I wanted to stop feeling I'd left things in my life undone, then I had to stop leaving them undone. I resolved to let myself ache over Ben, and when we embraced, it was hard to let him go. Harder to realize that all the time I'd let him take care of me, and hated him while he was doing it, I'd really been making him into my victim. Ben as victim. A new approach. But he was hurt, and I was going to have to pay for that.

The altitude, and the alcohol (all those free drinks in first class) made me giddy. And anxious. Since we'd boarded the plane I'd been in a fever, my mind urging time to pass faster than was physically possible. Worried. Worried that since it was so close, it wasn't going to happen.

Katie wanted me to calm down, kept reminding me that I wasn't moving back to New York, that this was just a vacation. Reminding me that I had a lot of options open to me, but whatever I'd end up doing, this trip was only the first step to clearing up my life.

"Christ, Katie, it may have taken a major accident to

get me to do this, but I think now that I'm doing it, I should get to be excited about it. Besides," I reminded her, "I'm seeing Coyote in a few hours."

I was seeing Coyote again. After four years. And I couldn't stop picturing Coyote's face, the way he must have looked when he walked into his office and sorted through his mail, and found my postcard. "I can be at the Right Bank at seven o'clock Saturday. Can you? Shrimpton." I kept giggling.

"That's what I mean, Mick," Katie said. "You can't think of Coyote as your only option. You've got to be careful not to set yourself up for a fall here, kiddo."

"You still don't believe that Coyote's as sincere as I am, do you?"

"You expect him to welcome you back, leave his wife—everything to just pick up where it left off?"

"I don't expect anything except that Coyote still loves me the way I love him. Right now, that's more than enough."

Just before the plane landed I made my way to the lavatory to brush my teeth and wash my face and comb my hair.

It was cold when we landed. Cold like it never got cold in California; cold so it slapped you in the face. When we were in the cab on our way into the city, it even started to snow. A "Welcome Home Snow" that turned to black slush as soon as it hit the ground. Very New York. The most beautiful thing I'd seen in a long time. It was six-thirty when we pulled up in front of the restaurant.

"Do you want me to wait?" Katie asked. "In case, just, you know. He doesn't show."

"Not even a possibility, Katie."

"You know him better than I do." Katie shrugged and kissed me before I climbed out onto Madison Avenue. "I'll be waiting at my apartment. I'll unpack for you."

"Thanks Katie." Then, "I love you."

"Love you, too, kiddo."

The Right Bank was the same as I remembered it: narrow, dark, with red-checkered tablecloths, and practically empty. I took a table near the back, by the door to the garden that couldn't be used in winter, and watched the snow fall over a mural of springtime Paris.

I forced my eyes to focus on the garden so that I wouldn't look at the entrance, wouldn't be staring at the door and appear overanxious when Coyote walked in. I would wait for the hand on my shoulder that would be Coyote's and then I would turn, collected, to smile up at him.

I felt the hand on my shoulder.

The waitress bent over and asked me if I wanted something to drink while I waited for my party to arrive.

I ordered a hot buttered rum.

It was 6:45, and looking at the snow fall in the Right Bank's garden was a real bore. I hated hot buttered rum.

I was starting to feel as though my life wasn't happening to me: How was it possible that I was in New York, at the Right Bank, waiting for Coyote? I felt as though I were in a movie, playing a scene in the soap, something. Ordinary noises were amplified: My cup clanked onto the table and the sole of my sneaker squeaked across the floor.

I looked at the door. Coyote would be walking through

it any minute. A watched pot never boils, so I looked at my cup. If he hadn't gotten my postcard, of course, he wouldn't know to meet me here. What were the chances he hadn't gotten it? Murphy's Law. Six fifty. If he didn't show by seven-thirty should I just go back to Katie's? The only excuse I would accept from him for not meeting me was death. His death. The door opened, let in the cold and two people I didn't know. Jesus, Mickey, you were damned sure of yourself, weren't you? All those lines you handed Katie. That Coyote still loves you the way you love him. That his not showing wasn't even a possibility. What if you've become just a fond, distant memory to him? What if you've become just a distant memory? Six fifty-five. I watched the second hand on my watch and was amazed at how time really did crawl sometimes. Slow motion. Life really did move in slow motion. Like my heartbeat was in slow motion. Like my hand, moving my cigarette to my mouth, taking its own sweet time. I could hear my lips opening to accommodate the filter. A gust of cold air coming in from the outside made me shiver.

I stood when I saw Coyote walk in. His eyes shifted, looking for me. I raised my hand to gesture to him to come and he shuffled toward me.

He stood in front of me, and we looked at each other. His eyes moved up and down, taking me in, and I was noticing that he wore his hair a little shorter, and he looked smaller than I remembered him, but he was still Coyote and seeing him still took my breath away.

"God," he said at last, and smiled. "You look like a thoroughbred." He moved to put his arms around me and I fell against him and breathed. Coconuts, his cologne, and Juicy Fruit.

"I've been mad at you."

"I've been mad at you, too."

"Hard staying mad all this time, isn't it?"

The waitress came over and we ordered a bottle of wine.

"You look older," he said when the wine came.

"So do you," I replied.

"No, Shrimp, I always did."

"Think of it this way. You're no longer twice as old as I am."

"Did you used to think of it like that?"

"I saw your book," I told him. "I haven't read it yet, though."

"Don't," he said. "It's not that good."

"Liked the dedication."

"Did you watch my show?"

He shook his head. "Not often."

He sipped his wine.

"You know that poster you did?"

I nodded.

"One of my students brought it in and hung it up in the projection booth. Seems you are his dream girl. I had to look at it every day."

"How are the girls?"

He chuckled.

"Big. Grown-up."

"Yeah?"

"Jane's . . . she's . . ." He used his hand to indicate

her size. "She takes piano lessons. Not bad. She's not bad."

"And Maggie?"

"She's . . . still Maggie." He chuckled again. "You know, can't get that kid down."

"So, what are you doing back in New York?"

Seeing you.

"Vacation."

He nodded.

"So, how long have you been in town?"

Forty-five minutes.

"Not long."

"You're still wearing your neck chain."

He started, embarrassed, and reached his hand to touch the silver piece around his neck.

"Yeah. Well. I don't wear it all the time anymore. I thought I'd wear it today. Give you a thrill."

I poured the last of the wine; we sipped it in silence.

"This is depressing me."

"What?"

"This." Coyote gestured at the table with both hands. "We can't talk. We're sitting here like an old married couple with nothing left to say to each other except small talk."

"You're happy now? With Shelley?"

"That was a low blow, Shrimpton."

"Why were you mad at me?"

"Because you didn't wait. You let me down. I thought you let me down."

"You let me down, Coyote."

"Because I didn't stay?"

"Right."

"I would've come back. You almost broke up my marriage."

"I didn't though, did I?"

"Problem was, you were too sweet. You never insisted on anything. Never gave me any ultimatums. You were too . . . good."

"I wasn't that good."

"Yeah. Still. You should have been meaner."

"A lot of help that information is to me now."

The waitress came over and wanted to know if we were enjoying the wine.

"I don't know why you shouldn't be happy with Shelley," I said. "All I know about her is that she wouldn't go to your father's funeral with you. You know, how bad is that?"

"Sums things up. She never had anyone die on her."

We started walking down Madison Avenue, toward Katie's place, where we would part because he had to get back home.

"What do you want from me?" Coyote asked.

"I don't know," I told him. "I was always pretty miserable with you."

He shot me a quick look. "Do you know why I loved you?"

"Why?"

"Well, first, you're beautiful. You may not like that, but that's the first reason. First place. Second, you have a great laugh. Third, you're smart."

"Very smart."

"Okay, *very* smart. Fourth, you just say what you

210

mean. No matter how much it hurts. What do you mean you were 'always miserable' with me? *Miserable?*"

I started to laugh.

We turned onto Fifty-seventh Street, arms around each other, clinging against the cold.

"*Always*," Coyote was saying, "*always* you were pretty miserable? No picnic for me, either, being with you, you know."

We were both giggling.

"You know, Shrimp," he said when we got to Katie's building, "even if you wanted me back, I'm not sure I'd be any better at leaving this time."

"Coyote, I'm not sure I'd be better at waiting."

"Well, that's fair. It's not enough, but I guess it's fair."

He kissed me goodbye. On the cheek. But neither of us would back away from the touch.

Inside Katie's apartment, Katie said she had to run out because she had to go to see somebody. Who? She'd think of someone to go see, she said, and shook her head at me and laughed as she headed for the door.

"So." I turned to Coyote, who was standing in the middle of the living room looking around and still wearing his coat.

"You hungry?" he shot at me.

I shrugged.

"I think we need a pizza," he said.

"I'll order one in." I went for the phone.

"I'll go get it," he volunteered too quickly.

Well, I thought, and replaced the receiver, if he needs

an excuse to bolt, picking up a pizza is a good one. I was nervous, too, so I wasn't sure I wasn't relieved.

"No," he said, "it's cold out there." He threw his coat over the couch. "Have one delivered."

"There's no Coke in here." Coyote stood in front of the refrigerator.

I took a bottle of red wine out of Katie's rack.

"Don't open that, Shrimp. That'll make two bottles of wine we've had tonight. We'll be, like, winos."

"There's nothing else to drink."

"Jesus." Coyote closed the refrigerator door. "Okay. One glass. I'll have one glass."

I uncorked the bottle.

"If you knew I was coming, you should have gotten some Coke."

"I didn't know you were coming," I said.

We ate the pizza. And we finished the wine. Katie's coffee table was littered with leftovers and empties.

I was curled up at one end of the couch, and Coyote was sprawled out at the other end. We were catching each other up on four years, and Coyote had his head bent back, laughing at my interpretations of the California experience. I watched him laugh and I thought that I was looking at the best sight of quite possibly my whole life. I didn't start to cry, but I was choked up and the emotion sobered up both of us.

We stared at each other for a while.

"So," said Coyote, "what do you want to do now?"

Kiss you. Have you hold me in your arms and kiss me back. As if you didn't know.

We kept staring, trying to decide the ramifications of

the next move. Would it seal a pact for recommitment, or would it just ruin any chance we had of getting over each other, obliterate any progress we'd made at being separate, and put us back at square one? Trouble. In either case, trouble.

His mouth moved over mine and his tongue made a slow circle around my lips and we both groaned softly.

I went to the bathroom and got undressed. I crawled under the sheets and blankets of Katie's bed.

"What the hell are you doing?" Coyote threw the covers back, to the foot of the bed. "What are you doing? Being shy? It's me, Shrimpton."

I couldn't get close enough to him.

"You know that thing I told you you did that got me really hot?" he asked when we had made love.

"Yeah?" I was resting my head on his patch of gray chest hair.

"You still do it," he said.

"And you're still not going to tell me what it is?" I sat up.

"Nope."

"You shit!" I dived onto him and began to tickle, but he flipped me and pinned me under him.

"Wanna fight, do you?" He straddled me, held my arms.

"No!" I begged for mercy, tried to push him off. "No more fights!"

"Oh, yeah? No more fights? Does that mean I shouldn't call you tomorrow?" he said, and attacked.

biblio

Le Fantôme
de Canterville

Oscar Wilde

Notes, questionnaires et Dossier Bibliocollège
par Isabelle **DE LISLE**,
professeur agrégé de Lettres
au collège Hoche (Versailles)

Traduction de Jules CASTIER

Crédits photographiques

Couverture : illustration originale de Dimitri Avramoglou. **p. 5 :** illustration originale de Dimitri Avramoglou. **p. 7, 19, 29, 43, 53, 65, 75 :** illustrations originales de Dimitri Avramoglou. **p. 12 :** *Vanité et trompe l'œil* de Jean-François De Le Motte © Josse. **p. 24 :** illustration de Donia Nachsen © The Art Archive. **p. 37 :** illustration originale de Dimitri Avramoglou. **p. 39 :** gravure de E. Zier © Jean-Loup Charmet. **p. 45 :** illustration originale de Dimitri Avramoglou. **p. 56 :** *Allégorie de la peinture* de Jean Restout © Josse. **p. 70 :** illustration originale de Dimitri Avramoglou. **p. 81 :** *L'Entrée au cimetière* de Caspar David Friedrich © AKG Paris. **p. 90 :** portrait d'Oscar Wilde, photo Downey © Photothèque Hachette Livre. **p. 92 :** portrait de la reine Victoria © Photothèque Hachette Livre. **p. 93 :** Disraeli à la chambre des communes © Photothèque Hachette Livre. **p. 94 :** *The Nonchalant Dandy* d'Edward Loevy © The Bridgeman Art Library. **p. 104 :** Illustration de Julian-Damazy © Jean-Loup Charmet.

Conception graphique

Couverture : *Rampazzo et Associés*

Intérieur : *ELSE*

Mise en page

Alinéa

Illustration des questionnaires

Harvey Stevenson

ISBN : 2.01.168209.6

© Hachette Livre, 2001, 43 quai de Grenelle, 75905 PARIS Cedex 15.
www.hachette-education.com

© Éditions Stock pour la traduction française.

Sommaire

Sommario

Introduction

Dans une Angleterre victorienne triomphante mais à la morale très rigide, un jeune Irlandais se fait remarquer dans les salons, à la fois par ses tenues recherchées et ses propos pleins d'humour. Il s'agit d'Oscar Wilde. Avant d'être condamné à la prison pour ses mœurs jugées scandaleuses et de mourir dans la misère à Paris, le jeune homme amuse, étonne, parfois choque la bonne société qu'il représente dans ses romans et pièces de théâtre.

Le Fantôme de Canterville, paru en 1891, la même année que le célèbre *Portrait de Dorian Gray*, est un court récit tout en nuances et en finesse. Mettant en scène une famille américaine installée en pleine Angleterre traditionnelle, il critique, grâce à toute la palette des procédés comiques, aussi bien la modernité des Américains que les vieilles habitudes anglaises ou la littérature de son temps.

Au premier plan évolue le fantôme, pur produit de la tradition aristocratique britannique. Comme il se doit, il hante un manoir caché au fond d'un immense parc. Il traverse les lambris et la porte fermée à clé de la bibliothèque ne l'arrête pas dès lors qu'il s'agit de maintenir la tache qui rappelle un crime vieux de plusieurs siècles. Lorsque sa main verte frappe à la fenêtre de l'office, le maître d'hôtel terrorisé se suicide. Quand il joue aux quilles c'est avec ses propres ossements ; quand il parcourt les couloirs du manoir de Canterville, c'est vêtu d'un linceul et traînant de lourdes chaînes…

Les clichés de l'horreur se trouvent réunis. Mais c'est avec humour qu'Oscar Wilde traite ce thème du château hanté. Le choix du vocabulaire, le jeu sur les mots et les procédés permettent le mélange étonnant des genres. La situation fantastique initiale est présentée avec légèreté ; l'évocation des crimes les plus atroces nous fait sourire ; le fantôme assassin se trouve confronté à deux collégiens américains que rien n'effraie.

Mais le comique n'est pas l'unique tonalité de ce conte car Oscar Wilde sait habilement glisser de l'humour à l'émotion. Ainsi, en quelques chapitres pleins de surprises, les tons se mêlent : le fantastique et l'horreur, la caricature et l'humour, le mystère et la tendresse. Le lecteur est tour à tour intrigué et inquiet, amusé puis ému, toujours séduit…

Chapitre 1

1   Lorsque Mr. Hiram B. Otis, le ministre américain, acheta le domaine de Canterville Chase, tout le monde lui dit qu'il faisait une folie car il n'y avait pas le moindre doute que le manoir fût hanté. À tel point, d'ailleurs, que Lord Canter-
5 ville lui-même, très scrupuleux en matière d'honneur, avait estimé de son devoir d'en dire un mot à Mr. Otis quand ils en étaient venus à discuter des conditions de vente.

  «Nous n'avons voulu y habiter, quant à nous, dit Lord Canterville, depuis que ma grand-tante, la duchesse douai-
10 rière[1] de Bolton, a été prise de convulsions[2] à la suite d'une peur épouvantable, dont elle ne s'est jamais tout à fait remise, lorsque deux mains de squelette se sont posées sur ses épaules au moment où elle s'habillait pour le dîner, et je me considère comme tenu de vous dire, Mr. Otis, que le
15 fantôme a été vu par diverses personnes de ma famille

notes

1. douairière : veuve de la haute aristocratie.
2. convulsions : violentes contractions, mouvements involontaires.

encore en vie, ainsi que par le recteur[1] de la paroisse, le révérend Augustus Dampier, qui est diplômé de Trinity College, à Cambridge. Après le regrettable accident survenu à la duchesse, aucun de nos jeunes domestiques n'a plus voulu rester auprès de nous, et Lady Canterville a passé plus d'une nuit blanche à cause des bruits mystérieux qui venaient du couloir et de la bibliothèque.

– Milord, répondit le ministre, je suis prêt à prendre le mobilier et le fantôme à leur valeur d'estimation. Je viens d'un pays moderne, où nous avons tout ce que l'argent peut acheter; et, avec tous nos fringants[2] jeunes gens qui viennent faire la noce en Europe, et qui enlèvent vos meilleures actrices et cantatrices, je gage que s'il y avait le moindre fantôme en Europe, nous l'aurions bien vite chez nous, dans un de nos musées publics, ou en tournée pour l'exhiber[3].

– Je crains que le fantôme n'existe bel et bien, dit Lord Canterville en souriant, et qu'il puisse résister aux propositions de vos imprésarios, si entreprenants soient-ils. Il est bien connu depuis trois siècles, exactement depuis 1584, et il fait toujours son apparition avant la mort d'un membre de notre famille.

– Ma foi, il en est de même du médecin de famille, tout bien considéré, Lord Canterville. Mais les fantômes n'existent pas, monsieur, et j'imagine que les lois de la nature ne vont pas se trouver suspendues pour l'aristocratie britannique.

– Vous êtes certes fort « nature », en Amérique, répondit Lord Canterville, qui ne comprit pas très bien la dernière

---

45 observation de Mr. Otis et si vous ne voyez pas d'inconvé-
nient à la présence d'un fantôme dans la maison, tout
va bien. Mais vous voudrez bien vous souvenir que je vous
ai averti. »

Quelques semaines après cet entretien, l'acquisition fut
50 effectuée, et à la fin de la saison le ministre et sa famille
s'installèrent à Canterville Chase.

Mrs. Otis, qui, sous le nom de Miss Lucretia R. Tappan, de
West 53 Street, avait été une beauté célèbre de New York,
était à présent une fort belle femme, entre deux âges, avec
55 de beaux yeux et un profil superbe. Beaucoup d'Américaines, lorsqu'elles abandonnent leur pays natal, adoptent
un air de mauvaise santé chronique, avec l'impression que
c'est là une forme de raffinement européen ; mais Mrs.
Otis n'était jamais tombée dans ce piège. Elle avait une
60 constitution magnifique, et une vitalité quasi animale.
Certes, par beaucoup de côtés, elle était tout à fait anglaise,
et elle constituait un excellent exemple de ce fait que nous
avons actuellement tout en commun avec l'Amérique,
hormis[1], bien entendu, la langue.

65 Son fils aîné, prénommé Washington par ses parents dans
un instant de patriotisme, qu'il n'avait jamais cessé de
regretter, était un jeune homme aux cheveux blonds, assez
beau garçon, qui s'était qualifié pour la diplomatie américaine en conduisant le cotillon[2] au casino de Newport
70 durant trois saisons consécutives, et il était connu, même à
Londres, pour être un excellent danseur. Les gardénias[3] et
la noblesse étaient ses seules faiblesses. Pour tout le reste, il
était extrêmement sensé.

---

notes

1. hormis : à l'exception de.   **2. cotillon :** danse.   **3. gardénias :** fleurs exotiques.

Miss Virginia E. Otis était une fillette de quinze ans, souple
et charmante comme un faon, avec un regard plein d'une
belle liberté dans ses grands yeux bleus. C'était une amazone[1] remarquable, et elle avait un jour fait la course sur
son poney avec le vieux Lord Bilton, parcourant deux fois
tout le circuit du parc, et gagnant d'une longueur et
demie, juste en face de la statue d'Achille, pour le plus
grand plaisir du jeune duc de Cheshire, qui avait sur-le-
champ demandé sa main, et avait été renvoyé en larmes le
soir même à Eton[2] par ses tuteurs.

Après Virginia venaient les jumeaux, qu'on appelait habi-
tuellement les « Stars and Stripes[3] », car ils recevaient
constamment des corrections. C'étaient des garçons charmants, et, à l'exception du digne ministre, les seuls répu-
blicains authentiques de la famille.

Canterville Chase étant situé à onze kilomètres d'Ascot, la
gare de chemin de fer la plus proche, Mr. Otis avait télé-
graphié pour qu'une voiture les y attendît, et ils se mirent
en route pleins d'entrain.

C'était une splendide soirée de juillet, et l'air était em-
baumé de l'odeur des forêts de pins. De temps à autre ils
entendaient un ramier[4] écoutant complaisamment son
propre roucoulement, ou apercevaient, profondément tapi
parmi les fougères bruissantes, le poitrail bruni du faisan.
De petits écureuils leur lançaient des regards curieux du
haut des hêtres, tandis qu'ils passaient, et les lapins déta-
laient à toute allure à travers les fourrés et par-dessus les
tertres[5] moussus, leur queue blanche dressée en l'air.

notes

1. *amazone :* femme qui monte à cheval avec les deux jambes du même côté.
2. *Eton :* célèbre collège anglais (pensionnat).
3. *Stars and Stripes :* étoiles et rayures (drapeau américain).
4. *ramier :* sorte de pigeon.
5. *tertres :* petites buttes.

Lorsqu'ils pénétrèrent dans l'avenue de Canterville Chase, toutefois, le ciel se couvrit de nuages, un calme bizarre parut s'emparer de l'atmosphère, un grand vol de corneilles passa
105 silencieusement au-dessus de leurs têtes, et, avant qu'ils n'eussent atteint la maison, il était tombé quelques grosses gouttes de pluie.

Debout sur le perron, pour les recevoir, se tenait une vieille femme, proprement habillée de soie noire, en bonnet et
110 tablier blancs. C'était Mrs. Umney, la gouvernante, que Mrs. Otis, à la prière instante[1] de Lady Canterville, avait consenti à maintenir dans sa situation antérieure. Elle leur fit à tous une profonde révérence à mesure qu'ils descendaient de voiture, et dit, d'une gentille voix à l'ancienne mode :
115 «Soyez les bienvenus à Canterville Chase, je vous prie. »

À sa suite, ils traversèrent le beau vestibule[2] Tudor[3] et entrèrent dans la bibliothèque, pièce longue et basse, lambrissée de chêne noir, au fond de laquelle il y avait une grande fenêtre à vitrail. Ils y trouvèrent le thé servi, et, après s'être
120 débarrassés de leurs manteaux, ils s'assirent et se mirent à regarder alentour, tandis que Mrs. Umney les servait.

Tout à coup, Mrs. Otis aperçut une tache rouge sombre sur le parquet, tout près de la cheminée, et sans la moindre idée de ce que cela pouvait être, elle dit à Mrs. Umney :
125 «Je crois bien qu'on a dû répandre là quelque chose.

– Oui, madame, répondit la vieille gouvernante d'une voix assourdie, on a répandu du sang en cet endroit.

– Mais c'est abominable, s'écria Mrs. Otis ; je n'aime pas du tout les taches de sang dans une pièce où l'on se tient.
130 Il faut la nettoyer tout de suite. »

notes

1. instante : pressante.
2. vestibule : entrée.

3. Tudor : qui date de l'époque du règne des Tudor (xve siècle).

Vanité et Trompe l'œil, peinture de Jean-François De Le Motte (2nde moitié du XVIIe siècle).

La vieille femme sourit, et répondit de la même voix basse et mystérieuse :

« C'est le sang de Lady Eleanore de Canterville, qui fut assassinée en cet endroit même par son propre mari, Sir Simon de Canterville, en 1575. Sir Simon lui survécut neuf ans, et disparut tout à coup dans des circonstances fort mystérieuses. Son corps n'a jamais été découvert, mais son esprit, coupable de ce meurtre, hante encore le manoir. Cette tache de sang a été très admirée par tous les visiteurs, et il est impossible de l'enlever.

– Tout ça, c'est de la blague, s'écria Washington Otis ; le Super-Kinettoy et Extra-Détersif Pinkerton enlèvera ça en un rien de temps. »

Et, avant que la gouvernante épouvantée eût eu le temps d'intervenir, il était à genoux, et frottait vivement le parquet avec un petit bâton qui ressemblait à un cosmétique[1] noir. Au bout de quelques instants, on ne voyait plus aucune trace de la tache de sang.

« Je savais bien que le Pinkerton en viendrait à bout », s'écria-t-il triomphalement, se retournant vers sa famille pleine d'admiration.

À peine eut-il prononcé ces mots, qu'un éclair terrible illumina la pièce sombre : un coup de tonnerre épouvantable les fit tous se dresser d'un bond, et Mrs. Umney s'évanouit.

« Quel climat monstrueux ! dit avec calme le ministre américain, tout en allumant un long cigare. Je gage que la vieille terre des ancêtres est tellement surpeuplée qu'ils ne peuvent faire des conditions météorologiques convenables

note

1. cosmétique : produit de beauté.

à tout le monde. J'ai toujours été d'avis que l'émigration[1]
était la seule chose qui convînt à l'Angleterre.

– Mon cher Hiram, s'écria Mrs. Otis, que pouvons-nous
faire d'une femme qui a des évanouissements ?

– Il faut les lui retenir sur ses gages[2], comme les bris de
vaisselle, répondit le ministre ; après cela, elle ne s'éva-
nouira plus. »

Au bout de quelques instants, Mrs. Umney revint à elle,
effectivement. Il était hors de doute, cependant, qu'elle
était extrêmement inquiète, et elle avertit d'un air sévère
Mr. Otis d'avoir à prendre garde à quelque malheur prêt à
s'abattre sur la maison.

« Monsieur, j'ai vu des choses, de mes propres yeux, dit-
elle, des choses qui feraient dresser les cheveux sur la tête
de n'importe quel chrétien, et nombreuses sont les nuits
où je n'ai pas fermé l'œil à cause des choses épouvantables
qui se passent ici. »

Cependant Mr. Otis et sa femme assurèrent chaleureuse-
ment à la brave vieille qu'ils n'avaient pas peur des reve-
nants. Après avoir appelé les bénédictions de la Providence
sur son nouveau maître et sa nouvelle maîtresse, et jeté les
bases d'une augmentation d'appointements[3], la vieille gouvernante s'en alla en chancelant vers sa chambre.

---

notes

1. émigration : fait de quitter son pays pour aller s'installer dans un autre pays.

2. gages : salaire.

3. appointements : salaire.

Au fil du texte

Avez-vous bien lu ?

1. Quel est le nom de la propriété achetée par les Otis ?

2. Où se situe cette propriété ?

3. Qui vend cette propriété ?

4. Quelle est la nationalité du vendeur ?

5. Quelle est la nationalité de l'acheteur ?

6. Le premier chapitre est un chapitre d'exposition★. Quelles sont les trois étapes de cette exposition ?

7. Quels sont les différents membres de la famille Otis ?

8. En quelle saison la famille Otis arrive-t-elle à Canterville ?

9. Donnez le nom et la fonction du personnage qui porte une robe de soie noire, un bonnet et un tablier blancs.

10. Qui est Eleanore de Canterville ?

exposition : présentation des éléments (décor, personnages…) nécessaires à la compréhension de l'intrigue.

énonciation : acte qui consiste à produire une parole (écrite ou orale). Le présent de l'énonciation est celui qui correspond au moment où l'on parle.

Étudier le vocabulaire et la grammaire

11. Dans le passage de la page 8 (lignes 32 à 42), relevez les verbes au présent de l'indicatif et précisez leur valeur (énonciation★, habitude, vérité générale).

12. Relisez le passage des pages 10 et 11 (lignes 93 à 107). Les deux paragraphes s'opposent nettement car l'atmosphère change radicalement. Pour montrer

cette opposition, relevez le vocabulaire mélioratif*
dans le premier paragraphe et le vocabulaire
péjoratif* dans le second paragraphe.

ÉTUDIER LE DISCOURS

13. Relevez une phrase qui ressemble à un message
publicitaire.

14. Quelles sont, dans la phrase relevée, les marques
du langage publicitaire ?

mélioratif :
qui exprime
un jugement
positif.

péjoratif :
qui exprime
un jugement
négatif.

15. Commentez la phrase : « Au bout de quelques
instants, on ne voyait plus aucune trace de la tache
de sang. » (lignes 147-148)

ÉTUDIER LE GENRE : FANTASTIQUE OU COMIQUE ?

16. Relevez dans le passage qui relate l'achat
du manoir (lignes 8 à 48) d'une part, les indices
qui laissent à penser que le fantôme existe bel et
bien et, d'autre part, les indices qui font supposer
que le fantôme n'existe pas.

17. Vous ferez le même relevé dans le passage
consacré à l'arrivée au manoir (lignes 93 à 107).

18. Vous effectuerez le même relevé à propos
de l'épisode de la tache de sang (lignes 122 à 171).

19. Afin de mettre en relief le ton comique
de ce passage, relevez les réactions des membres
de la famille Otis aux événements suivants :
a) Mrs. Umney affirme que la tache est une tache de sang.
b) Un coup de tonnerre éclate lorsque Washington
efface la tache.
c) La gouvernante s'évanouit.

LIRE L'IMAGE (PAGE 12)

20. Relevez dans le tableau et dans le chapitre les éléments qui évoquent la mort.

21. Dans quelle mesure la place du crâne explique la première partie du titre du tableau?

22. Expliquez la seconde partie du titre.

À VOS PLUMES!

23. Décrivez un jardin l'été puis évoquez-le en hiver.

24. Vous retrouvez, vingt ans après, le collège dans lequel vous avez fait vos études. Évoquez les transformations.

25. Relisez l'épisode de la tache de sang puis imaginez à votre tour un événement qui puisse être interprété de deux manières contradictoires: d'une part, on peut croire que le fantôme existe et d'autre part, on a l'impression que tout peut s'expliquer de manière naturelle.

Chapitre 2

1 L'orage se déchaîna toute cette nuit-là, mais il ne se produisit rien qui mérite d'être noté. Toutefois, le lendemain
matin, lorsqu'ils descendirent pour le petit déjeuner, ils
retrouvèrent la terrible tache de sang sur le parquet.

5 «Je ne crois pas que ce soit la faute de l'Extra-Détersif, dit
Washington, car je l'ai éprouvé avec tout. Ce doit être le
fantôme.»

Il effaça donc une seconde fois la tache, mais le lendemain
matin elle reparut encore. Le jour suivant elle était encore là,

10 bien que la bibliothèque eût été fermée à clef pour la nuit
par Mr. Otis lui-même, et qu'il eût emporté la clef à l'étage.
Toute la famille fut dès lors fort intéressée par cet événement; Mr. Otis commença à soupçonner qu'il avait été trop
dogmatique[1] dans sa dénégation[2] de l'existence des spectres,

15 Mrs. Otis manifesta son intention de faire partie de la
Société Spirite, et Washington prépara une longue lettre à

notes

1. dogmatique : catégorique.   **2. dénégation :** fait de nier.

MM. Myers et Podmore, au sujet de la « Permanence des taches sanglantes lorsqu'elles se rattachent à un crime ». Cette nuit-là, tous les doutes relatifs à l'existence objective[1]

20 des apparitions furent levés à tout jamais.

La journée avait été chaude et ensoleillée ; et, à la fraîcheur du soir toute la famille alla faire une promenade en voiture. Ils ne rentrèrent qu'à neuf heures, et prirent alors un souper léger. La conversation ne tomba nullement sur les fan-

25 tômes, de sorte qu'il n'y eut même pas ces conditions initiales d'attente qui précèdent si souvent la manifestation de phénomènes parapsychiques[2]. Les sujets dont il fut question, ainsi que je l'ai appris par la suite de la bouche de Mr. Otis, furent simplement de ceux qui constituent la

30 conversation habituelle des Américains cultivés des classes supérieures – tels que l'immense supériorité, comme actrice, de Miss Fanny Davenport sur Sarah Bernhardt ; la difficulté qu'il y avait à se procurer des épis de maïs vert, des galettes de sarrasin et de la bouillie de maïs, même dans les

35 meilleures maisons anglaises ; l'importance de Boston dans le développement de l'esprit universel ; les avantages du système d'enregistrement des bagages dans les voyages en chemin de fer ; et la douceur de l'accent de New York, en comparaison du parler traînard de Londres. Il ne fut absolument

40 pas question de surnaturel, et l'on ne fit en aucune façon allusion à Sir Simon de Canterville. À onze heures la famille se retira, et dès onze heures et demie toutes les lumières étaient éteintes.

Quelque temps après, Mr. Otis fut réveillé par un bruit

45 bizarre dans le couloir, à l'extérieur de sa chambre. On eût

---

notes

1. objective : réelle, incontestable.
2. parapsychique : se dit d'un phénomène psychique inexpliqué, paranormal.

dit un tintement de métal, et il semblait se rapprocher d'instant en instant. Il se leva immédiatement, frotta une allumette, et regarda l'heure. Il était exactement une heure. Mr. Otis était très calme, et se tâta le pouls, qui n'était nullement fébrile.

Le bruit étrange se prolongea encore, et il entendit en même temps distinctement un bruit de pas. Il chaussa ses pantoufles, prit dans sa mallette une petite fiole oblongue[1], et ouvrit la porte. Juste en face de lui il vit, au pâle clair de lune, un vieillard d'aspect terrible. Il avait des yeux rouges pareils à des charbons incandescents[2] ; une longue chevelure grise lui tombait sur les épaules en tresses emmêlées ; ses vêtements, d'une coupe ancienne, étaient salis et élimés[3]. De lourdes menottes et des fers rouillés lui pendaient aux poignets et aux chevilles.

« Cher monsieur, dit Mr. Otis, permettez-moi vraiment d'insister auprès de vous pour que vous huiliez ces chaînes : je vous ai apporté à cette fin un petit flacon de lubrifiant[4] Soleil Levant Tammany. On le dit totalement efficace dès la première application, et il y a, sur l'emballage, plusieurs attestations allant dans ce sens, émanant[5] de quelques-uns de nos ecclésiastiques[6] les plus éminents[7]. Je le laisse ici pour vous, à côté des veilleuses, et je me ferai un plaisir de vous en fournir encore au cas où vous en auriez besoin. »

Sur ces mots, le ministre des États-Unis posa le flacon sur une table à dessus de marbre, et, fermant sa porte, se retira dans sa chambre pour se reposer.

---

notes

1. oblongue : de forme allongée.
2. incandescents : rendus lumineux par une chaleur intense.

3. élimés : usés en surface.
4. lubrifiant : produit gras destiné à atténuer les frottements ou les grincements.

5. émanant de : provenant de.
6. ecclésiastiques : hommes d'Église.
7. éminents : célèbres pour leurs compétences.

Un instant, le fantôme de Canterville demeura absolument immobile, dans un accès d'indignation bien naturelle ; puis,
75 ayant lancé violemment le flacon sur le parquet poli, il s'enfuit le long du couloir, en poussant des gémissements sourds et en émettant une lueur verdâtre et fantomatique.

Mais, au moment précis où il atteignait le haut de l'escalier de chêne, une porte s'ouvrit brusquement, deux petits per-
80 sonnages apparurent, vêtus de longues robes blanches, et un gros oreiller lui frôla la tête avec un sifflement. Il n'y avait manifestement pas de temps à perdre ; aussi, adoptant à la hâte, comme moyen d'évasion, la quatrième dimension de l'espace, disparut-il à travers le lambris, et la maison devint-
85 elle absolument silencieuse.

Dès qu'il eut atteint un petit cabinet secret dans l'aile gauche, il s'appuya contre un rayon de lune pour reprendre haleine, et se mit en devoir de faire le point de sa situation. Jamais, au cours de sa carrière brillante et ininterrompue
90 depuis trois cents ans, il n'avait été aussi grossièrement insulté. Il songea à la duchesse douairière, qu'il avait frappée d'épouvante au moment où elle se tenait debout devant son miroir avec ses dentelles et ses diamants ; aux quatre servantes, qui avaient été saisies d'une crise d'hystérie[1] alors
95 qu'il les avait simplement regardées avec un rire grimaçant à travers les rideaux de l'une des chambres d'invités ; au recteur[2] de la paroisse, dont il avait soufflé la bougie tandis qu'il sortait de la bibliothèque, un soir, à une heure avancée, et qui avait été depuis lors soigné par Sir William Gull, pour
100 des troubles nerveux qui le martyrisaient ; et à la vieille Mme de Trémouillac, qui, s'étant réveillée un matin de

___
notes

1. hystérie : maladie nerveuse.   **2. recteur :** prêtre qui dirige la paroisse.

bonne heure et ayant aperçu un squelette assis dans un fauteuil auprès du feu et lisant son journal intime, avait dû garder le lit pendant six semaines avec une fièvre cérébrale, et

105 qui, après sa guérison, s'était réconciliée avec l'Église, et avait rompu ses relations avec ce sceptique[1] notoire[2], M. de Voltaire. Il se rappela cette nuit terrible où l'abominable Lord Canterville avait été trouvé étouffant dans son cabinet de toilette, pour avoir été contraint par le fantôme – cela il

110 le jura – à avaler le valet de carreau, qui lui était resté fiché en travers de la gorge, et dont il avoua, avant de mourir, s'être servi pour soutirer au jeu 50 000 livres à Charles James Fox, chez Crockford. Tous ses grands triomphes lui revinrent en mémoire, depuis le cas du maître d'hôtel qui s'était tué

115 d'un coup de pistolet dans l'office parce qu'il avait vu une main verte frappant au carreau, jusqu'à celui de la belle Lady Stutfield, qui fut contrainte définitivement de porter un ruban de velours noir autour de la gorge pour cacher la brûlure qu'avaient laissée cinq doigts sur sa peau blanche, et qui

120 finit par se noyer dans l'étang aux carpes à l'extrémité de l'Allée du Roi. Avec l'égotisme[3] enthousiaste du véritable artiste, il passa en revue ses exploits les plus célèbres, et eut un sourire amer en se remémorant sa dernière apparition en tant que « Ruben le Rouge, ou le Nourrisson Étranglé », ses

125 débuts comme « Gédéon le Décharné, le Suceur de Sang de Bexley Moor », et le succès prodigieux qu'il avait obtenu, par une splendide soirée de juillet, simplement en jouant aux quilles avec ses propres ossements sur le court de tennis gazonné. Et, après tout cela, quelques misérables Américains

130 modernes venaient lui offrir le lubrifiant Soleil Levant, et lui

---

notes

1. sceptique : personne qui ne croit en rien.
2. notoire : célèbre.

3. égotisme : intérêt porté à soi-même plutôt qu'aux autres.

lancer des oreillers à la tête ! C'était absolument intolérable. D'ailleurs, aucun fantôme de l'histoire n'avait jamais été traité ainsi. Aussi résolut-il de se venger, et il demeura jusqu'au jour plongé dans une profonde méditation.

Illustration de Donia Nachsen pour une édition anglaise du *Fantôme de Canterville* datant de 1931.

Au fil du texte

AVEZ-VOUS BIEN LU?

1. Relevez, page 20, une phrase qui montre que les habitants de Canterville n'ont plus aucun doute quant à l'existence du fantôme.

2. Quelles sont les propositions justes?

a) La tache de sang réapparaît bien que la porte de la bibliothèque soit fermée à clé.

b) La famille Otis a très peur du fantôme.

c) Le fantôme vient réveiller Mr. Otis dans sa chambre.

d) Le fantôme a un aspect effrayant.

e) Mr. Otis veut que le fantôme huile ses chaînes.

f) Les jumeaux lancent un seau d'eau sur le fantôme.

g) Le décalage entre la volonté de faire peur du fantôme et les réactions pragmatiques des Otis est source de comique.

Les questions 3 à 6 portent sur le passage des pages 22 à 24.

3. Où se trouve le fantôme?

4. Relevez les verbes qui montrent que le fantôme fait appel à ses souvenirs.

5. Relevez les trois phrases dans lesquelles le fantôme commente sa situation actuelle.

6. Relevez la phrase qui annonce les projets du fantôme.

ÉTUDIER LE VOCABULAIRE ET LA GRAMMAIRE

7. Trouvez deux mots contenant le même préfixe que « *égotisme* » (ligne 121) et utilisez-les dans une phrase qui en éclaire le sens.

8. Relevez les mots appartenant au champ lexical★ de la maladie dans les lignes 89 à 129.

9. Quels sont les différents temps de l'indicatif employés dans ce passage ?

10. Quelle est la valeur du temps composé qui est le plus utilisé ici ?

11. Relevez, dans les lignes 91 à 107, les propositions subordonnées relatives et donnez, pour chacune d'entre elles, l'antécédent du pronom relatif.

champ lexical (ou réseau lexical) : ensemble de mots se rapportant à une même notion.

ÉTUDIER UN THÈME : LE THÉÂTRE

12. Commentez les différents emplois des guillemets dans le chapitre.

13. Relevez, à la fin du chapitre, les différentes expressions appartenant au champ lexical du théâtre. Quelle est la signification de ce réseau lexical ?

ÉTUDIER L'ÉCRITURE

14. Pourquoi Oscar Wilde énumère-t-il des sujets de conversation sans lien les uns avec les autres ? (lignes 27 à 39)

15. Montrez que la description du fantôme contraste avec le ton adopté par Mr. Otis (lignes 51 à 69).

16. Nommez le procédé qu'utilise Oscar Wilde
à la fin du chapitre pour montrer l'accumulation
des exploits du fantôme.

17. Expliquez pourquoi les scènes terribles évoquées
par le fantôme ne font pas peur au lecteur.

LIRE L'IMAGE (PAGE 24)

18. Relevez dans le chapitre deux phrases qui pourrait
servir de légende à l'illustration.

19. Quels rôles joue le rayon de lune?

À VOS PLUMES!

20. À la manière d'Oscar Wilde, énumérez les exploits
du fantôme en commençant par «il songea à…».

21. Rédigez un paragraphe développant
un des exploits évoqués par le fantôme.

Chapitre 3

1   Le lendemain matin, quand les membres de la famille Otis
se retrouvèrent pour le petit déjeuner, ils parlèrent assez lon-
guement du fantôme. Le ministre des États-Unis fut naturellement un peu contrarié de constater que son cadeau
5   n'avait pas été accepté.
«Je n'ai nul désir, dit-il, de causer le moindre mal à ce fantôme, et je dois vous faire observer qu'étant donné le
nombre de siècles qu'il a passés dans ces murs, j'estime qu'il
n'est pas du tout poli de lui lancer des oreillers.»
10 Remarque fort juste, que les jumeaux, je regrette d'avoir à le
dire, accueillirent avec des éclats de rire.
«D'autre part, reprit-il, s'il refuse absolument de se servir du
lubrifiant Soleil Levant, il faudra que nous lui enlevions ses
chaînes. Il serait tout à fait impossible de dormir, avec un tel
15 tintamarre juste auprès de nos chambres.»
Pendant le reste de la semaine, toutefois, ils ne furent plus
dérangés, la seule chose qui retînt leur attention étant le
renouvellement constant de la tache de sang sur le parquet
de la bibliothèque. C'était là certes, un phénomène fort

20 étrange, car la porte était toujours fermée à clef, le soir, par Mr. Otis, et les fenêtres tenues soigneusement closes. La couleur de la tache qui tenait du caméléon suscita aussi force commentaires. Certains jours, au matin, elle était d'un rouge sombre (presque indien) ; puis elle virait au vermillon,
25 puis au pourpre généreux, et un jour qu'ils étaient descendus pour la prière familiale, selon les rites simples de la Libre Église Américaine Épiscopale Réformée, ils la trouvèrent d'un vert émeraude éclatant. Ces changements kaléidoscopiques amusèrent naturellement beaucoup la famille, et les
30 paris étaient librement ouverts, à ce sujet, tous les soirs. La seule personne qui ne participât point à la plaisanterie était la petite Virginia, qui, pour quelque raison inexpliquée, paraissait toujours passablement contrariée à la vue de la tache de sang, et qui faillit pleurer le jour où elle fut vert
35 émeraude.

La seconde apparition du fantôme eut lieu le dimanche soir. Peu après être allés se coucher, ils furent soudain alertés par un fracas épouvantable dans le vestibule. Étant redescendus précipitamment, ils constatèrent qu'une énorme armure
40 ancienne s'était détachée de son socle, et était tombée sur le dallage, tandis qu'assis dans un fauteuil à haut dossier, le fantôme de Canterville se frottait les genoux, le visage empreint[1] d'une expression de souffrance intense. Les jumeaux, qui avaient emporté leurs sarbacanes, lui décochèrent immédia-
45 tement deux boulettes, avec cette précision dans le pointage qui ne peut être obtenue que par une pratique longue et attentive sur la personne de son maître d'écriture – cependant que le ministre des États-Unis le menaçait de son revol-

note

1. empreint : profondément marqué par.

ver et le sommait, conformément à l'étiquette californienne,
de lever les mains en l'air! Le fantôme se dressa d'un bond,
avec un hurlement sauvage de colère, et les traversa comme
une brume, éteignant en passant la bougie de Washington
Otis, ce qui les laissa tous dans l'obscurité complète.

Lorsqu'il arriva en haut de l'escalier, il reprit ses esprits, et
résolut de lancer son célèbre éclat de rire démoniaque[1]. Il
l'avait, en plus d'une circonstance, trouvé extrêmement
utile. On dit que ce rire avait, en une seule nuit, fait gri-
sonner la perruque de Lord Raker, et il avait certainement
été cause que trois des gouvernantes françaises de Lady
Canterville avaient donné congé avant d'avoir terminé
leur premier mois. Il lança donc son rire le plus horrible,
au point que les vénérables voûtes résonnèrent de son
écho; mais à peine le dernier éclat s'était-il éteint, qu'une
porte s'ouvrit, et que Mrs. Otis sortit de sa chambre, vêtue
d'un peignoir bleu clair.

« Votre santé me paraît vraiment laisser à désirer, dit-elle ;
aussi vous ai-je apporté un flacon de l'élixir du docteur
Dobell. Si vous souffrez d'une indigestion, vous constaterez
que c'est un remède tout à fait excellent. »

Le fantôme la fusilla du regard, et s'apprêta immédiatement à se transformer en un gros chien noir, talent pour
lequel il était à juste titre renommé, et auquel le médecin
de la famille avait toujours attribué l'idiotie définitive de
l'oncle de Lord Canterville, l'Honorable J. Thomas
Horton. Toutefois, un bruit de pas se rapprochant le fit
hésiter dans son féroce dessein, de sorte qu'il se contenta
de devenir légèrement phosphorescent, et de disparaître

note
_____
1. démoniaque : diabolique.

avec un gémissement sépulcral[1], juste au moment où les jumeaux le rejoignaient.

80 Ayant regagné sa chambre, il perdit totalement contenance, et devint la proie de l'agitation la plus violente. La vulgarité des jumeaux, et le matérialisme grossier de Mrs. Otis lui étaient, bien entendu, extrêmement désagréables ; mais ce qui, à dire vrai, le contrariait le plus, c'était d'avoir été inca-
85 pable de revêtir l'armure. Il avait espéré que même des Américains modernes frémiraient à la vue d'un fantôme en armure, ne serait-ce, à défaut de raison plus sensée que par respect pour leur poète national Longfellow[2], grâce à la poésie gracieuse et attrayante de qui il avait quant à lui, charmé
90 bien des heures d'ennui, pendant que les Canterville étaient à Londres. De plus, c'était sa propre armure. Il l'avait portée avec beaucoup de succès au tournoi de Kenilworth, et elle lui avait valu les compliments les plus chaleureux de la Reine Vierge elle-même. Pourtant, en essayant de la revêtir,
95 il avait été complètement écrasé par le poids de l'énorme cuirasse et du heaume[3], et était tombé lourdement sur le sol dallé, s'écorchant sérieusement les deux genoux et se meurtrissant les jointures de la main droite.

Pendant les jours qui suivirent ces événements il fut extrê-
100 mement malade, et c'est à peine s'il quitta sa chambre, si ce n'est pour entretenir en bon état la tache de sang. Cependant, à force de soins, il guérit et résolut de faire une troisième tentative en vue d'effrayer le ministre des États-Unis et sa famille. Il choisit le vendredi 17 août pour effectuer
105 son apparition, et employa la majeure partie de cette journée à passer en revue sa garde-robe. Il se décida finalement

notes

1. sépulcral : qui provient du tombeau. **2. Longfellow :** poète critiqué par Oscar Wilde. **3. heaume :** casque enveloppant toute la tête.

pour un grand chapeau de feutre mou avec une plume rouge, un linceul[1] plissé aux poignets et au col, et un poignard rouillé.

110 Vers le soir il y eut un violent orage, et le vent était tellement déchaîné que toutes les fenêtres et les portes de la vieille maison tremblaient et claquaient. Bref, c'était précisément le genre de temps qu'il aimait. Voici quel était son plan de bataille : il devait se rendre sans bruit dans la

115 chambre de Washington Otis, lui adresser, du pied du lit, un baragouin[2] inintelligible, et s'enfoncer par trois fois le poignard dans la gorge aux sons d'une musique lente. Il en voulait tout particulièrement à Washington, car il savait fort bien que c'était lui qui avait l'habitude d'effacer la célèbre

120 tache de sang de Canterville avec de l'Extra-Détersif Pinkerton. Ayant ainsi amené le jouvenceau[3] téméraire et imprudent à un état de terreur abjecte, il devait alors se rendre dans la chambre occupée par le ministre des États-Unis et sa femme, et là, poser une main moite sur le front

125 de Mrs. Otis, cependant qu'il susurrerait[4], à l'oreille de son mari, les secrets effroyables du charnier[5].

En ce qui concerne la petite Virginia, il ne s'était pas encore entièrement décidé. Elle ne l'avait jamais insulté d'aucune façon, et elle était jolie et douce. Quelques

130 gémissements sourds issus de l'armoire, pensait-il, seraient largement suffisants, et si cela ne réussissait pas à la réveiller, il pourrait tirailler son couvre-pied avec des gestes saccadés de paralytique.

notes

1. linceul : pièce de tissu dans laquelle on ensevelit un mort.
2. baragouin : discours incompréhensible.
3. jouvenceau : jeune homme (Moyen Âge).

4. susurrer : murmurer très doucement.
5. charnier : lieu où sont entassés des cadavres.

Quant aux jumeaux, il était absolument décidé à leur donner une leçon. La première chose à faire, c'était, bien
entendu, de s'asseoir sur leur poitrine, de façon à produire
une sensation étouffante de cauchemar. Puis, comme leurs
lits étaient tout près l'un de l'autre, de se tenir debout entre
les deux, en prenant la forme d'un cadavre livide et froid
comme la glace, jusqu'à ce qu'ils fussent paralysés de peur, et
enfin de rejeter le linceul et de ramper autour de la pièce,
avec ses ossements tout blanchis et un seul œil qu'il ferait
rouler dans son orbite – tenant ainsi le rôle de «Daniel le
Muet, ou le Squelette du Suicidé», personnage sous la
forme duquel il avait en plus d'une circonstance produit un
effet sensationnel, et qu'il considérait comme valant largement son célèbre rôle de «Martin le Maniaque, ou le
Mystère Masqué».

À dix heures et demie, il entendit la famille aller se coucher.
Pendant quelque temps il fut dérangé par les éclats de rire
déchaînés des jumeaux, qui, avec la gaieté insouciante des
écoliers, s'amusaient manifestement avant de se retirer pour la
nuit; mais à onze heures et quart, tout était silencieux, et, aux
douze coups de minuit, il se mit en route. La chouette battait
des ailes contre les vitres, le corbeau croassait[1] du haut du
vieil if, et le vent errait en gémissant comme une âme en
peine autour de la maison; mais la famille Otis dormait, sans
se douter du sort qui l'attendait, et il entendit, dominant de
haut la pluie et le vent, le ronflement régulier du ministre des
États-Unis. Il sortit à pas de loup de derrière le lambris[2], avec
un sourire méchant aux coins de sa bouche cruelle et ridée,
et la lune se voila la face derrière un nuage quand il passa à

notes

1. croasser: crier, pour un corbeau.   **2. lambris:** boiserie.

pas de loup devant la grande fenêtre en encorbellement[1], où
ses propres armes, et celles de son épouse assassinée, étaient
165 blasonnées en azur et or. Il poursuivit son chemin sans bruit,
comme une ombre mauvaise, et l'obscurité elle-même semblait l'avoir en horreur tandis qu'il avançait. À ce moment, il
crut entendre un appel, et s'arrêta ; mais ce n'était que
l'aboiement d'un chien de la Ferme Rouge, et il reprit sa
170 marche, en marmottant d'étranges jurons du XVIe siècle et en
brandissant à tout instant le poignard rouillé dans l'air de
minuit. Enfin il atteignit l'angle du couloir qui menait à la
chambre de l'infortuné Washington. Un instant, il s'y arrêta,
cependant que le vent faisait voler ses longues boucles grises
175 autour de sa tête, et tordait en plis grotesques et fantastiques
l'horreur sans nom du linceul du mort. L'horloge sonna le
quart, et il se dit que l'heure était venue. Il eut un rire intérieur, et tourna le coin du couloir ; mais à peine l'eut-il fait
qu'il recula avec un gémissement pitoyable de terreur, et
180 cacha son visage blême dans ses longues mains osseuses.
Juste en face de lui se dressait un spectre horrible, immobile ainsi qu'une image taillée, et monstrueux comme le
rêve d'un dément[2] ! Sa tête était chauve et brunie, son
visage, rond, gras, et blanc ; et un rire hideux[3] semblait lui
185 avoir tordu les traits en une grimace éternelle. Des yeux,
s'échappaient à flots des rais de lumière écarlate, la bouche
était un large puits de feu, et un vêtement hideux, pareil au
sien, enveloppait de ses neiges silencieuses la forme titanesque[4]. Sur sa poitrine, était fixé un écriteau portant une
190 inscription étrange en caractères antiques, et cela ressem-

notes

1. **encorbellement :** se dit d'une fenêtre
accompagnée d'un petit balcon.
2. **dément :** atteint de folie.

3. **hideux :** très laid.
4. **titanesque :** gigantesque (les Titans
étaient des géants).

blait à un parchemin ignominieux[1], où aurait été inscrite une liste de péchés épouvantables, une sorte de calendrier du crime ; et, dans la main droite, l'apparition brandissait un glaive[2] d'acier brillant.

195 N'ayant encore jamais vu de fantôme, il fut naturellement fort épouvanté, et, après un second coup d'œil lancé en hâte sur l'effarante apparition, il s'enfuit vers sa chambre en trébuchant dans son suaire[3], tandis qu'il courait dans les couloirs. Finalement il laissa tomber le poignard rouillé dans les

200 bottes du ministre, où il fut retrouvé le lendemain matin par le valet. Une fois dans ses appartements, il se jeta sur un petit grabat[4], et enfouit son visage sous les couvertures. Au bout de quelque temps, toutefois, le vieux courage des Canterville reprit le dessus, et il résolut d'aller parler à l'autre

205 fantôme lorsqu'il ferait jour. Aussi, dès que l'aube eut commencé à tacher d'argent les collines, retourna-t-il vers l'endroit où il avait aperçu pour la première fois le fantôme menaçant, ayant le sentiment qu'après tout deux fantômes valaient mieux qu'un seul, et que, grâce à l'aide de son nou-

210 vel ami, il pourrait en toute sécurité se colleter avec[5] les jumeaux. Une fois sur place, cependant, un spectacle terrible s'offrit à sa vue. Il était manifestement arrivé un malheur au spectre, car la lumière s'était totalement évanouie de ses yeux creux, le glaive luisant était tombé de sa main, et il s'appuyait

215 au mur dans une attitude tendue et incommode. Le fantôme s'élança en avant et le saisit dans ses bras, lorsque, à sa grande horreur, la tête se détacha et roula à terre, le corps prit une position couchée, et il se retrouva en train d'étreindre un

---

notes

1. ignominieux : honteux.
2. glaive : épée à deux tranchants.

3. suaire : pièce de toile dans laquelle on ensevelit un mort.

4. grabat : mauvais lit.
5. se colleter avec : affronter.

rideau de lit en basin[1] blanc, tandis qu'un balai, un couperet
220 de cuisine, et un navet creux gisaient à ses pieds! Incapable
de comprendre cette transformation curieuse, il saisit le panneau avec une hâte fébrile, et il y lut, à la lumière grise du
matin, ces mots effrayants :

Iceluy[2] phantasme[3] des Otis
225 *Seul spectre véritable et original*
Méfiez-vous des contrefaçons
Tous autres sont faux

Comme un éclair, la vérité se fit jour dans son esprit. On
s'était moqué de lui, il avait été joué, floué! Le vieux regard
230 des Canterville passa dans ses yeux ; il serra ses gencives
édentées ; et, levant ses mains flétries au-dessus de sa tête, il
jura, selon la phraséologie[4] pittoresque de la vieille école,
que «quand Chantecler aurait fait retentir par deux fois son
cor joyeux, la geste[5] de sang s'accomplirait, et le Meurtre se
235 mettrait en chemin, de sa démarche silencieuse ».
À peine eut-il proféré ce serment effroyable, que, du haut
du toit aux tuiles rouges d'une ferme lointaine, un coq
chanta. Il partit d'un long rire, bas et amer, et attendit.
D'heure en heure, il prolongea son attente, mais le coq,
240 pour quelque raison étrange, ne chanta plus. Enfin, à sept
heures et demie, l'arrivée des servantes le contraignit à
abandonner son effrayante veille, et il regagna doucement sa
chambre, songeant à son vain espoir et à son dessein[6]
contrecarré[7]. Là, il consulta plusieurs livres de chevalerie

---

notes

1. **basin :** sorte d'étoffe de coton.
2. **iceluy :** c'est le (terme du Moyen Âge).
3. **phantasme** (s'écrit aussi *fantasme*) :
fantôme ; le sens moderne est différent.
4. **phraséologie :** manière de parler.
5. **geste :** action, aventure (Moyen Âge).
6. **dessein :** projet.
7. **contrecarré :** mis en échec.

245 ancienne, qu'il affectionnait beaucoup, et constata que, chaque fois qu'on avait fait usage de son serment, Chantecler avait toujours chanté une seconde fois.

« Que la vilaine beste périsse de male[1] mort, marmotta-t-il. Fut un temps où, de mon fier épieu, je l'eusse embrochée par 250 la gorge, et l'eusse fait chanter pour moi, fût-ce en la mort ! » Il se retira alors dans un confortable cercueil de plomb, où il demeura jusqu'au soir.

Gravure réalisée en 1885 pour illustrer une nouvelle de Maupassant intitulée *La Main*.

note

1. *male* : mauvaise (Moyen Âge).

Au fil du texte

AVEZ-VOUS BIEN LU?

1. Après le Pinkerton et le lubrifiant Soleil Levant, quel est le troisième produit «miracle» proposé par les Américains au fantôme?

2. Quels sont les différents mauvais tours joués au fantôme par les jumeaux?

métaphore: comparaison qui fonctionne sans outil (sans *comme*). L'élément comparé n'est pas donné, c'est au lecteur de deviner.

3. Pour chacun de ces tours, quels sont les accessoires employés et quelles sont les réactions du fantôme?

4. Relevez les expressions qui montrent que le dernier mauvais tour se déroule la nuit.

5. Pourquoi le fantôme quitte-t-il sa chambre? (page 34)

6. Quelle est l'expression qui indique que le fantôme se retrouve face à un autre fantôme?

7. Relevez, dans le portrait du «spectre horrible» (page 35), les termes qui expriment son immobilité. Après avoir lu la fin du chapitre, vous dégagerez l'intérêt de ce champ lexical.

ÉTUDIER DES PROCÉDÉS DE STYLE

8. Relevez deux comparaisons (pages 34-35) et précisez à chaque fois le comparant, le comparé et l'outil de comparaison.

9. Relevez deux métaphores★ dans le paragraphe consacré à la description du faux fantôme (lignes 181 à 194).

10. Relevez deux personnifications★ d'éléments naturels (pages 34-35).

ÉTUDIEZ UNE TONALITÉ : L'HORREUR

11. Relevez cinq expressions montrant que les différents projets du fantôme sont violents.

12. Étudiez les circonstances de l'action (heure, décor, etc.) dans les lignes 149 à 160.

13. L'horreur repose sur l'utilisation de différents champs lexicaux. Recopiez puis complétez le tableau suivant en relevant des mots ou des expressions dans l'ensemble du chapitre.

La laideur	La cruauté	L'évocation du passé	Le destin	La mort

personnification : procédé qui consiste à représenter un élément sous les traits d'un être humain.

caricature : portrait qui accentue les traits pour ridiculiser un personnage.

parodie : imitation d'un genre littéraire dont les caractéristiques sont accentuées dans le but de les critiquer.

14. Quel est l'effet produit par l'emploi de ces différents réseaux lexicaux ?

15. Comme à la fin du chapitre 2, l'accumulation d'éléments horribles produit un effet comique ; ce passage (lignes 149 à 180) est une caricature★, une parodie★. Relevez les éléments qui rendent la scène comique.

LIRE L'IMAGE (PAGE 39)

16. Qu'y a-t-il d'horrible dans cette scène ?

17. Quel rôle jouent les ombres dans cette gravure ?

Chapitre 4

1 Le lendemain, le fantôme se sentit très faible et fatigué. La surexcitation terrible des quatre dernières semaines commençait à faire sentir son effet. Ses nerfs étaient complètement à vif, et il sursautait au moindre bruit. Durant cinq
5 jours, il garda la chambre, et se décida enfin à abandonner la question de la tache de sang sur le parquet de la bibliothèque. Puisque la famille Otis n'en voulait pas, c'est que manifestement elle ne la méritait point. C'étaient de toute évidence des gens habitués à vivre sur un plan d'existence
10 bas et matérialiste[1], et tout à fait incapables d'apprécier la valeur symbolique des phénomènes extra-sensoriels[2]. La question des apparitions, et du développement des corps astraux, était, bien entendu, fantasmagorique, tout autre chose, et cela ne dépendait pas vraiment de lui. Il était de
15 son devoir solennel d'apparaître dans le couloir une fois par

notes

1. matérialiste : attaché à tout ce qui est matériel, pratique, quotidien.

2. extra-sensoriels : se dit des phénomènes qui échapperaient à la perception ordinaire des sens.

43

semaine, et de lancer des cris inarticulés, du fond de la grande fenêtre en encorbellement, le premier et le troisième mercredi de chaque mois, et il ne voyait pas comment il aurait pu se dérober honorablement à ses obligations. Il est
20 vrai que sa vie avait été fort mauvaise, mais, d'un autre côté, il était très consciencieux pour tout ce qui touchait au surnaturel. Aussi traversa-t-il le couloir, chacun des trois samedis suivants, comme d'habitude, entre minuit et trois heures, en prenant toutes les précautions possibles pour n'être ni vu
25 ni entendu. Il ôtait ses bottes, posait les pieds aussi légèrement que possible sur les vieilles lames de parquet vermoulues[1], s'enveloppait d'un vaste manteau de velours noir, et prenait soin de se servir du lubrifiant Soleil Levant pour huiler ses chaînes. Je dois avouer que c'est avec beaucoup de
30 réticence[2] qu'il se résolut à adopter ce dernier procédé.
Un soir, cependant, tandis que la famille était en train de dîner, il se glissa dans la chambre de Mr. Otis, et emporta le flacon. Il se sentit d'abord un peu humilié, mais, par la suite, il fut assez avisé pour se rendre compte que cette
35 invention n'était pas sans présenter de grands avantages, et, dans une certaine mesure, elle fut utile à son dessein. Malgré toutes ces précautions, il ne s'en tira pas sans égratignures. Des ficelles étaient continuellement tendues en travers du couloir, et il s'y prenait les pieds dans l'obscu-
40 rité ; un jour, alors qu'il s'était habillé pour le rôle d'« Isaac le Noir, ou le Chasseur des Bois de Hogley », il fit une chute grave, pour avoir marché sur une pente savonnée, que les jumeaux avaient installée depuis l'entrée de la chambre aux Tapisseries jusqu'au sommet de l'escalier de

notes

1. vermoulu : dont le bois est rongé par de petits vers.
2. réticence : hésitation, manque de conviction.

45 chêne. Cette dernière insulte le mit dans une rage telle qu'il résolut de tenter un suprême effort pour raffermir sa dignité et son rang, et il se décida à rendre visite aux jeunes Étoniens[1] insolents la nuit suivante, dans son célèbre rôle de « Rupert le Téméraire, ou le Comte sans Tête ».

50 Il y avait plus de soixante-dix ans qu'il n'avait paru sous ce déguisement, exactement depuis qu'il avait, par ce moyen, tellement effrayé la jolie Lady Barbara Modish, qu'elle avait soudain rompu ses fiançailles avec le grand-père de l'actuel Lord Canterville, pour s'enfuir à Gretna Green

55 avec le beau Jack Castleton, déclarant que rien au monde ne l'amènerait à s'allier à une famille qui permettait à un fantôme aussi horrible de déambuler[2] sur la terrasse, au crépuscule. Le pauvre Jack fut plus tard tué en duel, d'un coup de pistolet, par Lord Canterville, sur le pré commu-

60 nal de Wandsworth, et Lady Barbara mourut de chagrin à Tunbridge Wells avant que l'année fût écoulée : ç'avait donc, à tous points de vue, été un grand succès. Toutefois, ce rôle supposait une présentation physique extrêmement difficile, s'il m'est permis d'employer cette expression

65 empruntée au théâtre à propos de l'un des plus grands mystères du surnaturel, ou, pour faire usage d'un terme plus scientifique, du monde supranaturel ; et il lui fallut largement trois heures pour faire ses préparatifs. Enfin, tout fut prêt, et il fut fort content de son aspect. Les grosses

70 bottes de cuir à l'écuyère qui allaient avec le costume étaient bien un tantinet[3] trop grandes pour lui, et il ne put trouver que l'un des deux pistolets d'arçon ; mais, dans l'ensemble, il fut pleinement satisfait, et, à une heure et

---

notes

1. Étoniens : élèves du collège de Eton.

2. déambuler : marcher sans but précis.

3. un tantinet : un petit peu.

quart, il se glissa hors du lambris et descendit tout doucement le couloir.

Lorsqu'il arriva à la chambre occupée par les jumeaux –
désignée, je dois le dire en passant, sous le nom de chambre
Bleue, en raison de la couleur de ses tentures –, il trouva la
porte entrebâillée.

Désirant faire une entrée remarquée, il l'ouvrit toute grande,
d'un geste violent, lorsqu'un lourd broc d'eau lui tomba dessus, le trempant jusqu'aux os, et manquant de quelques centi-
mètres seulement son épaule gauche. Au même instant, il
entendit des éclats de rire étouffés provenant du lit à
colonnes. Le choc qu'en ressentit son système nerveux fut si
grand qu'il s'enfuit dans sa chambre à toutes jambes ; le lendemain, il fut immobilisé par un gros rhume. La seule chose
qui le consolait dans toute l'affaire, c'était de n'avoir pas
emporté sa tête, car s'il l'avait fait, les conséquences auraient
pu être très graves.

Il renonça dès lors à tout espoir d'effrayer jamais cette grossière famille américaine, et se contenta, en général, de rôder
le long des couloirs, chaussé de pantoufles de lisière[1], avec
un épais cache-nez rouge autour de la gorge, de peur des
courants d'air, et une petite arquebuse[2], pour le cas où il
aurait été attaqué par les jumeaux.

Le coup final qu'il reçut se produisit le 19 septembre. Il était
descendu dans le vestibule d'honneur, se sentant assuré que
là, du moins, il ne serait aucunement molesté[3], et s'amusait à
faire des réflexions satiriques sur les grandes photographies,
par Saroni, du ministre des États-Unis et de sa femme, qui
avaient à présent pris la place des portraits de famille des

---

notes

1. pantoufles de lisière : pantoufles
cousues dans une étoffe grossière.

2. arquebuse : arme à feu en usage au XVIe siècle.
3. molesté : brutalisé.

Canterville. Il était vêtu simplement mais proprement d'un long linceul, maculé[1] de terreau de cimetière ; il s'était attaché la mâchoire avec une bande de linge jaune, et portait une petite lanterne et une pelle de fossoyeur. En fait, il était costumé pour le rôle de «Jonas sans Tombe, ou le Voleur de Cadavres de Chertsey Barn», une de ses créations les plus remarquables, et l'une de celles dont les Canterville avaient toutes les raisons de se souvenir, car c'était là l'origine véritable de leur querelle avec leur voisin, Lord Rufford. Il était environ deux heures et quart du matin, et, pour autant qu'il pouvait s'en rendre compte nul ne remuait. Cependant, tandis qu'il se dirigeait lentement vers la bibliothèque pour voir s'il restait quelques traces de la tache de sang, deux personnages bondirent tout à coup sur lui du fond d'un recoin sombre, agitant follement les bras au-dessus de leur tête, et lui hurlant «Bou !» à l'oreille.

Saisi de panique, ce qui, vu les circonstances, était bien naturel, il se précipita dans l'escalier, mais trouva Washington Otis qui l'y attendait, muni de la grande seringue du jardin. Se voyant ainsi encerclé de toutes parts par ses ennemis, et presque aux abois[2], il disparut dans le gros poêle de fonte, qui, heureusement pour lui, n'était pas allumé, et il fut obligé de rentrer chez lui par les carneaux[3] et les cheminées, arrivant dans sa chambre dans un état affreux de saleté, de désordre, et de désespoir.

Après cela, on ne le vit plus en expédition nocturne. Les jumeaux se tinrent en embuscade[4] à plusieurs reprises pour

notes

1. maculé : taché.
2. aux abois : se dit de quelqu'un qui se sent menacé, pris dans une situation sans issue.

3. carneaux : parties d'un conduit de cheminée.
4. embuscade : piège destiné à prendre quelqu'un par surprise.

130 le surprendre, et parsemèrent tous les soirs les couloirs de coques de noix, au grand ennui de leurs parents et des domestiques, mais ce fut en vain. Il était bien manifeste qu'il se sentait tellement blessé dans ses sentiments, qu'il refusait d'apparaître. Mr. Otis, en conséquence, se remit à son

135 important travail sur l'histoire du Parti démocrate, auquel il se consacrait depuis plusieurs années ; Mrs. Otis organisa un merveilleux pique-nique aux palourdes[1], qui fit sensation dans le comté ; les gamins s'adonnèrent à des parties de la crosse, d'euchre, de poker, et autres jeux nationaux améri-

140 cains ; et Virginia parcourut les chemins sur son poney, accompagnée par le jeune duc de Cheshire, qui était venu passer la dernière semaine de ses vacances à Canterville Chase. Il fut généralement admis que le fantôme était parti, et, en vérité, Mr. Otis écrivit une lettre en informant Lord

145 Canterville, qui, en réponse, exprima la grande satisfaction que lui causait cette nouvelle, et adressa ses compliments à la digne épouse du ministre.

Les Otis, cependant, se trompaient, car le fantôme était toujours dans la maison ; et, bien qu'il fût maintenant presque

150 réduit à l'état d'invalide[2], il n'était nullement disposé à en rester là, d'autant moins qu'il avait appris que, parmi les invités, se trouvait le jeune duc de Cheshire, dont le grand-oncle, Lord Francis Stilton, avait un jour parié cent guinées avec le colonel Carbury qu'il ferait une partie de dés avec le

155 fantôme de Canterville, et avait été retrouvé le lendemain matin étendu sur le parquet de la salle de jeu, dans un tel état d'impotence[3] paralytique que, bien qu'il vécût jusqu'à un

---

notes

1. *pique-nique aux palourdes :* pique-nique au cours duquel on fait griller des coquillages appelés palourdes sur des pierres (coutume américaine).

2. *invalide :* infirme.
3. *impotence :* infirmité.

âge avancé, il ne fut plus capable de dire autre chose que
«Double Six».

160 L'histoire s'était ébruitée[1] à l'époque, bien que, naturellement, par respect envers les sentiments des deux familles,
l'on eût fait tout son possible pour l'étouffer; et l'on trou-
vera un récit détaillé de tous les événements qui s'y rattachent dans le troisième volume des *Souvenirs du Prince*
165 *Régent et de ses Amis*, de Lord Tattle.

Le fantôme était donc naturellement très désireux de montrer qu'il n'avait pas perdu son influence sur les Stilton, à
qui, en vérité, il était apparenté de loin, sa propre cousine
germaine ayant épousé en secondes noces le sire de
170 Bulkeley, de qui, comme chacun sait, descend toute la
lignée des ducs de Cheshire. Aussi prit-il ses dispositions
pour apparaître devant le petit amoureux de Virginia sous la
forme de sa célèbre création : « Le Moine Vampire, ou le
Bénédictin Exsangue » – vision tellement horrible que,
175 lorsque la vieille Lady Startup en avait été témoin, ce qui
était arrivé un soir fatal de Saint-Sylvestre, en l'an 1764 elle
s'était mise à pousser des cris perçants, qui avaient abouti à
une apoplexie[2] violente, si bien qu'elle était morte au bout
de trois jours, après avoir déshérité les Canterville, qui
180 étaient ses parents les plus proches, et laissé tout son argent
à son apothicaire de Londres… Au dernier moment, toutefois, la terreur que lui inspiraient les jumeaux l'empêcha de
quitter sa chambre; le petit duc dormit donc en paix sous le
grand dais[3] emplumé de la chambre Royale, et rêva de
185 Virginia.

notes

1. *ébruiter:* répandre, propager une rumeur.   3. *dais:* baldaquin, sorte de plafond
2. *apoplexie:* évanouissement soudain dû   au-dessus d'un lit ou d'un trône.
en général à une hémorragie cérébrale.

Au fil du texte

AVEZ-VOUS BIEN LU?

1. Quels sont les différents mauvais tours joués par les jumeaux au fantôme? Comment réagit la victime?

2. *« Durant cinq jours, il garda la chambre... »* : retrouvez cette expression et expliquez la cause de la grande faiblesse du fantôme.

3. Parmi les propositions suivantes, relevez celles qui sont exactes.
a) Le fantôme s'en prend surtout aux jumeaux.
b) Le fantôme terrorise le duc de Cheshire.
c) À la fin du chapitre, le fantôme renonce à agir contre les Otis.
d) Mr. Otis, à la fin du chapitre, pense que le fantôme est parti.
e) Le fantôme a joué aux dés avec le grand-oncle du duc de Cheshire.

ÉTUDIER LE VOCABULAIRE ET LA GRAMMAIRE

4. Relevez, dans les pages 48 et 49, les verbes au passé simple et proposez, selon une méthode que vous choisirez, une classification des terminaisons.

5. Relevez les indicateurs de temps qui justifient la présence du passé simple au début du chapitre.

6. Quel est le temps dominant dans le premier paragraphe du chapitre?

7. Relevez trois verbes au présent de l'indicatif dans ce premier paragraphe. Quelle est ici la valeur de ce temps ?

8. Relevez les compléments du nom en soulignant la préposition qui les introduit (lignes 103 à 111).

9. Pourquoi les compléments du nom sont-ils si nombreux dans ce passage ?

ÉTUDIER UN THÈME :
LE FANTÔME RIDICULE

10. Relevez trois expressions qui montrent que le fantôme est bien un personnage surnaturel.

11. Relevez cinq expressions qui donnent, au contraire, l'impression que le fantôme est un personnage tout à fait ordinaire.

12. Quel est l'effet produit par ces deux impressions contradictoires ?

À VOS PLUMES !

13. Jouez, vous aussi, avec l'imparfait et le passé simple : dans un premier paragraphe, vous décrirez à l'imparfait une pièce du manoir des Canterville ; puis, votre second paragraphe sera au passé simple et commencera par : « Soudain, une lueur apparut au fond de la cheminée… ».

14. À votre tour, rédigez un passage comique en jouant sur les contrastes : un personnage immense et très peureux, un personnage tout petit et très courageux, un enfant au sourire angélique qui a commis les pires bêtises…

Chapitre 5

1   Quelques jours après ces événements, Virginia et son cava-
     lier aux cheveux bouclés se promenèrent à cheval à travers
     les prés de Brockley, où elle fit un accroc[1] si désastreux à
     son amazone en sautant une haie, qu'elle résolut, en ren-
5   trant, de monter par l'escalier de service afin qu'on ne la
     vît pas. Alors qu'elle passait en courant devant la chambre
     aux Tapisseries, dont la porte était ouverte, il lui sembla
     voir quelqu'un dans la pièce, et, croyant que c'était la
     femme de chambre[2] de sa mère, qui s'y installait parfois
10   avec son ouvrage, elle y entra pour lui demander de faire
     une reprise à sa jupe.
     Mais, à sa grande surprise, c'était le fantôme de Canterville
     en personne ! Il était assis à la fenêtre, observant l'or en
     ruine des feuilles jaunissantes tourbillonner dans l'air, et les
15   feuilles rouges danser follement dans la longue avenue. Sa
     tête était appuyée dans sa main, et toute son attitude expri-

notes

1. accroc : déchirure.   **2. femme de chambre :** domestique au service d'une femme.

mait un abattement extrême. En vérité, il avait l'air si triste et en si piteux[1] état, que la petite Virginia, dont la première pensée avait été de s'enfuir et de s'enfermer à clef dans sa chambre, fut remplie de pitié, et résolut d'essayer de le consoler. Sa démarche était si légère, et si profonde la mélancolie du fantôme, qu'il ne s'aperçut pas de sa présence avant qu'elle lui eût parlé.

«Je vous plains bien sincèrement, dit-elle, mais mes frères rentrent demain à Eton, et alors, si vous vous conduisez bien, personne ne vous tracassera.

– Il est absurde de me demander de me bien conduire, répondit-il, se retournant vers la jolie fillette qui avait osé lui adresser la parole, absolument absurde. Il faut que je secoue mes chaînes, et que je gémisse à travers les trous des serrures, et que j'erre pendant la nuit, si c'est là ce que vous voulez dire. C'est ma seule raison d'être.

– Ce n'est nullement là une raison d'être, et vous savez que vous avez été très méchant. Mrs. Umney nous a dit, le jour même de notre arrivée, que vous aviez tué votre femme.

– Oh! je le reconnais volontiers, dit le fantôme d'un ton irrité, mais ce fut là strictement une affaire de famille, qui ne regardait personne d'autre.

– C'est fort mal de tuer qui que ce soit, dit Virginia, qui avait par moments une charmante gravité, héritée de quelque lointain ancêtre de la Nouvelle-Angleterre[2].

– Oh! comme je déteste la sévérité facile de l'éthique[3] abstraite! Ma femme était fort laide, elle ne faisait jamais empeser[4] convenablement mes collerettes, et n'entendait

---

notes

1. *piteux :* pitoyable.
2. *Nouvelle-Angleterre :* région d'Amérique dominée par les Anglais au XVIIe siècle.
3. *éthique :* morale.
4. *empeser :* amidonner un vêtement pour lui donner du poids et de la tenue.

45 rien à la cuisine. Voyons ! Je me souviens d'un daim que j'avais abattu dans les bois de Hogley, un daguet[1] magnifique, et savez-vous comment elle l'a fait servir à table ?... Enfin, peu importe, à présent, car tout cela est passé ; et j'avais beau l'avoir tuée, je ne trouve pas que ç'ait été bien

50 gentil de la part de ses frères de me faire mourir de faim.

— Vous faire mourir de faim ? Oh ! monsieur le Fantôme — je veux dire : Sir Simon —, avez-vous faim ? J'ai un sandwich dans mon sac. Le voulez-vous ?

— Non, merci ; je ne mange jamais rien, à présent ; mais c'est

55 bien aimable à vous, néanmoins, et vous êtes beaucoup plus gentille que le reste de votre affreuse famille, si grossière, si vulgaire, et si malhonnête !

— Assez ! s'écria Virginia, en frappant du pied le parquet, c'est vous qui êtes grossier, affreux et vulgaire ; et quant à la mal-

60 honnêteté, vous savez fort bien que vous avez volé les couleurs dans ma boîte, pour essayer de raviver[2] cette ridicule tache de sang dans la bibliothèque. Vous avez commencé par prendre tous mes rouges, y compris le vermillon, de sorte que je n'ai plus pu faire de couchers de soleil ; puis vous avez

65 pris le vert émeraude et le jaune de chrome, et finalement il ne m'est plus rien resté que l'indigo et le blanc de Chine, si bien que je n'ai pu faire rien d'autre que des clairs de lune, qui sont toujours déprimants à regarder, et qui ne sont pas faciles du tout à peindre. Je ne vous ai jamais dénoncé, bien

70 que je fusse fort contrariée, et toute cette histoire était ridicule : car qui a jamais entendu parler de sang vert émeraude ?

— Enfin, voyons, dit le fantôme, d'un air assez penaud, que vouliez-vous que je fisse ? Il est fort difficile de se procurer

notes

1. daguet : jeune cerf.   **2. raviver :** redonner de la couleur, rendre plus vif.

Allégorie de la peinture par Jean Restout (1692-1768).

du sang, à notre époque, et puisque votre frère est à l'origine
75 de toute l'affaire avec son Extra-Détersif, je n'ai vu aucune
raison de ne pas m'approprier[1] vos couleurs. Quant à la
teinte c'est toujours une affaire de goût : les Canterville ont
du sang bleu, par exemple – le plus bleu qui soit en
Angleterre ; mais je sais que, vous autres Américains, vous ne
80 vous intéressez pas aux choses de ce genre.

– Vous n'en savez absolument rien, et ce que vous auriez de
mieux à faire, ce serait d'émigrer, pour vous cultiver l'esprit.
Mon père ne sera que trop heureux de vous accorder un
passage gratuit, et bien qu'il y ait des droits élevés sur les spi-
85 ritueux[2] de toute nature, il n'y aura pas de difficultés à la
douane, car les fonctionnaires y sont tous démocrates. Une
fois à New York, vous aurez certainement beaucoup de succès. Je connais des tas de gens qui donneraient cent mille
dollars pour avoir un grand-père, et bien plus encore pour
90 avoir un fantôme de famille.

– Je crois que cela ne me plairait pas, l'Amérique.

– Sans doute parce que nous n'avons pas de ruines ni de
curiosités, dit Virginia d'un ton sarcastique[3].

– Pas de ruines ? Pas de curiosités ? répondit le fantôme. Vous
95 avez votre marine et vos façons.

– Bonsoir ; je vais aller demander à papa d'obtenir pour les
jumeaux huit jours de congé supplémentaires.

– Je vous en prie, ne partez pas, Miss Virginia ! s'écria-t-il. Je
suis si solitaire et si malheureux, et je ne sais vraiment que
100 faire ! Je voudrais m'endormir, et je ne le puis pas.

---

notes

1. s'approprier : prendre pour soi ce qui
n'appartient à personne ou ce qui
appartient à quelqu'un d'autre.

2. spiritueux : alcools ; en anglais, ce mot
désigne également les fantômes. Oscar Wilde
joue ici sur le double sens du mot.
3. sarcastique : qui se moque méchamment.

– Voilà qui est complètement absurde ! Vous n'avez tout simplement qu'à vous mettre au lit et à souffler la bougie. Il est très difficile, parfois, de rester éveillé, en particulier à l'église, mais il n'y a absolument aucune difficulté à s'endor105 mir. Voyons, les bébés eux-mêmes savent faire cela, et ils ne sont pas très malins.

– Il y a trois cents ans que je n'ai pas dormi, dit-il tristement, et les beaux yeux bleus de Virginia s'agrandirent, pleins d'étonnement, oui, je n'ai pas dormi depuis trois cents
110 ans, et je suis si fatigué ! »

Virginia devint toute grave, et ses petites lèvres frémirent, pareilles à des pétales de rose. Elle s'approcha, et, s'agenouillant tout contre lui, leva les yeux sur son vieux visage flétri.

115 « Pauvre, pauvre fantôme, murmura-t-elle ; n'avez-vous nul endroit où vous puissiez dormir ?

– Au loin, là-bas, au-delà des bois de pins, répondit-il, d'une voix lente et rêveuse, il y a un petit jardin. L'herbe y croît, longue et drue[1] ; il y a là les grosses étoiles blanches de la
120 fleur de ciguë[2], et le rossignol y chante toute la nuit. Toute la nuit, il chante, et la lune froide, pareille à un globe de cristal, penche ses regards sur ce jardin ; et l'if étend ses bras géants au-dessus des dormeurs. »

Les yeux de Virginia s'embuèrent de larmes, et elle se cacha
125 la tête dans les mains.

« Vous voulez dire le Jardin de la Mort, chuchota-t-elle.

– Oui, la Mort. Comme la Mort doit être belle ! Reposer dans la terre molle et brune, tandis que les herbes vous ondulent au-dessus de la tête, et écouter le silence. N'avoir

notes

1. drue : épaisse.   **2. ciguë :** fleur dont le poison est mortel.

130 pas d'hier, et pas de demain. Oublier le temps, oublier la vie, être en paix... Vous pouvez m'aider. Vous pouvez m'ouvrir le portail de la maison de la Mort, car l'Amour est toujours avec vous, et l'Amour est plus fort que la Mort. »

Virginia se mit à trembler ; elle fut parcourue d'un frisson 135 glacial, et pendant quelques instants il y eut un silence. Elle avait l'impression d'être au milieu d'un rêve terrible.

Puis le fantôme se remit à parler, et sa voix ressemblait aux soupirs du vent :

« Avez-vous lu la vieille prophétie[1] sur la fenêtre de la biblio-140 thèque ?

– Oh ! souvent, s'écria la fillette, levant les yeux, je la connais fort bien. Elle est peinte avec de drôles de lettres noires, et elle est difficile à lire. Il n'y a que six vers :

Quand celle aux cheveux d'or aura su arracher
145   *Les mots d'une prière aux lèvres du péché*
Quand l'amandier stérile[2] aura repris ses charmes
      Et qu'un petit enfant aura donné ses larmes,
      Alors, cette maison redeviendra tranquille
      Et la paix reviendra devers les Canterville.

150 Mais je ne sais pas ce qu'ils signifient.

– Ils signifient, dit-il tristement, qu'il faut que vous pleuriez sur mes péchés, parce que je n'ai point de larmes, et que vous priiez avec moi pour mon âme, parce que je n'ai point de foi, et alors, si vous avez toujours été douce, sage, et gen-155 tille, l'Ange de la Mort aura pitié de moi. Vous verrez des formes effarantes dans l'obscurité, et des voix mauvaises vous parleront tout bas à l'oreille, mais elles ne vous feront

notes

1. prophétie : prédiction.   **2. stérile :** qui ne peut se reproduire.

pas de mal, car contre la pureté d'une enfant les puissances de l'Enfer ne peuvent rien. »

160 Virginia ne répondit rien, et le fantôme se tordit les mains en signe de désespoir farouche, tandis qu'il abaissait son regard sur la tête penchée et dorée de la fillette. Tout à coup elle se redressa, toute pâle, avec une lueur étrange dans les yeux.

165 « Je n'ai pas peur, dit-elle avec fermeté, et je demanderai à l'Ange d'avoir pitié de vous. »

Il se leva de son siège avec un léger cri de joie, et, lui prenant la main, se pencha sur elle avec une grâce d'un autre temps, et la baisa. Il avait les doigts froids comme de la
170 glace, et les lèvres brûlantes comme du feu, mais Virginia n'hésita pas, tandis qu'il lui faisait traverser la pièce plongée dans la pénombre. Sur les tapisseries vertes et fanées étaient brodés de petits chasseurs. Ils sonnaient de leurs cors garnis d'aiguillettes, et, de leurs petites mains, lui faisaient signe de
175 revenir. « Reviens, petite Virginia criaient-ils, reviens ! » Mais le fantôme lui agrippa la main plus étroitement, et elle ferma les yeux pour ne pas les voir. Des animaux horribles, à la queue de lézard et aux yeux protubérants[1], clignaient vers elle du haut de la cheminée sculptée, et murmuraient :
180 « Prends garde, petite Virginia, prends garde ! Il se peut que nous ne te revoyions plus jamais ! », mais le fantôme avança plus vite de sa démarche glissée, et Virginia ne les écouta pas. Quand ils eurent atteint le fond de la pièce, il s'arrêta, et marmotta quelques mots qu'elle fut incapable de com-
185 prendre. Elle ouvrit les yeux, et vit le mur qui s'évanouissait lentement comme une brume, et, devant elle, une grande

note
---
1. protubérants : en relief.

caverne noire. Un vent froid et mordant les enveloppa, et elle sentit quelque chose qui tirait sa robe. «Vite, vite, s'écria le fantôme, sinon, il sera trop tard!» En un instant, le 190 lambris s'était refermé sur eux, et la chambre aux Tapisseries était vide.

Au fil du texte

AVEZ-VOUS BIEN LU?

1. Parmi les affirmations suivantes, relevez celles qui sont justes.

a) Virginia demande à la femme de chambre de repriser sa tenue d'amazone.

b) Virginia aborde le fantôme car elle a pitié de lui.

c) Le fantôme a assassiné sa femme pour des raisons financières.

d) Le fantôme a été assassiné par ses deux beaux-frères.

e) Virginia peint des clairs de lune car il ne lui reste plus que du blanc et de l'indigo dans sa boîte de couleurs.

f) Le fantôme pense qu'il est difficile de rester éveillé.

g) Le fantôme demande à Virginia de l'aider à trouver la paix de la mort.

h) Virginia récite au fantôme la prophétie écrite sur le mur du salon.

i) Le fantôme demande à Virginia de jouer le rôle de l'Ange de la Mort.

j) Virginia accepte avec enthousiasme de suivre le fantôme.

(Les questions 2 à 4 portent sur les deux dernières pages du chapitre.)

2. Relevez deux passages qui montrent que certains personnages tentent de retenir Virginia.

3. Relevez trois phrases qui expriment le fait que le fantôme cherche à entraîner Virginia.

4. Relevez deux phrases qui prouvent que Virginia est d'accord pour suivre le fantôme.

ÉTUDIER LE VOCABULAIRE ET LA GRAMMAIRE

5. Étudiez le champ lexical des sensations en relevant les noms, les adjectifs et les verbes qui évoquent des sensations visuelles, auditives et tactiles.

6. Combien la prophétie inscrite sur la fenêtre compte-t-elle de phrases ? Justifiez votre réponse.

7. Relevez les propositions subordonnées de cette prophétie en soulignant le mot subordonnant qui les introduit. Quelles sortes d'indications donnent ces propositions ?

surnaturel:
qui ne se produit pas dans la nature, dans la réalité.

8. Dans le passage « *Sur les tapisseries… caverne noire* » (l. 172 à 187), relevez un complément circonstanciel de lieu, de temps, de moyen, de manière, de but et de comparaison. Vous préciserez à chaque fois sa nature grammaticale.

9. Pourquoi les compléments circonstanciels sont-ils si nombreux dans ce passage ?

ÉTUDIER UN THÈME: LE SURNATUREL

10. Relevez les éléments inquiétants dans la réponse du fantôme (lignes 117 à 123).

11. Quels sont les éléments surnaturels★ de ce passage ?

12. À la fin du texte, à partir de « *Elle ouvrit les yeux…* », relevez les éléments qui contribuent à créer un mystère.

13. Pourquoi la fin du chapitre 5 produit-elle un effet dramatique et inquiétant alors que la fin du chapitre 2 a une tonalité comique ?

À VOS PLUMES!

14. En vous inspirant de l'évocation du *«petit jardin»*, rédigez à votre tour un paragraphe évoquant ainsi un lieu abandonné et mystérieux (forêt, grenier, cave, grotte, maison...).

15. Reprenez le lieu abandonné que vous avez choisi pour rédiger le paragraphe demandé ci-dessus et décrivez-le de manière exagérée, parodique.

16. En conservant le ton mystérieux de la fin de ce chapitre, imaginez la progression de Virginia et du fantôme en direction du Jardin de la Mort.

LIRE L'IMAGE (PAGE 56)

17. Expliquez le titre.

18. En considérant les lignes du dessin, expliquez l'impression de douceur.

19. Quelle impression crée le regard baissé de la jeune fille?

20. Relevez, dans le chapitre, trois passages qui montrent que Virginia présente des points communs avec la jeune fille du tableau.

Chapitre 6

1   Une dizaine de minutes plus tard, la cloche sonna pour le thé, et, comme Virginia ne descendait pas, Mrs. Otis dépêcha là-haut l'un des laquais[1], pour la prévenir. Il revint au bout d'un petit moment, disant qu'il ne trouvait nulle part
5   Miss Virginia. Comme elle avait l'habitude de sortir tous les soirs au jardin afin de cueillir des fleurs pour orner la table, au dîner, Mrs. Otis ne fut pas inquiète tout d'abord ; mais lorsque six heures sonnèrent, sans que parût Virginia, elle fut sérieusement agitée, et envoya les garçons à sa
10   recherche, cependant qu'elle-même, avec Mr. Otis, fouillait chacune des pièces de la maison. À six heures et demie les garçons rentrèrent, disant qu'ils ne trouvaient nulle part trace de leur sœur. Ils étaient tous, à présent, dans un état de violente surexcitation, et ne savaient que faire, lorsque
15   Mr. Otis se rappela tout à coup qu'il avait, quelques jours auparavant, autorisé une bande de romanichels[2] à camper

notes

1. laquais : serviteur.
2. romanichel : nom péjoratif donné aux tsiganes, aux gens du voyage.

dans le parc. Aussi se mit-il immédiatement en route pour Blackfell Hollow, où il savait qu'ils se trouvaient, accompagné de son fils aîné et de deux des valets de ferme. Le petit
20 duc de Cheshire, qui était absolument fou d'inquiétude, supplia instamment[1] qu'on lui permît d'y aller, lui aussi, mais Mr. Otis ne voulut pas l'y autoriser, car il craignait l'éventualité d'une altercation[2]. En arrivant sur les lieux, toutefois, il constata que les romanichels étaient partis, et il
25 était manifeste que leur départ avait été assez soudain, car le feu était encore allumé, et plusieurs assiettes jonchaient[3] l'herbe. Ayant dépêché Washington et les deux hommes pour fouiller les environs, il se hâta de rentrer à la maison, et envoya des télégrammes à tous les inspecteurs de police du
30 comté, leur disant de rechercher une fillette qui avait été enlevée par des chemineaux ou des romanichels. Il fit alors amener son cheval, et après avoir insisté pour que sa femme et les trois garçons se missent à table pour dîner, il s'éloigna le long de la route d'Ascot avec un palefrenier[4].
35 À peine, cependant, eut-il parcouru deux ou trois kilomètres, qu'il entendit quelqu'un qui galopait derrière lui pour le rejoindre, et, se retournant, il vit le petit duc qui arrivait sur son poney, le sang aux joues, et sans chapeau.

«Je regrette vivement, Mr. Otis, haleta le gamin, mais il m'est
40 impossible de dîner tant que Virginia n'est pas retrouvée. Je vous en supplie, ne me grondez pas; si vous aviez autorisé nos fiançailles, l'an dernier, nous n'aurions jamais eu tout ce tracas. Vous n'allez pas me renvoyer, dites? Je ne peux pas partir! Je ne le veux pas!»

---

notes

1. instamment: avec insistance.
2. altercation: dispute.
3. joncher: être éparpillé sur le sol.

4. palefrenier: employé(e) chargé de l'entretien des chevaux.

45 Le ministre ne put s'empêcher de sourire en voyant le jeune
et charmant garnement, et fut vivement touché du dévoue-
ment qu'il témoignait envers Virginia ; aussi, se penchant sur
son cheval, il lui tapota l'épaule avec bonté, et lui dit :

« Ma foi, Cecil, puisque vous ne voulez pas faire demi-tour,
50 je suppose qu'il faut que vous m'accompagniez ; mais il faut
que je vous trouve un chapeau à Ascot.

– Oh ! peu importe mon chapeau ! C'est Virginia qu'il me
faut ! » s'écria le petit duc, en riant, et ils se dirigèrent au
galop vers la gare du chemin de fer.

55 Mr. Otis s'y enquit[1] auprès du chef de gare pour savoir si
l'on n'avait pas vu, sur le quai, une personne répondant au
signalement de Virginia ; mais il ne reçut aucune réponse
affirmative. Toutefois, le chef de gare lança des télégrammes le long de la voie, dans les deux sens, et lui donna
60 l'assurance qu'on exercerait une surveillance sérieuse pour
la retrouver ; et, après avoir acheté un chapeau pour le petit
duc, chez un drapier[2] qui mettait les volets à sa devanture,
Mr. Otis poursuivit sa route jusqu'à Bexley, village situé à
quelque six kilomètres de là, et qui, lui dit-on, était un lieu
65 de ralliement bien connu des romanichels, car il y avait un
vaste pré communal tout proche. Là, ils réveillèrent l'agent
de police rural, mais ne purent lui tirer aucun rensei-
gnement, et, après avoir parcouru à cheval toute l'étendue
du pré, ils firent prendre à leurs montures le chemin du
70 retour, et arrivèrent à Canterville Chase vers onze heures,
recrus de fatigue[3] et presque au désespoir. Ils trouvèrent
Washington et les jumeaux qui les attendaient à la loge
d'entrée, munis de lanternes, car l'avenue était sombre.

notes

1. s'y enquit : (du verbe *s'enquérir*) se renseigner.

2. drapier : marchand de tissu.
3. recrus de fatigue : épuisés.

On n'avait pas découvert la moindre trace de Virginia. Les
75 romanichels avaient été rejoints dans les prairies de Broley,
mais elle n'était pas avec eux, et ils expliquèrent leur
brusque départ en disant qu'ils s'étaient trompés dans la
date de la foire de Chorton, et étaient partis précipitamment, de peur d'y arriver trop tard. Ils avaient même été
80 fort contrariés en apprenant la disparition de Virginia, car
ils étaient reconnaissants à Mr. Otis de les avoir autorisés à
camper dans son parc, et quatre d'entre eux étaient restés
pour prendre part aux recherches. On avait dragué[1] l'étang
aux carpes, et tout le domaine avait été fouillé à fond, mais
85 sans résultat. Il était évident que, pour cette nuit-là tout au
moins, Virginia était perdue pour eux ; et c'est dans un état
d'abattement des plus profonds que Mr. Otis et ses garçons
se dirigèrent à pied vers la maison, suivis du palefrenier
conduisant les deux chevaux et le poney. Dans le vestibule,
90 ils trouvèrent un groupe de serviteurs effarés, et, étendue
sur un canapé dans la bibliothèque, la pauvre Mrs. Otis,
presque folle de terreur et d'inquiétude, se faisant poser sur
le front des compresses d'eau de Cologne par la vieille
gouvernante. Mr. Otis insista sur-le-champ pour qu'elle
95 mangeât quelque chose, et commanda qu'on servît à souper à tout le monde.
Ce fut un repas mélancolique, car à peu près personne ne
dit mot, et les jumeaux eux-mêmes étaient consternés et
abattus, car ils aimaient beaucoup leur sœur. Lorsqu'ils
100 eurent fini, Mr. Otis, en dépit des supplications du petit
duc, leur ordonna à tous d'aller se coucher, disant qu'on ne
pouvait rien faire de plus ce soir-là, et qu'il télégraphierait

note

1. draguer : racler le fond d'un cours d'eau, d'un port…

dès le lendemain à Scotland Yard pour qu'on envoyât immédiatement quelques détectives sur les lieux.

105 Juste au moment où ils sortaient de la salle à manger, minuit commença à sonner lourdement au clocher, et lorsque retentit le dernier coup, ils entendirent un fracas et un cri perçant et soudain, un coup de tonnerre épouvantable ébranla la maison, les sons d'une musique supraterrestre[1]
110 flottèrent dans l'air, un panneau au sommet de l'escalier s'enfonça brusquement dans le mur avec un bruit violent, et la petite Virginia, très pâle et toute blanche, parut sur le palier, portant à la main une cassette[2]. Il ne leur fallut qu'un instant pour monter jusqu'auprès d'elle, à pas précipités.
115 Mrs. Otis l'étreignit passionnément dans ses bras, le duc la couvrit de baisers violents, et les jumeaux exécutèrent une sauvage danse guerrière autour du groupe.

«Grand Dieu! Mon enfant, où donc étais-tu? dit Mr. Otis, non sans colère, croyant qu'elle leur avait fait quelque farce
120 stupide. Cecil et moi, nous avons battu la campagne à ta recherche, et ta mère a été mortellement effrayée. Il ne faut plus jouer de tours semblables!

– Sauf au fantôme! Sauf au fantôme! hurlèrent les jumeaux, tout en gambadant en tous sens.
125 – Ma chérie à moi, Dieu soit loué, tu es retrouvée! Il ne faudra plus jamais me quitter, murmura Mrs. Otis, tandis qu'elle embrassait l'enfant tremblante, et lissait l'or de ses cheveux emmêlés.

– Papa, dit Virginia avec calme, j'étais auprès du fantôme. Il
130 est mort, et il faut que vous veniez le voir. Il avait été bien méchant, mais il a regretté sincèrement tout ce qu'il avait

---

notes

1. supraterrestre: surnaturel.
2. cassette: petit coffre pouvant contenir de l'argent et des bijoux.

fait, et il m'a donné, avant de mourir, cette boîte de bijoux magnifiques. »

Toute la famille la dévisagea, muette de stupéfaction, mais elle était parfaitement grave et sérieuse ; et, se retournant, elle les conduisit, par l'ouverture du lambris, le long d'un étroit couloir secret, Washington fermant la marche avec une bougie allumée qu'il avait saisie sur la table. Ils arrivèrent finalement à une grande porte de chêne, garnie de clous rouillés. Quand Virginia la toucha, elle s'ouvrit en arrière sur ses lourdes paumelles[1], et ils se trouvèrent dans une petite pièce basse, au plafond voûté, avec une fenêtre minuscule munie de barreaux. Encastré dans le mur, il y avait un énorme anneau de fer, auquel était enchaîné un squelette, étendu de tout son long sur le sol de pierre, et qui paraissait essayer de saisir, de ses longs doigts décharnés, un plat et une cruche à eau de forme démodée qui étaient placés juste hors de sa portée. La cruche avait évidemment été remplie d'eau jadis, car elle était recouverte à l'intérieur d'une moisissure verte. Il n'y avait rien sur le plat, si ce n'est de la poussière amoncelée. Virginia s'agenouilla à côté du squelette, et, joignant ses petites mains se mit à prier silencieusement, cependant que les autres contemplaient, saisis d'étonnement, la tragédie terrible dont le secret leur était à présent révélé.

« Tiens ! s'écria tout à coup l'un des jumeaux, qui avait regardé par la fenêtre pour essayer de découvrir dans quelle aile de la maison la chambre était située. Tiens ! Le vieil amandier tout desséché a fleuri ! Je vois distinctement les fleurs, au clair de lune.

---

note

1. paumelles : panneau pivotant sur des gonds.

– Dieu lui a pardonné, dit gravement Virginia, se relevant, et son visage parut s'illuminer d'une lumière splendide.
– Quel ange vous êtes ! » s'écria le jeune duc, et il lui passa le bras autour du cou et l'embrassa.

Au fil du texte

Avez-vous bien lu?

1. Relevez trois phrases qui montrent que le duc de Cheshire est très affecté par la disparition de Virginia.

2. Quelle est la piste suivie par Mr. Otis?

3. Quels sont les indices en faveur de cette piste?

4. Quels sont les éléments qui conduisent Mr. Otis à abandonner cette piste?

antéposé: placé avant.

5. En quoi consiste «*la tragédie terrible*» vécue par Sir Simon?

Étudier le vocabulaire et la grammaire

6. Relevez les indicateurs de temps dans les lignes 1 à 19.

7. Combien rencontre-t-on d'adjectifs qualificatifs et de participes passés employés comme adjectifs dans les lignes 134 à 164?
a) entre 5 et 10;   b) entre 10 et 15;   c) plus de 15.

8. Relevez, dans le passage précédemment délimité, accompagnés du nom qu'ils déterminent, huit adjectifs qualificatifs antéposés★. Quelle est la particularité commune à tous ces adjectifs?

9. Donnez la fonction des adjectifs suivants: «*muette*» (ligne 134), «*grave*» (ligne 135), «*grande*» (ligne 139), «*basse*» (ligne 142), «*verte*» (ligne 150) et «*terrible*» (ligne 154).

10. Relevez les adverbes en *-ment* employés dans ce même passage (lignes 134 à 164) et précisez l'adjectif à partir duquel l'adverbe est formé.

ÉTUDIER LA PLACE DU CHAPITRE DANS LE RÉCIT

11. Quels sont les personnages présents au moment où Virginia est retrouvée ?

12. Relevez l'expression qui montre que ce chapitre lève le voile sur l'origine du fantôme.

13. Dans quelle mesure ce chapitre constitue-t-il le dénouement ?

14. Quelle place occupe le surnaturel dans ce chapitre ?

À VOS PLUMES !

15. Imaginez que vous deviez tourner un film sur le passage au cours duquel Virginia guide les autres personnages jusqu'à la découverte de la cellule du fantôme. Après avoir décrit le décor que vous avez choisi, présentez les séquences successives de votre film en détaillant les mouvements des personnages.

Chapitre 7

1   Quatre jours après ces curieux incidents, une procession
     funèbre partit de Canterville Chase vers onze heures du
     soir. Le corbillard était traîné par huit chevaux noirs, dont
     chacun portait sur la tête un gros toupet[1] de plumes d'au-
5   truche, et le cercueil de plomb était recouvert d'un somp-
     tueux poêle[2] de pourpre, sur lequel était brodé en or
     l'écusson de Canterville. À côté du corbillard et des voi-
     tures marchaient les domestiques, portant des torches allu-
     mées, et toute la procession était merveilleusement
10   impressionnante.
     Lord Canterville, qui conduisait le deuil, était venu tout
     exprès du pays de Galles pour assister aux obsèques[3], et il
     avait pris place dans la première voiture avec la petite
     Virginia. Puis venaient le ministre des États-Unis et sa
15   femme, puis Washington et les trois garçons, et dans la der-

notes

1. toupet : bouquet de plumes.
2. poêle : drap recouvrant le cercueil.

3. obsèques : funérailles, cérémonie
d'enterrement.

nière voiture se trouvait Mrs. Umney. Le sentiment général était que, comme elle avait été effrayée par le fantôme durant plus de cinquante années de sa vie, elle avait le droit de l'accompagner à sa dernière demeure. Une fosse pro-
20 fonde avait été creusée dans l'angle du cimetière, juste sous le vieil if, et l'office funèbre fut dit d'une manière fort impressionnante par le révérend Augustus Dampier.
La cérémonie terminée, les domestiques, conformément au vieil usage conservé dans la famille des Canterville,
25 éteignirent leurs torches, et, au moment où le cercueil était descendu dans la tombe, Virginia s'avança et y déposa une grande croix faite avec des fleurs d'amandier blanches et roses. Au même instant, la lune sortit de derrière un nuage et inonda de ses silencieux rais[1] d'argent le petit cimetière,
30 et, du fond d'un boqueteau[2] lointain, un rossignol se mit à chanter. Virginia songea à la description que lui avait faite le fantôme du Jardin de la Mort, ses yeux s'embuèrent de larmes, et c'est à peine si elle prononça une parole au cours du trajet de retour.
35 Le lendemain matin, avant que Lord Canterville fût reparti pour Londres, Mr. Otis eut un entretien avec lui, au sujet des bijoux que le fantôme avait donnés à Virginia. Ils étaient absolument magnifiques, en particulier certain collier de rubis avec une monture vénitienne, qui était véritablement
40 un échantillon superbe du XVIe siècle, et leur valeur était si considérable que Mr. Otis se sentait saisi de scrupules, se demandant s'il pouvait permettre à sa fille de les accepter…
« Milord, dit-il, je sais que dans ce pays la main morte doit s'appliquer aux bijoux aussi bien qu'aux terres, et il me

---

notes

1. rais : rayons.   **2. boqueteau :** petit groupe d'arbres isolé.

45 paraît parfaitement évident que ces joyaux sont, ou devraient être, des biens d'héritage de votre famille. Je me vois obligé, en conséquence, de vous prier de les emporter à Londres, et de les considérer simplement comme une portion de vos biens, qui vous a été restituée dans certaines cir-
50 constances étranges. Quant à ma fille, elle n'est qu'une enfant, et elle ne témoigne encore, je suis heureux de le dire, que peu d'intérêt pour de semblables accessoires d'un luxe oiseux[1]. J'ai appris également, par Mrs. Otis, qui, je puis le dire, s'y connaît assez bien en matière d'art – car elle a eu
55 l'avantage de passer plusieurs hivers à Boston étant jeune fille –, que ces bijoux sont d'une grande valeur marchande, et atteindraient un prix considérable si on les mettait en vente. Dans ces conditions, Lord Canterville, vous reconnaîtrez qu'il me serait absolument impossible d'admettre qu'ils
60 demeurent en la possession d'un membre de ma famille ; et, certes, tous les vains hochets et jouets de ce genre, quelque convenables ou nécessaires qu'ils soient à la dignité de l'aristocratie britannique, seraient complètement déplacés chez ceux qui ont été élevés dans les principes sévères, et, je crois,
65 immortels, de la simplicité républicaine. Peut-être devrais-je ajouter que Virginia est très désireuse que vous lui permettiez de conserver la boîte, à titre de souvenir de votre ancêtre infortuné mais fourvoyé[2]. Comme elle est extrêmement vieille, et par suite en assez mauvais état, il vous paraî-
70 tra peut-être possible d'accéder à cette requête. Pour ma part, j'avoue que je suis fort surpris de voir un de mes enfants exprimer de la sympathie envers le médiévisme[3] sous une forme quelconque, et je ne puis me l'expliquer

notes

1. oiseux : douteux.
2. fourvoyé : dans l'erreur.

3. médiévisme : intérêt pour ce qui a trait au Moyen Âge.

que par le fait que Virginia est née dans l'un de vos fau-
75 bourgs de Londres, peu après que Mrs. Otis fut revenue
d'un court voyage à Athènes. »

Lord Canterville écouta avec beaucoup de gravité le discours du digne ministre, tirant de temps à autre sa moustache grise afin de dissimuler un sourire involontaire, et
80 lorsque Mr. Otis eut terminé, il lui serra cordialement la
main, et dit :

« Cher monsieur, votre charmante petite fille a rendu à
mon malheureux ancêtre, Sir Simon, un service important,
et ma famille et moi, nous avons une lourde dette envers
85 elle pour les merveilleuses qualités de courage et de cœur
dont elle a fait preuve. Les bijoux sont manifestement à
elle, et, parbleu ! je crois que si j'étais assez dénaturé[1] pour
les lui enlever, le vieux scélérat aurait quitté sa tombe d'ici
quinze jours, et m'en ferait voir de dures ! Quant à leur
90 qualité d'héritage, rien n'est héritage qui n'ait été men-
tionné comme tel dans un testament ou un document
juridique, et l'existence de ces bijoux est restée totalement
inconnue. Je vous assure que je n'ai pas plus de droits sur
eux que votre maître d'hôtel, et quand Miss Virginia sera
95 adulte je gagerais qu'elle sera contente d'avoir de jolies
choses à porter. D'ailleurs, vous oubliez, Mr. Otis, que vous
avez pris les meubles et le fantôme à leur valeur d'estimation, et que tout ce qui a appartenu au fantôme est passé
aussitôt en votre possession, car, quelque activité que Sir
100 Simon ait pu manifester dans le couloir, la nuit, au point de
vue juridique, il était effectivement mort, et vous avez
acquis ses biens par un achat régulier. »

---

note

1. dénaturé : inhumain, sans scrupule.

Mr. Otis fut fort contrarié du refus de Lord Canterville et le pria de revenir sur sa décision, mais l'aimable pair[1] tint bon, et amena en fin de compte le ministre à permettre à sa fille de garder le présent que lui avait fait le fantôme ; et quand, au printemps de 1890, la jeune duchesse de Cheshire fut présentée à la Cour à l'occasion de son mariage lors de la première réception de la Reine, ses bijoux provoquèrent l'admiration générale. Car Virginia reçut la couronne ducale, qui est la récompense de toutes les bonnes petites filles américaines, et fut épousée par son jeune amoureux dès qu'il atteignit sa majorité.

Ils étaient tous les deux si charmants, et ils s'aimaient tellement, que tout le monde fut ravi de ce mariage, sauf la vieille marquise de Dumbleton, qui avait essayé de s'approprier le duc pour une de ses sept filles non mariées et qui, dans cette intention, n'avait pas donné moins de trois grands dîners coûteux, et – chose étrange à dire – Mr. Otis lui-même. Mr. Otis aimait beaucoup le jeune duc, à titre personnel, mais, théoriquement, il était opposé aux titres, ou, pour se servir de ses propres paroles, « n'était pas sans appréhender[2] que, au milieu des influences énervantes d'une aristocratie avide[3] de plaisirs, les principes authentiques de la simplicité républicaine ne fussent oubliés ». Toutefois, ses objections furent complètement écartées, et je crois que lorsqu'il descendit la nef de l'église Saint-George, dans Hanover Square, avec sa fille appuyée à son bras, il n'y avait pas, dans toute l'Angleterre, d'homme plus fier que lui.

Le duc et la duchesse, quand la lune de miel fut terminée, se rendirent à Canterville Chase, et, le lendemain de leur

notes

1. pair : membre de la Chambre des lords en Angleterre.

2. appréhender : craindre.

3. avide : qui désire violemment quelque chose.

arrivée, ils firent une promenade, l'après-midi, au cimetière solitaire proche des bois de pins. Il y avait eu de grosses difficultés, au début, au sujet de l'épitaphe[1] à inscrire sur la

135 tombe de Sir Simon, mais on avait décidé, en fin de compte, d'y graver simplement les initiales du vieux gentilhomme, avec le verset de la fenêtre de la bibliothèque.

La duchesse avait apporté des roses magnifiques, qu'elle effeuilla sur la tombe, et après qu'ils s'y furent arrêtés

140 quelque temps, ils entrèrent dans le sanctuaire[2] en ruine de l'ancienne abbaye. La duchesse s'assit sur un pilier écroulé, tandis que son mari s'étendait à ses pieds, fumant une cigarette et levant ses regards sur ses beaux yeux. Tout à coup, il jeta sa cigarette, lui prit la main, et lui dit : « Virginia, une

145 femme ne doit pas avoir de secrets pour son mari.

– Mon cher Cecil ! Je n'ai pas de secrets pour toi.

– Mais si, tu en as un, répondit-il en souriant : tu ne m'as jamais raconté ce qui t'est arrivé quand tu étais enfermée avec le fantôme.

150 – Je ne l'ai jamais confié à personne, dit gravement Virginia.

– Je le sais, mais tu pourrais me le dévoiler, à moi.

– Je t'en prie, ne me le demande pas, Cecil, je ne puis te le dire. Pauvre Sir Simon ! Je lui dois beaucoup. Oui, ne ris pas, Cecil, c'est vrai. Il m'a fait voir ce qu'est la Vie, ce que

155 signifie la Mort, et pourquoi l'amour est plus puissant que l'une et que l'autre. »

Le duc se leva et embrassa sa femme avec amour.

« Tu peux garder ton secret tant que j'aurai ton cœur, murmura-t-il.

160 – Cela, tu l'as toujours eu, Cecil.

---

notes

1. épitaphe : inscription gravée sur une tombe. **2. sanctuaire :** lieu sacré.

– Et tu le révéleras quelque jour à nos enfants, n'est-ce
pas ? »
Virginia rougit.

L'Entrée au cimetière de Caspar David Friedrich (1774-1840).

Au fil du texte

Avez-vous bien lu?

1. À quelle heure ont lieu les obsèques de Sir Simon?

2. Que dépose Virginia dans la tombe à la fin de la cérémonie?

3. De quelle époque datent les bijoux que le fantôme a donnés à Virginia?

4. En quelle année Virginia épouse-t-elle le duc de Cheshire?

5. Quelle est l'épitaphe gravée sur la tombe de Sir Simon?

6. Virginia, en définitive, gardera-t-elle les bijoux?

Étudier le vocabulaire et la grammaire

7. Quelle est la couleur des pierres du collier de rubis offert par le fantôme à Virginia? Citez d'autres pierres précieuses en précisant leur couleur.

8. Dans le passage allant des lignes 35 à 42, relevez les adjectifs possessifs et les adjectifs indéfinis en précisant le nom qu'ils déterminent.

9. Dans le même passage, relevez les articles et les articles définis contractés en précisant le nom qu'ils déterminent.

10. Dans les lignes 46 à 50: «*je me vois obligé… étranges*», relevez les mots ne comptant qu'une ou deux lettres et précisez pour chacun d'eux leur nature.

ÉTUDIER LA PLACE DE CE CHAPITRE DANS LE CONTE

11. Pour montrer que ce dernier chapitre résout les problèmes posés au début du récit, répondez aux questions que le lecteur était en droit de se poser à la fin du premier chapitre :

a) Le fantôme existe-t-il ?

b) Si le fantôme existe bel et bien, troublera-t-il l'existence de la famille Otis ?

c) Comment les Otis cohabiteront-ils avec un fantôme ?

d) Comment se résoudra l'opposition entre les Anglais et les Américains ?

ÉTUDIER LE GENRE DU TEXTE

12. Comparez le ton de ce chapitre à celui du premier chapitre.

13. Citez la phrase du chapitre 5 qui marque un changement de ton dans le récit.

14. Dans quelle mesure le dénouement de cette histoire est-il bien celui d'un conte ?

À VOS PLUMES !

15. Écrivez un conte mettant en scène un fantôme au XXIe siècle.

LIRE L'IMAGE (PAGE 81)

16. Quelle phrase du chapitre pourrait servir de légende à ce tableau ?

17. Quels sont les éléments verticaux dans ce tableau ?

18. Quel rôle symbolique joue la porte ?

Retour sur l'œuvre

LA PROGRESSION DU RÉCIT

1. Numérotez chaque événement afin de reconstituer l'ordre chronologique.

☐ Virginia épouse le duc de Cheshire.

☐ L'amandier fleurit.

☐ La famille Otis découvre le squelette de Sir Simon.

☐ Les Otis arrivent à Canterville

☐ Mr. Otis propose au fantôme du lubrifiant Soleil Levant.

☐ Les jumeaux imaginent un faux fantôme pour effrayer Sir Simon.

☐ La gouvernante s'évanouit.

☐ Virginia déchire sa tenue d'amazone.

☐ On enterre Sir Simon.

☐ Virginia a disparu.

LE GENRE

2. Attribuez à chaque mot sa définition.

- Le fantastique
- L'humour
- Le comique
- Le surnaturel
- Le dénouement
- Une péripétie
- L'épilogue

A. Situation dans laquelle se produit un événement qui ne peut pas avoir lieu dans la réalité.

B. Résolution du problème posé par la situation initiale.

C. Présentation de la situation des personnages quelque temps après le dénouement.

D. Un événement qui fait progresser l'intrigue.

E. Registre littéraire caractérisé par une hésitation entre une interprétation réaliste et une interprétation surnaturelle d'un événement.

F. Registre littéraire qui provoque le rire ou le sourire du destinataire.

G. Procédé qui consiste à traiter à la légère un sujet grave.

LES PERSONNAGES

3. Inscrivez dans la grille suivante les personnages du conte en vous aidant des définitions.

Horizontalement

1. Prénom de Mrs. Otis.
2. Prénom de Mr. Otis.
3. Prénom de Miss Otis.
3 bis. Prénom du duc de Cheshire.
4. Surnom des jumeaux.
5. Nom de la gouvernante.

Verticalement

I. Prénom du fantôme.
II. Prénom de l'aîné des Otis.
III. Nom d'un pasteur diplômé de Cambridge (chap. 1).
IV. Nom d'une Lady condamnée à porter un ruban de velours noir autour du cou (chap. 2).
V. Nouveau nom de Virginia.

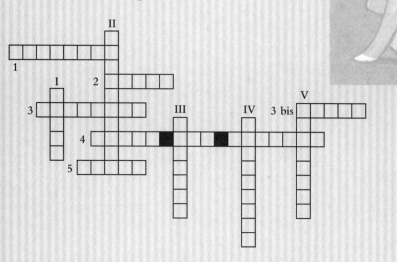

LA PARODIE DE L'HORREUR

4. Le fantôme évoque ses exploits passés comme le ferait un ancien acteur de théâtre. En associant les expressions suivantes, reconstituez les titres des grands succès de Sir Simon.

Ruben le Rouge…   ...ou le Voleur de Cadavres
                               de Chertsey Barn

Daniel le Muet…   ...ou le Suceur de Sang
                               de Bexley Moor

Gédéon le Décharné…   ...ou le Comte sans Tête

Le Moine Vampire…   ...ou le Squelette du Suicidé

Jonas sans Tombe…   ...ou le Bénédictin Exsangue

Martin le Maniaque…   ...ou le Nourisson Étranglé

Rupert le Téméraire…   ... ou le Mystère Masqué

Dossier
Bibliocollège

Schéma narratif

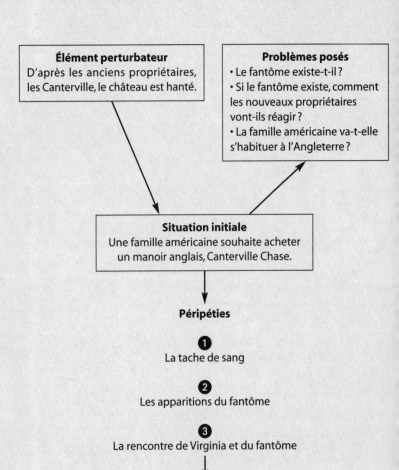

Élément perturbateur
D'après les anciens propriétaires, les Canterville, le château est hanté.

Problèmes posés
• Le fantôme existe-t-il ?
• Si le fantôme existe, comment les nouveaux propriétaires vont-ils réagir ?
• La famille américaine va-t-elle s'habituer à l'Angleterre ?

Situation initiale
Une famille américaine souhaite acheter un manoir anglais, Canterville Chase.

Péripéties

❶ La tache de sang

❷ Les apparitions du fantôme

❸ La rencontre de Virginia et du fantôme

Situation finale
• Le fantôme ne hante plus le château.
• La famille américaine s'est habituée à l'Angleterre : Virginia, républicaine américaine, épouse le jeune duc de Cheshire, aristocrate anglais.

Le récit est construit autour d'une série de péripéties que l'on peut regrouper chronologiquement en trois épisodes.

❶ La tache de sang

• Mrs. Umney affirme que la tache de sang date d'un meurtre commis en 1575 et que le meurtrier hante le manoir.

• Washington efface la tache de sang avec un détersif.
→ La famille Otis pense que le fantôme n'existe pas.

• La tache réapparaît même lorsque la porte est fermée à clé.
→ La famille Otis en déduit que le fantôme existe bel et bien.

❷ Les apparitions du fantôme

• Mr. et Mrs. Otis proposent divers produits miracle au fantôme afin qu'il cesse de les déranger.

• Les jumeaux martyrisent le fantôme :
– ils lui lancent des oreillers à la figure ;
– ils lui tirent dessus avec des sarbacanes ;
– ils fabriquent un faux fantôme pour l'effrayer ;
– ils lui font tomber un seau d'eau sur la tête.
→ Le fantôme finit par renoncer à terroriser les Otis.

❸ La rencontre de Virginia et du fantôme

• Virginia rencontre le fantôme et accepte de l'aider à mourir en l'accompagnant dans le Jardin de la Mort.

• Elle réapparaît quelques heures plus tard avec une cassette remplie de bijoux.

• L'amandier refleurit, signe, selon la prophétie, que le fantôme a enfin trouvé la paix.
→ Le fantôme est enterré quelque temps plus tard.

Il était une fois Oscar Wilde

Oscar Wilde est un écrivain irlandais qui a vécu dans la seconde moitié du XIXe siècle. Célèbre pour ses costumes audacieux et son humour autant que pour ses œuvres, il a été l'idole des milieux mondains de Grande-Bretagne et d'Amérique avant d'être rejeté à cause de sa vie privée jugée scandaleuse.

Un jeune homme brillant

Oscar Wilde est né à Dublin le 16 octobre 1854. Son père était un chirurgien renommé et sa mère est un écrivain engagé qui a défendu la cause de la Jeune Irlande. Il fait sa scolarité au Trinity College de Dublin et il obtient une bourse pour étudier en Angleterre au Magdalen College d'Oxford où il reste quatre ans. En 1878, il remporte un prix de poésie.

Un écrivain mondain

Oscar Wilde s'installe à Londres où il fréquente les milieux intellectuels et mondains. Ses *Poèmes* publiés en 1881 connaissent un grand succès même s'ils ne sont pas très originaux ; mais l'on s'intéresse surtout beaucoup à sa manière de se vêtir et à son comportement. En 1882, il part donner une série de conférences aux États-Unis où il va connaître un vrai triomphe. Le 29 mai 1884, il épouse Constance Lloyd dont il aura deux fils.

Un conteur

Devenu rédacteur en chef d'un magasine *The Woman's World (Le Monde de la femme)*, il publie un recueil de contes intitulé *The Happy Prince (Le Prince heureux)*. Il écrit de nombreux articles comme critique d'art et, en 1891, fait paraître un roman, *Le Portrait de Dorian Gray*, qui sera jugé scandaleux. Il écrit également un recueil de contes *Lord Arthur Savile's crime and Other Stories (Le Crime de Lord Arthur Savile et autres histoires)*. *Le Fantôme de Canterville* fait partie de ce recueil.

Un auteur de théâtre

En 1892, sa pièce *Lady Windermere's Fan (L'Éventail de Lady Windermere)* est mise en scène. Il fera jouer également *A Woman of no importance (Une Femme sans importance)*, *An Ideal Husband (Un Mari idéal)* et *The Importance of being Earnest (De l'importance d'être constant)*. On apprécie l'absurdité des situations et l'humour des répliques.

Le scandale

Oscar Wilde a une liaison avec Lord Alfred Douglas. Il est arrêté et condamné à deux ans de travaux forcés pour atteinte aux bonnes mœurs. Il purge sa peine à la prison de Reading où il écrit *De Profundis*, une longue lettre adressée à Lord Alfred Douglas ; ce texte sera publié après sa mort
Il s'exile à Paris en 1898 et compose *The Ballad of the Reading Gaol (La Ballade de la geôle de Reading)*. Il mène une vie misérable et solitaire et meurt à l'hôtel d'Alsace, rue des Beaux-Arts, le 30 novembre 1900.

Dates clés

1891 :
publication du *Portrait de Dorian Gray* et du *Fantôme de Canterville*.

1895-1897 :
Oscar Wilde est en prison.

1898 :
exil à Paris.

1900 :
Oscar Wilde meurt dans la misère à Paris.

L'Angleterre d'Oscar Wilde : l'ère victorienne

Oscar Wilde, né en 1854 et mort en 1900, n'aura connu qu'un seul régime politique (la monarchie parlementaire) et qu'une seule reine : Victoria.

UNE REINE EXCEPTIONNELLE

Victoria est née en 1819 à Londres. En 1837, à la mort de son oncle Guillaume IV, elle monte sur le trône. En 1840, elle épouse le prince Albert de Saxe-Cobourg. Reine de Grande-Bretagne et d'Irlande, elle devient impératrice des Indes en 1876. Elle meurt en 1901 ; son règne aura duré 63 ans et aura profondément marqué l'histoire de la Grande-Bretagne. Elle a toujours su s'impliquer personnellement dans le gouvernement et notamment dans la politique extérieure, tout en se montrant respectueuse du régime parlementaire et en écoutant les conseils de ses ministres, le plus célèbre étant le conservateur Disraeli. Son règne a été une période de grande prospérité économique et de grand rayonnement.

Le ministre Benjamin Disraeli en 1868, à la Chambre des communes, assemblée parlementaire britannique qui exerce le pouvoir législatif.

C'est également une époque de grande transformation économique et sociale, marquée par l'essor d'une bourgeoisie industrielle très active et par des crises dues à l'émergence d'une classe ouvrière. Le droit de grève est reconnu ainsi que l'existence des syndicats (1875). En 1893, apparaît le parti travailliste*.

LA SOCIÉTÉ VICTORIENNE

Oscar Wilde, comme ses personnages du *Fantôme de Canterville*, évolue dans une société rigide. La morale est sévère et l'on ne pardonnera pas à l'auteur ses mœurs. Dans cette société victorienne, l'aristocratie joue un rôle dominant ; mais elle ne craint pas toujours de s'allier avec la haute bourgeoisie industrielle. Ainsi, il n'est pas choquant de voir le jeune duc de Cheshire épouser une républicaine américaine.

Cette haute société, que fréquente Oscar Wilde, se retrouve dans des lieux à la mode tels Ascot, un célèbre champ de courses. Elle inscrit ses enfants dans des collèges réputés : Eton où sont pensionnaires les jumeaux Otis en est un exemple.

Washington, le fils aîné de la famille Otis, qui est assez beau garçon et excellent danseur, incarne sans doute un personnage de la bonne société victorienne : le dandy*. Les dandys se font remarquer par leur extravagance et le soin particulier apporté à leur tenue vestimentaire. Héritiers peut-être des précieux* de l'époque de Molière, ils affichent, en Angleterre comme en France, une élégance exagérée et provocante. Habitué des salons et apprécié pour son humour et son originalité (dans la limite du respect de la morale victorienne), Oscar Wilde était un dandy.

À retenir

Dandy : mondain qui, sans dépasser les limites admises par la morale, se fait remarquer par son élégance et son originalité.

Précieux : personnes très à la mode dans les salons du XVIIe siècle.

Le Dandy nonchalant peint en 1901 par E. Loevy.

ANGLAIS ET AMÉRICAINS

Dans *Le Fantôme de Canterville*, deux familles s'opposent :
les Canterville, modèles de l'aristocratie anglaise
traditionnelle, et les Otis, une famille américaine à l'esprit
pratique. Ainsi Oscar Wilde évoque, à travers son récit,
le fossé qui sépare les deux pays de langue anglaise.
Si le peuplement des États-Unis est majoritairement
anglais, l'Indépendance américaine a marqué le début
d'un fossé entre deux manières d'être : la tradition et
le modernisme.

En effet, les Anglais et les Américains sont à la fois
proches et différents. C'est en considérant l'histoire
des États-Unis que l'on comprend mieux ce qui unit
et ce qui sépare ces deux peuples. La colonisation
du « Nouveau Monde » a commencé au XVIIe siècle.
Au milieu du XVIIIe siècle, les différentes colonies
comptent environ 1 200 000 habitants. Se faisant au
détriment des populations indigènes, la colonisation
est marquée, dès le début, par la rivalité des Anglais
et des Français.

Dans la seconde moitié du XVIIIe siècle, le conflit se durcit et
la France se voit finalement obligée de céder ses colonies.
Les colons anglais vont, par la suite, progressivement se
révolter contre l'autorité de l'Angleterre : c'est la guerre
de l'Indépendance (1776-1783). Le 4 juillet 1776,
l'indépendance des États-Unis est proclammée.
La France soutient les Américains et, c'est en 1783,
par le *traité de Versailles*, que l'Angleterre reconnaît enfin
l'indépendance des États-Unis.

Le Fantôme de Canterville: un conte?

LES CARACTÉRISTIQUES DU CONTE*

Le conte appartient tout d'abord au genre narratif. C'est une histoire, un récit : le temps s'écoule, des événements s'enchaînent.

Comme la nouvelle*, le conte est un texte court ; il est publié, avec d'autres contes, dans un recueil. C'est le cas des *Contes de ma mère l'Oye* de Charles Perrault ou des *Contes du chat perché* de Marcel Aymé. En général, *Le Fantôme de Canterville* est accompagné d'autres textes : *Le Crime de Lord Arthur Savile*, *Le Millionnaire modèle* et *Le Sphinx sans secret*.

À la différence de la nouvelle, le conte présente nécessairement des événements merveilleux, surnaturels : la baguette magique de la marraine de Cendrillon, les bottes de sept lieues, la princesse qui dort cent ans…

Comme la fable*, le conte a souvent une dimension didactique, c'est-à-dire qu'il suppose ou exprime clairement une morale. Certains contes sont mêmes écrits pour faire passer des idées ; on dit que ce sont des contes philosophiques. On peut citer *Zadig*, *Micromégas* ou *Candide*, que Voltaire a écrits au XVIIIe siècle.

UNE HISTOIRE MERVEILLEUSE

Un certain nombre d'éléments font que l'on peut dire que *Le Fantôme de Canterville* est bien un conte. Tout d'abord, le merveilleux est présent avec le personnage surnaturel du fantôme. Sir Simon peut accomplir des exploits terrifiants comme passer à travers les murs ou encore enlever sa tête.

L'histoire se termine bien : le fantôme est pardonné et Virginia, qui a fait preuve de bonté et de courage, est récompensée par les bijoux et par son mariage avec le jeune duc. Les qualités de la jeune fille sont reconnues, ce qui donne au texte une dimension morale.

UN CONTE ORIGINAL

Il est évident cependant que *Le Fantôme de Canterville* ressemble en fait fort peu aux contes de Perrault ou de Grimm.

Tout d'abord, le « il était une fois » traditionnel n'a pas sa place dans le récit d'Oscar Wilde car l'histoire est contemporaine de l'auteur. Il y est question de phénomènes historiques connus tels que l'opposition des Anglais et des Américains.

Mais surtout, *Le Fantôme de Canterville* joue sur plusieurs tonalités : après un premier chapitre qui crée une sorte de climat fantastique* autour de la question de l'existence du fantôme, le récit devient plutôt humoristique et parodique*, puis, à la fin, prend une tonalité plus dramatique et émouvante, davantage proche des contes de référence. Ainsi, le mélange des tonalités rend ce récit difficile à classer dans un genre ou dans un autre.

On peut certes parler de conte, étant donné la brièveté de l'histoire et la présence du merveilleux. Mais il faut alors entendre le mot au sens large et non dans le sens traditionnel qui correspond aux récits de Perrault ou de Grimm. On peut dire qu'Oscar Wilde renouvelle le genre du conte en y introduisant une dimension historique : le contexte anglais et américain de son époque.

À retenir

fantastique :
qui introduit des phénomènes surnaturels dans le réel, hésitation entre le réel et le merveilleux.

parodique :
qui imite un genre en en grossissant les traits afin de le ridiculiser.

Le Fantôme de Canterville: un conte?

UN CONTE PARODIQUE

Mais si *Le Fantôme de Canterville* mélange ainsi les tonalités et joue à la fois sur les registres de l'émotion, du fantastique et du comique, c'est aussi parce qu'Oscar Wilde utilise le personnage de Sir Simon et le décor du manoir pour se moquer d'un genre : l'horreur. Les détails horribles – du rire grimaçant ou démoniaque en passant par la main verte frappant au carreau – s'accumulent et les exploits du fantôme sont évoqués comme les titres d'une mauvaise littérature fantastique (« *Daniel le Muet, ou le Squelette Suicidé* », « *Martin le Maniaque ou le Mystère Masqué* », etc.). En rendant le fantôme fragile et ordinaire et en caricaturant les clichés de l'horreur, Oscar Wilde écrit une œuvre parodique.

Histoires de fantômes...

Qui sont-ils ?

Un voile blanc, des chaînes, des cris et des grincements, des courants d'air, des chouettes, une maison abandonnée… Voici quelques-uns des nombreux symboles qui sont associés aux fantômes dans la littérature ou au cinéma. Dans beaucoup de romans policiers, les bandits imaginent un scénario de maison hantée pour effrayer les occupants : le fantôme est un être surnaturel qui fait peur.

Il y a plusieurs raisons à cela :

– Le fantôme est un être mystérieux ; on le devine plus qu'on ne le voit ; c'est un être de la nuit le plus souvent ; il semble à la fois absent et présent, ce qui est inquiétant.

– Le fantôme appartient au monde de l'horreur : squelettes et têtes coupées, taches de sang… Oscar Wilde s'appuie sur les clichés du genre pour écrire son *Fantôme de Canterville*.

– Le fantôme est surtout associé à la mort. Il est un être qui a vécu et qui n'a pas pu bénéficier du repos de la mort.

Les rites funéraires et les fantômes

Une des caractéristiques des sociétés humaines, par opposition aux sociétés animales (les fourmis, les abeilles…), est l'existence de rites funéraires. La croyance dans un monde de l'au-delà suppose que s'accomplissent après un décès un certain nombre de rites destinés à favoriser le passage vers l'autre monde. En Égypte ancienne, le mort ne peut trouver la paix que s'il a été purifié et momifié. Dans l'Antiquité grecque, le mort qui n'a pas été enterré est condamné à devenir un fantôme ; son esprit va errer, torturé, à la surface de la terre, sans pouvoir rejoindre les enfers*. C'est ainsi que la jeune Antigone se bat pour recouvrir de terre le corps d'un de ses frères ; en effet Polynice a été condamné par le Roi à être privé de sépulture, ce qui signifie qu'il devra errer éternellement sans trouver le repos.

Plus proche de nous, dans notre tradition européenne, il n'était pas rare d'ôter une tuile d'un toit pour faciliter le départ de l'âme Et, il n'y a pas si longtemps, on redoutait les feux follets dans les cimetières car l'on croyait que ces lumières dues à la combustion des gaz provenant de la décomposition des corps, n'étaient autres que les esprits errants des morts.

Le plus souvent le fantôme est un être qui n'a pas pu trouver le repos car les rites funéraires n'ont pas été accomplis ou ont mal été accomplis. C'est de cette tradition que s'inspire Oscar Wilde lorsqu'il présente la triste fin de Sir Simon. Le meurtrier a été en effet puni par ses beaux-frères, condamné à mourir de faim et de soif ; enfermé dans un cachot oublié, Sir Simon ne reçoit pas de sépulture. Elle n'aura lieu qu'après l'intervention de Virginia.

À retenir

Les enfers : lieu où séjournent les âmes des morts dans la mythologie gréco-latine.

LES IMAGES DU FANTÔME

Appartenant à l'univers des morts, le fantôme est un être à la fois mystérieux et menaçant. De nombreux textes évoquent, sans faire clairement allusion aux rites funéraires et à leurs conséquences, des personnages surnaturels indéfinissables, ombres inquiétantes, souvenirs puissants ou doubles de l'individu.

En effet, les fantômes, parce qu'ils appartiennent au monde inconnu de la mort, sont souvent représentés comme des formes floues ou sans force, des créatures lointaines.

Les fantômes sont des âmes, ils peuvent donc être totalement invisibles, ou n'être qu'une présence diaphane ou blanche. Ils peuvent aussi apparaître tels qu'ils sont : un squelette vivant.

Quel que soit son aspect, le fantôme est, au départ, un être inquiétant. Il possède des pouvoirs surnaturels dus au fait que la réalité n'est plus pour lui un obstacle : le temps n'existe plus, les contraintes du corps non plus ; les murs peuvent être traversés…

Mais ces êtres surnaturels et menaçants qui peuplent notre imaginaire ont été apprivoisés. Le drap blanc devient un attribut familier, presque rassurant. Certains fantômes, comme Casper, sont même très souriants. Et les fantômes qui hantent Poudlard, la célèbre école de sorciers de Harry Potter, sont plus pitoyables que terrifiants.

Ainsi le fantôme, ombre inquiétante ou squelette horrible, est devenu un personnage imaginaire familier au même titre que les fées ou les sorcières.

Groupement de textes :
Mystérieuses apparitions

Les fantômes ont toujours hanté notre imaginaire. Dans la mythologie grecque, comme dans nos récits imprégnés de christianisme, nous rencontrons – ou parfois devinons simplement – ces êtres mystérieux qui appartiennent au monde des morts.

L'ODYSSÉE, D'HOMÈRE

Ulysse doit interroger l'âme du devin Tirésias pour connaître les étapes de son retour à Ithaque. Après s'être livré à des sacrifices rituels, il voit apparaître les âmes des morts : celle de Tirésias, celle de sa mère, mais aussi celles de célèbres suppliciés tels Tantale ou Sisyphe.

Là Périmède et Eurylochos maintinrent les victimes ; moi cependant, ayant tiré du long de ma cuisse mon coutelas aigu, je creusai une fosse d'une coudée en long et en large ; tout autour je versai des libations pour tous les morts : une première de lait mêlé de miel ; une seconde de doux vin ; une troisième d'eau ; par-dessus, je répandis la blanche farine d'orge. J'adressai une ardente prière aux têtes vaines des morts ; à mon retour en Ithaque, je leur sacrifierais en ma demeure une génisse stérile, ma plus belle, et je remplirais d'offrandes le bûcher. Pour Tirésias seul, j'immolerais à part un bouc tout noir, le plus fort du troupeau. Quand j'eus imploré par vœux et prières ces tribus de morts, je saisis les bêtes et leur coupai la gorge au-dessus de la fosse, et le sang noir y coulait.

Les âmes des morts se rassemblaient du fond de l'Érèbe : jeunes épousées, jeunes hommes, vieillards éprouvés par la vie, tendres vierges dont le cœur novice n'avait pas connu d'autre douleur, et combien de guerriers blessés par les javelines armées de bronze, victimes d'Arès, avec leurs armes ensanglantées ! Ils venaient en foule de toute part autour de la fosse, élevant une prodigieuse clameur, et moi, la crainte blême me saisissait. Alors, je pressai mes compagnons d'écorcher les bêtes, qui gisaient, égorgées par le bronze impitoyable, de les rôtir, et de prier les dieux, le puissant Hadès et l'effroyable Perséphone. Moi, ayant tiré du long de ma cuisse mon épée aiguë, je restais là et j'empêchais les morts, têtes débiles, d'approcher du sang, avant que j'eusse interrogé Tirésias.

Homère, *Odyssée*, chant XI, Garnier-Flammarion (trad. M. Dufour), 2001.

BARBE BLEUE DE CHARLES PERRAULT

La jeune épouse de Barbe bleue explore sa nouvelle maison en l'absence de son mari. Ce dernier lui a confié un trousseau de clés en lui interdisant formellement d'utiliser l'une d'entre elles.

Étant arrivée à la porte du cabinet, elle s'y arrêta quelque temps, songeant à la défense que son Mari lui avait faite, et considérant qu'il pourrait lui arriver malheur d'avoir été désobéissante ; mais la tentation était si forte qu'elle ne put la surmonter : elle prit donc la petite clef et ouvrit en tremblant la porte du cabinet. D'abord elle ne vit rien, parce que les fenêtres étaient fermées ; après quelques moments, elle commença à voir que le plancher était tout couvert de sang caillé, et que dans ce sang se miraient les corps de plusieurs femmes mortes et attachées le long des murs (c'étaient toutes les femmes que la Barbe bleue avait épousées et qu'il avait égorgées l'une après l'autre). Elle pensa mourir de peur, et la clef du cabinet qu'elle venait de retirer de la serrure lui tomba de la main. Après avoir un peu repris ses esprits, elle ramassa la clef, referma la porte, et monta à sa chambre pour se remettre un peu ; mais elle n'en pouvait venir à bout, tant elle était émue. Ayant remarqué que la clef du cabinet était tachée de sang, elle l'essuya deux ou trois fois, mais le sang ne s'en allait point ; elle eut beau la laver, et même la frotter avec du sablon et avec du grais, il y demeura toujours le sang, car la clef était Fée, et il n'y avait pas moyen de la nettoyer tout à fait : quand on ôtait le sang d'un côté, il revenait de l'autre.

Charles Perrault, *Les Contes de ma mère l'Oye* (1697).

Illustration du *Horla* par Julian Damazy.

Le Horla de Maupassant

Le narrateur du *Horla* de Guy de Maupassant est profondément troublé par des événements étranges : il ne sait plus si une créature mystérieuse habite sous son toit ou s'il est en train de sombrer dans la folie.

Je me promenais à deux heures, en plein soleil, dans mon parterre de rosiers… dans l'allée des rosiers d'automne qui commencent à fleurir.

Comme je m'arrêtais à regarder un *géant des batailles* qui portait trois fleurs magnifiques, je vis, je vis distinctement, tout près de moi, la tige d'une de ces roses se plier, comme si une main invisible l'eût tordue, puis se casser comme si cette main l'eût cueillie ! Puis la fleur s'éleva, suivant la courbe qu'aurait décrite un bras en la portant vers une bouche, et elle resta suspendue dans l'air transparent, toute seule, immobile, effrayante tache rouge à trois pas de mes yeux.

Éperdu, je me jetai sur elle pour la saisir ! Je ne trouvai rien, elle avait disparu. Alors je fus pris d'une colère furieuse contre moi-même ; car il n'est pas permis à un homme raisonnable et sérieux d'avoir de pareilles hallucinations.

Mais était-ce bien une hallucination ? Je me retournai pour chercher la tige, et je la retrouvai immédiatement sur l'arbuste, fraîchement brisée, entre les deux autres roses demeurées à la branche.

Alors, je rentrai chez moi l'âme bouleversée ; car je suis certain, maintenant, certain comme de l'alternance des jours et des nuits, qu'il existe près de moi un être invisible, qui se nourrit de lait et d'eau, qui peut toucher aux choses, les prendre et les changer de place, doué par conséquent d'une nature matérielle, bien qu'imperceptible pour nos sens, et qui habite comme moi, sous mon toit…

Guy de Maupassant, *Le Horla* (1887).

LES NUITS D'ALFRED DE MUSSET

Dans sa *Nuit de décembre*, Alfred de Musset évoque successivement différents épisodes malheureux de sa vie ; à chaque fois, une ombre est présente à ses côtés.

LE POÈTE

Du temps que j'étais écolier,
Je restai un soir à veiller
Dans notre salle solitaire.
Devant ma table vint s'asseoir
Un pauvre enfant vêtu de noir,
Qui me ressemblait comme un frère.

Son visage était triste et beau.
À la lueur de mon flambeau,
Dans mon livre ouvert il vint lire.
Il pencha son front sur ma main,
Et resta jusqu'au lendemain,
Pensif, avec un doux sourire.

Comme j'allais avoir quinze ans,
Je marchais un jour, à pas lents,
Dans un bois, sur une bruyère.
Au pied d'un arbre vint s'asseoir
Un jeune homme vêtu de noir,
Qui me ressemblait comme un frère.

Je lui demandai mon chemin ;
Il tenait un luth d'une main,
De l'autre un bouquet d'églantine.
Il me fit un salut d'ami,
Et, se détournant à demi,
Me montra du doigt la colline.

À l'âge où l'on croit à l'amour,
J'étais seul dans ma chambre un jour,
Pleurant ma première misère.
Au coin de mon feu vint s'asseoir
Un étranger vêtu de noir,
Qui me ressemblait comme un frère.

Il était morne et soucieux ;
D'une main il montrait les cieux,
Et de l'autre il tenait un glaive.
De ma peine il semblait souffrir,
Mais il ne poussa qu'un soupir,
Et s'évanouit comme un rêve.

À l'âge où l'on est libertin,
Pour boire un toast en un festin,
Un jour je soulevai mon verre.
En face de moi vint s'asseoir
Un convive vêtu de noir,
Qui me ressemblait comme un frère.

Il secouait sous son manteau
Un haillon de pourpre en lambeau,
Sur sa tête un myrte stérile ;
Son bras maigre cherchait le mien,
Et mon verre en touchant le sien,
Se brisa dans ma main débile.

Un an après, il était nuit,
J'étais à genoux près du lit
Où venait de mourir mon père.
Au chevet du lit vint s'asseoir
Un orphelin vêtu de noir,
Qui me ressemblait comme un frère.

Ses yeux étaient noyés de pleurs ;
Comme les anges de douleurs,
Il était couronné d'épine ;
Son luth à terre était gisant,
Sa pourpre de couleur de sang,
Et son glaive dans sa poitrine.

Je m'en suis si bien souvenu,
Que je l'ai toujours reconnu
À tous les instants de ma vie.
C'est une étrange vision,
Et cependant, ange ou démon,
J'ai vu partout cette ombre amie.

Qui donc es-tu, toi que dans cette vie
Je vois toujours sur mon chemin?
[…]

LA VISION

Je ne suis ni dieu ni démon,
Et tu m'as nommé par mon nom
Quand tu m'as appelé ton frère;
Où tu vas, j'y serai toujours,
Jusques au dernier de tes jours,
Où j'irai m'asseoir sur ta pierre.

Le ciel m'a confié ton cœur.
Quand tu seras dans la douleur,
Viens à moi sans inquiétude.
Je te suivrai sur le chemin;
Mais je ne puis toucher ta main,
Ami, je suis la Solitude.

Alfred de Musset, *Les Nuits* (1835-1837).

« VÉRA » DE VILLIERS DE L'ISLE-ADAM

Le comte d'Athol est désespéré, son épouse, Véra, vient de mourir.
Il rentre chez lui, entouré par ses sinistres serviteurs.

Chancelant, il monta les blancs escaliers qui conduisaient à
cette chambre où, le matin même, il avait couché dans un cercueil de velours et enveloppé de violettes, en des flots de
batiste, sa dame de volupté, sa pâlissante épousée, Véra, son
désespoir. […]
Les heures passèrent.
Il regardait, par la croisée, la Nuit qui s'avançait dans les cieux:
et la nuit lui apparaissait *personnelle*; elle lui semblait une reine
marchant, avec mélancolie, - dans l'exil, et l'agrafe de diamant
de sa tunique de deuil, Vénus, seule, brillait, au-dessus des
arbres, perdue au fond de l'azur.
- C'est Véra, pensa-t-il.

À ce nom, prononcé tout bas, il tressaillit en homme qui s'éveille ; puis, se dressant, regarda autour de lui.

Les objets, dans la chambre, étaient maintenant éclairés par une lueur jusqu'alors imprécise, celle d'une veilleuse, bleuissant les ténèbres, et que la nuit, montée au firmament, faisait apparaître ici comme une autre étoile. C'était la veilleuse aux senteurs d'encens, d'un iconostase, reliquaire familial de Véra. Le triptyque, d'un vieux bois précieux, était suspendu, par sa sparterie russe, entre la glace et le tableau. Un reflet des ors de l'intérieur, tombait, vacillant, sur le collier, parmi les joyaux de la cheminée.

Le plein-nimbe de la Madone en habits de ciel brillait. [...] Depuis l'enfance, Véra plaignait, de ses grands yeux, le visage maternel et si pur de l'héréditaire madone, et, de sa nature, hélas ! ne pouvant lui consacrer qu'un *superstitieux* amour, le lui offrait parfois, naïve, pensivement, lorsqu'elle passait devant la veilleuse.

Le comte, à cette vue, touché de rappels douloureux jusqu'au plus secret de l'âme, se dressa, souffla vite la lueur sainte, et, à tâtons, dans l'ombre, étendant la main vers une torsade, sonna. Un serviteur parut : c'était un vieillard vêtu de noir ; il tenait une lampe, qu'il posa devant le portrait de la comtesse. Lorsqu'il se retourna, ce fut avec un frisson de superstitieuse terreur qu'il vit son maître debout et souriant comme si rien ne se fût passé.

- Raymond, dit tranquillement le comte, *ce soir, nous sommes accablés de fatigue, la comtesse et moi* ; tu serviras le souper vers dix heures. – À propos, nous avons résolu de nous isoler davantage, ici, dès demain. Aucun de mes serviteurs, hors toi, ne doit passer la nuit dans l'hôtel. Tu leur remettras les gages de trois années, et qu'ils se retirent. – Puis, tu fermeras la barre du portail ; tu allumeras les flambeaux en bas, dans la salle à manger ; tu nous suffiras. – Nous ne recevrons personne à l'avenir.

Villiers de l'Isle-Adam, « Véra » *in Contes cruels* (1883).

LE CHÂTEAU DES CARPATHES
DE JULES VERNE

Franz de Télek ne s'est pas consolé de la mort mystérieuse de la jeune fille qu'il devait épouser. En effet, la Stilla, une célèbre cantatrice, est morte sur scène le jour de son dernier concert. Voyageant pour tenter d'oublier son chagrin, il est amené à s'approcher d'un château dans lequel semblent se produire d'étranges phénomènes.

Le plateau d'Orgall était déjà obscur. L'ombre élargie du massif, en remontant vers le sud, dérobait l'ensemble des constructions, dont les contours ne présentaient plus qu'une silhouette incertaine. Bientôt, rien n'en serait visible, si aucune lueur ne jaillissait des étroites fenêtres du donjon.

«Mon maître... venez donc!» répéta Rotzko.

Et Franz allait enfin le suivre, lorsque, sur le terre-plein du bastion, où se dressait le hêtre légendaire, apparut une forme vague...

Franz s'arrêta, regardant cette forme, dont le profil s'accentuait peu à peu.

C'était une femme, la chevelure dénouée, les mains tendues, enveloppée d'un long vêtement blanc.

Mais ce costume, n'était-ce pas celui que portait la Stilla dans cette scène finale d'*Orlando*, où Franz de Télek l'avait vue pour la dernière fois?

Oui! et c'était la Stilla, immobile, les bras dirigés vers le jeune comte, son regard si pénétrant attaché sur lui...

«Elle!... Elle!...» s'écria-t-il.

Et, se précipitant, il eût roulé jusqu'aux assises de la muraille, si Rotzko ne l'eût retenu...

L'apparition s'effaça brusquement. C'est à peine si la Stilla s'était montrée pendant une minute...

Peu importait! Une seconde eût suffi à Franz pour la reconnaître, et ces mots lui échappèrent:

«Elle... elle... vivante!»

[...]

Était-ce possible ? La Stilla que Franz de Télek ne croyait jamais revoir, venait de lui apparaître sur le terre-plein du bastion !... Il n'avait pas été le jouet d'une illusion, et Rotzko l'avait vue comme lui !... C'était bien la grande artiste, vêtue de son costume d'Angélica, telle qu'elle s'était montrée au public à sa représentation d'adieu au théâtre San-Carlo !

L'effroyable vérité éclata aux yeux du jeune comte. Ainsi, cette femme adorée, celle qui allait devenir comtesse de Télek, était enfermée depuis cinq ans au milieu des montagnes transylvaines ! Ainsi, celle que Franz avait vue tomber morte en scène, avait survécu !

**Mais la fin du roman donne à cette apparition étrange
une explication différente :**

Personne, sans doute, puisque le jeune comte avait perdu la raison, n'aurait jamais eu l'explication des derniers phénomènes dont le château des Carpathes avait été le théâtre, sans les révélations qui furent faites dans les circonstances que voici : […]

En premier lieu, sur les demandes pressantes de Rotzko, Orfanik affirma que la Stilla était morte, et – ce sont les expressions mêmes dont il se servit –, qu'elle était enterrée et bien enterrée depuis cinq ans dans le cimetière du *Campo Santo Nuovo*, à Naples.

Cette affirmation ne fut pas le moindre des étonnements que devait provoquer cette étrange aventure. En effet, si la Stilla était morte, comment se faisait-il que Frantz eût pu entendre sa voix dans la grande salle de l'auberge, puis la voir apparaître sur le terre-plein du bastion, puis s'enivrer de son chant, lorsqu'il était enfermé dans la crypte ?... Enfin, comment l'avait-il retrouvée vivante dans la chambre du donjon ?

Voici l'explication de ces divers phénomènes, qui semblaient devoir être inexplicables.

On se souvient de quel désespoir avait été saisi le baron de Gortz, lorsque le bruit s'était répandu que la Stilla avait pris la résolution de quitter le théâtre pour devenir comtesse de Télek. L'admirable talent de l'artiste, c'est-à-dire toutes ses satisfactions de dilettante, allaient lui manquer.

Ce fut alors que Orfanik lui proposa de recueillir, au moyen d'appareils phonographiques, les principaux morceaux de son répertoire que la cantatrice se proposait de chanter à ses représentations d'adieu. Ces appareils étaient merveilleusement perfectionnés à cette époque, et Orfanik les avaient rendus si parfaits que la voix humaine n'y subissait aucune altération, ni dans son charme, ni dans sa pureté.

Le baron de Gortz accepta l'offre du physicien. Des phonographes furent installés successivement et secrètement au fond de la loge grillée pendant le dernier mois de la saison. C'est ainsi que se gravèrent sur leurs plaques, cavatines, romances d'opéras ou de concerts, entre autres, la mélodie de Stéphano et cet air final d'*Orlando* qui fut interrompu par la mort de la Stilla.

Voici en quelles conditions le baron de Gortz était venu s'enfermer au château des Carpathes, et là, chaque soir, il pouvait entendre les chants qui avaient été recueillis par ces admirables appareils. Et non seulement il entendait la Stilla, comme s'il eût été dans sa loge, mais – ce qui peut paraître absolument incompréhensible –, il la voyait comme si elle eût été vivante, devant ses yeux.

C'était un simple artifice d'optique.

On n'a pas oublié que le baron de Gortz avait acquis un magnifique portrait de la cantatrice. Ce portrait la représentait en pied avec son costume blanc de l'Angélica d'*Orlando* et sa magnifique chevelure dénouée. Or, au moyen de glaces inclinées suivant un certain angle calculé par Orfanik, lorsqu'un foyer puissant éclairait ce portrait placé devant un miroir, la Stilla apparaissait, par réflexion, aussi « réelle » que lorsqu'elle était pleine de vie et dans toute la splendeur de sa beauté. C'est grâce à cet appareil, transporté pendant la nuit sur le terre-plein du bastion, que Rodolphe de Gortz l'avait fait apparaître, lorsqu'il avait voulu attirer Franz de Télek ; c'est grâce à ce même appareil que le jeune comte avait revu la Stilla dans la salle du donjon, tandis que son fanatique admirateur s'enivrait de sa voix et de ses chants.

Jules Verne, *Le Château des Carpathes* (1892).

LE FANTÔME DE L'OPÉRA
DE GASTON LEROUX

Les fantômes sont des êtres surnaturels et la famille Otis, au début du récit d'Oscar Wilde, n'admet pas l'existence de tels êtres. On peut également se poser la question de l'existence d'un fantôme à l'Opéra de Paris…

Et c'est vrai que, depuis quelques mois, il n'était question à l'Opéra que de ce fantôme en habit noir qui se promenait comme une ombre du haut en bas du bâtiment, qui n'adressait la parole à personne, à qui personne n'osait parler et qui s'évanouissait, du reste, aussitôt qu'on l'avait vu, sans qu'on pût savoir par où ni comment. Il ne faisait pas de bruit en marchant, ainsi qu'il sied à un vrai fantôme. On avait commencé par en rire et par se moquer de ce revenant habillé comme un homme du monde ou comme un croque-mort, mais la légende du fantôme avait bientôt pris des proportions colossales dans le corps de ballet. Toutes prétendaient avoir rencontré plus ou moins cet être extra-naturel et avoir été victimes de ses maléfices. Et celles qui en riaient le plus fort n'étaient point les plus rassurées. Quand il ne se laissait point voir, il signalait sa présence ou son passage par des événements drolatiques ou funestes dont la superstition quasi générale le rendait responsable. Avait-on à déplorer un accident, une camarade avait-elle fait une niche à l'une de ces demoiselles du corps du ballet, une houpette à poudre de riz était-elle perdue ? Tout était de la faute du fantôme, du fantôme de l'Opéra !

Au fond, qui l'avait vu ? On peut rencontrer tant d'habits noirs à l'Opéra qui ne sont pas des fantômes. Mais celui-là avait une spécialité que n'ont point tous les habits noirs. Il habillait un squelette.

Du moins, ces demoiselles le disaient.

Et il avait, naturellement, une tête de mort.

Tout cela était-il sérieux ? La vérité est que l'imagination du squelette était née de la description qu'avait faite du fantôme, Joseph Buquet, chef machiniste, qui, lui, l'avait réellement vu. Il

s'était heurté, – on ne saurait dire «nez à nez», car le fantôme
n'en avait pas, – avec le mystérieux personnage dans le petit
escalier qui, près de la rampe, descend directement aux «des-
sous». Il avait eu le temps de l'apercevoir une seconde, – car le
fantôme s'était enfui, – et avait conservé un souvenir inef-
façable de cette vision.

Et voici ce que Joseph Buquet a dit du fantôme à qui voulait
l'entendre : «Il est d'une prodigieuse maigreur et son habit
noir flotte sur une charpente squelettique. Ses yeux sont si
profonds qu'on ne distingue pas bien les prunelles immobiles.
On ne voit, en somme, que deux grands trous noirs comme
aux crânes des morts. Sa peau qui est tendue sur l'ossature
comme une peau de tambour, n'est point blanche, mais vilai-
nement jaune ; son nez est si peu de chose qu'il est invisible de
profil, et *l'absence* de ce nez est une chose horrible *à voir*. Trois
ou quatre longues mèches brunes sur le front et derrière les
oreilles font office de chevelure.»

En vain Joseph Buquet avait-il poursuivi cette étrange apparition. Elle avait disparu comme par magie et il n'avait pu retrouver sa trace.

Ce chef machiniste était un homme sérieux, rangé, d'une imagination lente, et il était sobre. Sa parole fut écoutée avec stu-
peur et intérêt, et aussitôt il se trouva des gens pour raconter
qu'eux aussi avaient rencontré un habit noir avec une tête de
mort.

Gaston Leroux, *Le Fantôme de l'Opéra*, Gallimard, 1943.

«LA BOUTIQUE DU COIN» DE CYNTHIA ASQUITH

Le narrateur a beaucoup apprécié l'accueil chaleureux
que lui ont réservé deux jeunes antiquaires et il retourne
dans la «Boutique du coin».

Il m'est impossible de décrire à quel point l'endroit paraissait
différent. J'imagine que les plombs avaient sauté car à présent,
l'obscurité de la grande pièce n'était atténuée que par deux
chandelles à la flamme vacillante et dans cette lueur incer-

taine, la forme sombre des meubles, autrefois brillamment éclairés, se dessinait, impressionnante et mystérieuse, en projetant des ombres étranges et presque menaçantes. Le feu s'était éteint et seule une braise à peine rougeoyante témoignait qu'il avait récemment brûlé là. C'était d'ailleurs la seule trace qu'il avait laissée car il régnait dans les lieux un froid lugubre, tel que je n'en avais jamais connu auparavant. Dire d'ailleurs que ce spectacle «jetait un froid» eût été ridiculement insuffisant pour exprimer mon impression. Rétrospectivement, la rue me semblait presque agréable. Au moins, le vent glacial était-il revigorant. D'une manière ou d'une autre, le magasin était devenu à présent aussi sombre qu'il m'avait paru lumineux lors de ma première visite. J'éprouvai une très forte envie de m'en aller immédiatement, mais l'obscurité se dissipa quelque peu tandis que le vieil homme s'affairait à allumer des chandelles un peu partout.

«Voulez-vous voir quelque chose?» demanda-t-il de sa voix chevrotante en s'approchant de moi, une bougie à la main. [...]
À ma première visite, si vous vous souvenez bien, j'avais été surpris par la propreté inattendue de l'endroit. Or il me vint l'idée singulière que ce vieil homme semblait avoir accumulé en lui toute la poussière qu'on aurait pu s'attendre à trouver en un tel lieu. À la vérité, il avait l'air à peine plus solide qu'un simple amas de poussière et de toiles d'araignée qu'un souffle ou un effleurement aurait suffi à disperser.

Il était difficile d'imaginer que cet incroyable petit vieux pût être l'employé de deux jeunes femmes d'apparence si prospère. «C'est sûrement quelque vieux serviteur qu'elles gardent auprès d'elles par charité», pensai-je.

«Voulez-vous voir quelque chose?» répéta le vieil homme.
Sa voix n'avait guère plus d'intensité que le bruit d'une toile d'araignée qu'on déchire, mais elle exprimait une curieuse insistance, presque implorante, et ses yeux me fixaient d'un regard dévorant, malgré leur pâleur. J'avais envie de partir immédiatement. La simple proximité du vieil homme m'affligeait, me démoralisait complètement. Malgré tout, je murmurai involontairement: «Oui, merci, je vais jeter un coup d'œil» et je me surpris à suivre sa silhouette gracile, examinant avec

distraction divers objets qu'éclairait la flamme vacillante de la bougie.

Le silence glacé – que seul le glissement las de ses pantoufles sur le sol parvenait à rompre – me portait sur les nerfs.

« Il fait froid ce soir, lançai-je.

– Froid, dites-vous? Froid? Oui, c'est vrai qu'il fait froid », répondit-il d'une voix neutre qui traduisait une parfaite indifférence.

Depuis combien d'années ce pauvre vieux bonhomme traînait-il ainsi son infortune? pensai-je.

« Il y a longtemps que vous faites ce travail? lui demandai-je en contemplant d'un œil morne un lit à baldaquin.

– Oh! très, très, très longtemps. »

Cynthia Asquith, « La Boutique du coin », in Histoires de Fantômes,
Le Livre de Poche Jeunesse, 1985.

Bibliographie et filmographie

D'AUTRES ŒUVRES D'OSCAR WILDE

Le Prince heureux et autres contes, 1888.
Le Portrait de Dorian Gray, 1891.

DES RÉCITS PRÉSENTANT DES PERSONNAGES EXTRAORDINAIRES

Marcel Aymé, *Le Passe-Muraille*, Gallimard, 1943.
H. G. Wells, *L'Homme invisible*, 1897.
J. K. Rowling, *Harry Potter à l'école des sorciers*, Folio Junior, 1998.

DES RÉCITS FANTASTIQUES

Théophile Gautier, *La Cafetière et autres contes fantastiques*, Bibliocollège, 2000.
Mérimée, *La Vénus d'Ille*, 1837 (en Bibliocollège).
Guy de Maupassant, *Le Horla et six contes fantastiques*, Bibliocollège, 2000.
Gogol, *Récits de Pétersbourg*, 1897.
Histoires de fantômes, Le Livre de Poche Jeunesse, 1985.

FILMS

Fantôme à vendre de René Clair, 1936.
Le Fantôme de Canterville de Jules Dassin, 1944.
Sylvie et son fantôme de Claude Autan-Lara, 1945.
Un nommé Joe de Victor Flemming, 1943.
Always de Steven Spielberg, 1989 (remake du film précédent).
Le Ciel peut attendre de Warren Beatty, 1978.
Ghost de Jerry Zucker, 1990.

Notes

Imprimé en Italie par «La Tipografica Varese S.p.A.»
Dépôt légal : 11590-08/01 - Collection : 46 - Edition : 01 - **16/8209/5**